CURRENT ISSUES IN THE PSYCHOLOGY OF RELIGION

CURRENT ISSUES IN THE PSYCHOLOGY OF RELIGION

Proceedings of the third symposium on the
psychology of religion in Europe

edited by

J.A. VAN BELZEN & J.M. VAN DER LANS

AMSTERDAM 1986

CIP-GEGEVENS KONINKLIJKE BIBLIOTHEEK, DEN HAAG

Proceedings

Proceedings of the third symposium on the psychology of
religion in Europe / ed. by J.A. van Belzen & J.M. van
der Lans. — Amsterdam : Rodopi.
ISBN 90-6203-758-5 geb.
SISO 202 UDC [159.9:2](4)
Trefw.: godsdienstpsychologie ; Europa ; opstellen
©Editions Rodopi B.V., Amsterdam 1986
Printed in The Netherlands

Preface

The Third International Conference for European Psychologists of Religion was held in Nijmegen (The Netherlands) in August 1985. Among the participants were over sixty scientists from eight European countries (Belgium, Federal Republic of Germany, Finland, Great Britain, the Netherlands, Poland, Sweden and Switzerland). Moreover, two Australian colleagues were present.
These proceedings contain all the papers that were presented to the conference. Also included are two statements (by J. van der Lans and A. Vergote) pertaining to the matter of how to define the discipline's object of study. These statements were presented to the conference in order to stimulate a plenary discussion on the question "is it the task of psychologists of religion to study behavior related to world-view systems in general, or should, on the other hand, the discipline's object be restricted to revelational systems only?".

As was the case with both previous conferences (1979 and 1982), the majority of the papers were research-reports (18 empirical reports, as against 6 theoretical contributions and 3 review-studies). Clearly, the questionnaire is by far the most popular research-instrument utilized among psychologists of religion. Attention has recently been drawn to the fact that experimental laboratory studies are extremely rare in the psychology of religion. Surprisingly, however, the proceedings of the three symposia show that the same is true for two other research methods which one might expect to be suitable for psychologists of religion, viz. case-studies and content-analysis of religious texts.

The time span of three symposia in six years may be too short to give evidence of changes within the discipline, but the trend seems to be a shift from studies of religious experience and mysticism (very popular a decade ago) to research on the ideological dimension of religious behavior. This parallels the increasing influence of cognitive theories in general psychology, especially in social and developmental psychology.
Three topics seem to have been almost totally absent from our conferences, although in the past at least two of them have been adressed by psychologists of religion. Religious studies of ethnic groups have been popular in the United States between 1950 and 1970 (the "religion of the Blacks"-studies), but have never been an important issue in Europe. Perhaps the growing influence of Islam in western Europe will stimulate such research in the near future.
A second topic which is absent in the proceedings is the study of symbolism. In the history of our discipline such studies have always been of central importance. Their absence is all the more surprising since they might bridge the gap between the experiential and ideological studies of religiosity. Because symbols have both experiential and cognitive aspects,

their study might prove to be a unifying factor and might prevent the discipline from breaking into several unrelated sub-disciplines.

A third topic deserving more attention is the study of gender differences. Although theories of gender differences have in the past been formulated by psychologists of religion, and although such differences have been found indeed in empirical studies, almost no studies exist in which this has been the central focus. One reason for this omission might be the fact that until recently psychologists of religion have been exclusively male. The growing number of female colleagues might stimulate research on differences between male and female religiosity.

The absence of the above mentioned topics in our proceedings indicates that at this moment they are not being investigated by (European) psychologists of religion. The ability to signal this ommission might in itself justify the time and energy spent on organising the conference and producing these proceedings. The central function of our conferences is not only to allow investigators to meet each other and discuss specific research (and theoretical) problems, but also to inform each other about the general topics in which we are currently involved. "Work in progress", however, necessarily implies other work is not in progress. As long as the result of our conferences is that neglected topics in the psychology of religion are signalled, we think that the conferences will have a vital function for our discipline.

The Editors

Contents

Research in social and developmental psychology of religion

Contributors

Belzen, J.A. van
Psychologisch Laboratorium, Montessorilaan 3,
NL-6525 CG Nijmegen, The Netherlands

Bergling, K.
Rosenvägen 21 A, S-752 52 Uppsala, Sweden

Bocquet, E.
Faculteit der Psychologie en Pedagogische Wetenschappen,
Tiensestraat 102, B-3000 Leuven

Brown, L.B.
School of Psychology, Kensington, NSW 2033, Australia

Clark, J.H.
Department of Psychology, University of Manchester,
Manchester M 13 9 PL, Great Britain

Derks, F.
Psychologisch Laboratorium, Montessorilaan 3,
NL-6525 CG Nijmegen, The Netherlands

Donders, C.
Wanningstraat 14, NL-1071 LB Amsterdam, The Netherlands

Fraeye, M. de.
Predikherenstraat 56, B-3000 Leuven, Belgium

Gerritsen, A.
Psychologisch Laboratorium, Montessorilaan 3,
NL-6525 CG Nijmegen, The Netherlands

Grzymala-Moszczynska, H.
Institute for the Science of Religions, Jagiellonian University,
Westerplatte St. 3/9, Cracow, Poland

Heimbrock, H.G.'
Universität Köln, Gronewaldstraße 2, D-5000 Köln 41, W-Germany

Hoenkamp-Bisschops, A.
Catholic Theological Faculty, Oliemolenstraat, Postbus 4406,
NL-6401 CX Heerlen, The Netherlands

Holm, N.G.
Sirkkalag. 26 A 17, 20700 Åbo 70, Finland

Jaspard, J.M.
Centre de Psychologie de la Religion, Voie du Roman Pays,
B-1348 Louvain-la-Neuve, Belgium

Kassel, M.
Am Kanonengraben 8, D-4400 Münster, W-Germany

Lans, J.M. van der.
Psychologisch Laboratorium, Montessorilaan 3,
NL-6525 CG Nijmegen, The Netherlands

Lupton, H.E.
Staff Office, Saint Martin's College, Manchester, Lancaster LA2 5NU,
Great Britain

Oosterwijk, J.W.
Catholic Theological Faculty, Oliemolenstraat, Postbus 4406,
NL-6401 CX Heerlen, The Netherlands

Pieper, J.Z.T.
Catholic Theological Faculty, Oliemolenstraat, Postbus 4406,
NL-6401 CX Heerlen, The Netherlands

Schreuder, O.
Sociologisch Instituut, Thomas van Aquinostraat 4,
NL-6500 HK Nijmegen, The Netherlands

Scobie, G.E.W.
Department of Psychology, University of Glasgow, Bute Gardens,
Adam Smith Building, Glasgow, Scotland, G12 8RT, Great Britain

Szmyd, J.
ul. Majora 3/7, 31-422 Cracow, Poland

Uden, M.H.F. van.
Catholic Theological Faculty, Oliemolenstraat, Postbus 4406,
NL-6401 CX Heerlen, The Netherlands

Uleyn, A.J.R.
Psychologisch Laboratorium, Montessorilaan 3,
NL-6525 CG Nijmegen, The Netherlands

Vergote, A.
Tiensestraat 102, B-3000 Leuven, Belgium

Weima, J.
    Catholic Theological Faculty, Academielaan 9, NL-5037 ET Tilburg,
    The Netherlands

Wikström, O.
    Rödhakevägen 5 A, 752 52 Uppsala, Sweden

Wit, H.F. de.
    Vakgroep Theoretische Psychologie, Vrije Universiteit, De Boelelaan
    1081, postbus 7161, NL-1081 HV Amsterdam, The Netherlands

Address of welcome (by Prof. Dr. V. Welten, President of the Subfaculty for Psychology and Head of the Department for the Psychology of Culture and Religion)

Ladies and gentlemen,

It's a pleasure for me to welcome you at this third symposion for psychologists of religion in Europe. Although it is a bit difficult to speak of a tradition yet, since it's only for the third time such a symposion is held, we nevertheless can say that traditionally professor Willem Berger opened these symposia. That I stand here before you to open this conference is a break with this short tradition. This most of us, including myself, regret. As some of you may know, the government of the Netherlands lowered the age of retirement for professors last year, and so Willem Berger had to leave in December. Fortunately he is among us, and in your name I thank him for being here.

I know you are wondering if there will be a successor for Willem Berger, will there be another professor for the psychology of religion in Nijmegen? I can't give you an answer to this question at the moment. The financial resources of the university are cut down more and more, and the number of professors in the subfaculty of psychology have to be decreased from eighteen in 1980 to eleven and a half in 1995. You can understand that in such a situation there is a strong tendency to economize at the expense of the psychology of religion. On the other hand, it is unlikely that the only catholic university of the Netherlands will give up the only chair of psychology of religion. One thing is certain: the department of culture and religion of this subfaculty will stay responsible for the teaching and the research of the psychology of religion in the future, and so our department will, if required by you, go on with the organization of these symposia every three years.

Herewith I come to another subject. By studying the lists of the participants of the symposia of 1979, 1982 and this year, I noticed that there is a continuity in participation. Of the fifty-five participants of this year, only fifteen are here for the first time, and twenty-two, that is 40%, are here for the third time. Almost 50% of the 28 guests from other countries is here for the third time, another 25% of them is here for the second time. My conclusion is that these symposia fill the need of meeting each other, and that they gave and give an important opportunity for international contact in the field of psychology of religion. It is good to see how scientists meet each other in symposia like this one in a time of secularization and cultural change. The problems of religion and philosophy of life are diverse and form a challenge for your research activities. Speaking of secularization and dechristianization, these are processes which are only obviously present in the western world. Among you there are some who live in a society in which there is no question of such changes. On the contrary, there is a prosperous religious life in all ranks of society. This raises the question of the relation between culture and religion.

When Willem Berger held an oration on 'Mythos and logos' at the occasion of his leave-taking from this university, he posed the question about the compatibility of a religious life and a scientific orientation. Or, in other words, the question about the compatibility of a sensibility for the mystery of the human condition and the rationality with which we investigate nature and the material basis of our existence. There is an analogous problem with regard to the relation between culture and religious life. Some years ago I read an article written by Kaufmann and Stachel, two German sociologists, who argued that a prosperous religious and christian life is only possible in a situation of oppression, there where christianity is in a minority position. According to them the media are an important factor in the process of dechristianization. They pose the thesis that when the television is being watched for more than two hours a day, the development and conservation of a christian spirituality is impossible.[1] The implications of their thesis are important for the psychology of religion. The question if there is an incompatibility between on the one hand an open and modern way of life, and on the other hand a christian spirituality and a mature religiosity, is a crucial question for all who are concerned about the problems of religion. And this applies to those who have only a scientific interest in the psychology of religion, and to those who have a living faith. On this day, the 26th of August 1985, it is exactly 75 years ago that William James died. He is considered to be the founder of the psychology of religion. I think that his book on the variaties of religious experience is of topical interest. For the question can be raised which are the variaties of religious experience that are compatible with the modern way of life. I hope that our conference will give a contribution to our insight in this important issue.

---

[1] Kaufmann, Fr. und Stachel, G. Religiöse Sozialisation. In: Christlicher Glaube in moderner Gesellschaft, Teilband 15. Freiburg: Herder, 1980, p. 117-164.

Religions in Australia.

L.B. Brown
University of New South Wales

An English novelist (Lodge, 1984) has recently argued that academic conferences have many similarities to classical religious pilgrimages. There is travel, self-improvement, and the discipline (of preparing a paper), as well as feasting and the pleasure of the company of new and old friends. It has certainly been a welcome pilgrimage for Dr O'Connor and me, as the two Australians here, coming to this Symposium from a country that is roughly the area of the United States with the population of Holland, and with religious traditions that were, like its population, largely imported from Europe. The Australian way of life is essentially European, despite striking differences in the physical, natural and social environment with its kangaroos, koala bears, Australian Rules football, with the Sydney Opera House dominating a sky-line in which one has difficulty finding a Church tower among the commercial buildings.

The first English settlers arrived in Australia in 1788 with Chaplains to control the convicts who formed the majority of those who were sent out. The Aboriginals they found there, and who had lived in Australia since time immemorial, were deliberately neglected and even persecuted. They were thought to be too primitive to be incorporated into the life that was to be established, in contrast to the more benign attitudes of the New Zealand settlers to the Maoris. But Australia seemed a strange place to the first British people who went there. To make it familiar they produced paintings that made the landscape look like England, and built English houses and social institutions.

The traditional British patterns of life became so well established that they have continued with comparatively little change, despite the successive waves of migration which, especially since the Second World War, have substantially reduced the proportion of the population that derives from Britain. The source of Australia's migrants has moved steadily eastwards, first across Europe and after the Vietnam War into South East Asia. Since 1974 a 'multi-cultural Australia' has been Government policy. These groups of people with their new attitudes have altered the patterns of religious identity and affiliation in Australia, and simple contrasts between Catholics and Protestants are no longer adequate to describe what it means 'to be religious' there.

Social scientific research.

There has been far more historical and sociological research into the patterns of religiousness in Australia than into any of the anthropological or psychological questions that might be asked. It is not that psychology is not well established there, although Australians may not be very reflective about themselves, but it is hard to decide what lies behind any explicit religious structures, or what is expected of them. While it may be comparatively easy to analyse the structures themselves, a latent argument in this paper is that such structures must be transformed before they can be put to work by individuals.

Australian sociologists have applied and tested their received theories to religion, although Mol (1985) now says he is not satisfied with the results. Two recent collections of essays have examined various facets of Australian religion from a sociological perspective (Harris, Hynd and Milliken, 1982, and Black and Glasner, 1983), while Wilson (1983), a sociologically trained Anglican bishop, has asked 'Can God survive in Australia?', as if a specific answer were possible. He seems to believe that it depends on what you mean by religion. There are now three extensive bibliographies (Hynd, 1982, Mason and Fitzpatrick, 1982, and Rossiter, 1984), the first two with a general coverage and the other two concerned with religious education. Because of sectarian pressures, especially among Catholics, and the prestige that attaches to some 'private' schools, religious education is an important issue that any Government or Party must deal with. (While at least limited State aid to parish and private schools has been accepted, the question of religious education in State schools continues to arouse strong feelings, both for and against, because of the secular pressures on them. These tensions in education suggest that religion, if not God, is alive in Australia even if life in parishes presents problems (Dempsey, 1983) because they embody the principles of inter-group conflict that psychologists have become familiar with.

The Churches in Australia have recently discovered or accepted social surveys, and they bought into the Australian Values Study in 1983, which was carried out by the Morgan Gallup Poll to replicate parallel studies in 23 other countries, mostly in Europe. That the commercial polling organisations regularly include questions about Church attendance and religious belief in their surveys shows that those forms of religious observance are still important social indicators, despite what some see as the declining influence of the Church, which was directly attributed by Wilson (1983) to secularisation and urbanisation. Mol (1985, p.63) qualifies that conclusion by arguing that 'the more our religious organisations move towards the exclusive end of the continuum the higher their attendance rate and the more they go in the opposite direction the more tenuous, apparently, is the hold on their membership'. Conflicting interpretations like these could provide data for a psychology of religious explanations, since attempts to find direct support for general

2

interpretations of 'religion' have been unsuccessful. Yet Bouma (1983, pp23–4) shows, 'most Australians still claim to be religious and identify with one of the mainstream denominations' (and blasphemy is still a charge that can be pursued, although no charges have been laid for at least 20 years (Watson and Purnell, 1981)).

Religious behaviour

Since 1860 about one quarter of Australians (22 per cent in 1981) claim to have attended Church in the last week, and half of the population rarely or never attends Church.

A salient feature of Australian religion now is a steady increase in the proportion of the population whose answer to the Census question about religion is that they have 'no religion', with 11 per cent in that category in 1981. Other indicators of religiousness are, of course, highly variable, and the decline in Church attendance from 1971 to 1976 has been followed by an increase since 1981.

Although the total proportion of Anglicans has declined, an increasing number of them say they have attended Church in the last week, and while the proportion of Catholics continues to increase their frequency of Church attendance has recently declined. Although Anglicans and Catholics together make up about half the population of Australia, other striking trends are the increasing number of categories found in answers to the broad Census question on religion, and the greater number of Jehovah's Witnesses, Pentecostals and Latter Day Saints, as well as Muslims, Buddhists and Hindus, and Atheists, Nihilists, and Non–believers (cf. Price, 1981). Dorothy Harris' (1982) analysis of this material, called 'Counting Christians', should, she says 'encourage the Church to abandon its fond dream of an imperium over residential Australia' (p. 283).

Religious values and belief.

Closer to more strictly psychological questions are the data about religious belief. The Australian Values Study, based on a random sample of 1,228 adults, shows that more people in Australia than in Europe accept that the Ten Commandments apply to them, with 75 per cent in Australia and 62 per cent in Europe who accept that 'Thou shalt not commit adultery', compared with the 28 per cent who agreed that 'Thou shalt keep holy the Sabbath Day'. A recognisably moral base for religion is shown in this material by the fact that the first three commandments were accepted be fewer people than were the other seven.

Many other studies have reported similar findings about the strength of religious belief. The stability of them across both time and samples always strikes me as uncanny, suggesting stereotyped if not orthodox responses (in Deconchy's, 1980, sense), and the percentages accepting statements of Christian doctrine are similar to those who believe in English proverbs. Harper's magazine in the United States reported in June, 1985, that 78 per cent accepted that 'A stitch in time saves nine', 73 per cent that 'A bird in the hand....', 57 per cent that 'What's good for the goose is good for the gander', and 38 per cent accepted that 'The grass is always greener.....'. Those responses parallel answers to political questions in an Australian study published as a Sentry Holdings Report in 1984. It shows that 82 per cent identify both with an established religious denomination and with one of the three major political parties, 40 per cent claim 'considerable interest' in both religion and politics, 28 per cent trust Church leaders, 25 per cent trust State governments and that 23 per cent trust the Federal Government. God was rated as being 'important in your life' by 42 per cent and as 'not important' by 25 per cent in the Australian Values Study, while 33 per cent said they 'fairly often' took moments for prayer or contemplation, 44 per cent did not do that at all or only rarely, and 14.6 per cent said they were often aware of a presence of power beyond themselves while 53 per cent had never had that experience.

Several conclusions seem to emerge from these kinds of findings. They show varying levels of agreement with statements that are drawn from a broad body of social knowledge about religious and other issues. Such knowledge is assumed of those who answer closed response questions (unless they do that at random). Because of that these questions must be pitched at a consensus, tapping the most convergent and unreflective responses. They do not capture the essence of anyone's private religiousness. Furthermore, since the same questions have been asked repeatedly over the last 40 years, they have become the doctrinal issues that our society allows us to use, at least in surveys if not in our everyday conversation. Because of this we have prepared answers ready which, when analysed are expected to support ecclesiastical and political, as well as sociological and even psychological conclusions about religion. The questions are themselves reflexive, in that they identify what we 'should' believe so that the answers to them become tests of what a 'religious' person is or might be expected to believe. Because they are in the public domain, these survey questions draw on our socially rather than personally represented knowledge, not to say beliefs, and while the reliability of answers to these questions is hardly an issue their validity is difficult to establish, and their implications are usually taken for granted. We also have no clear idea about what to compare them with. In this sense religion stands apart.

What does it mean to know that, in the Australian Values Study, 36.7 per cent said they never go to Church, 17.3 per cent go once a year or less, 10.9 per cent go only on 'special occasions', 6.5 per cent go once a month, 15.5 per cent once a week and 5.8 per cent go more often that that?

Perhaps these percentages should be compared with the frequency of making bets, which is stereotyped as an Australian preoccupation, watching soccer, football or cricket (rather than actually playing those games), or attending meetings of political' parties. Since voting is compulsory in Australia, there is little interest beyond simple rule-following in the percentages who do or do not cast a vote. Similarly, there may be little that is specific to religion (or to Australia) and psychologically meaningful in religious surveys, since religion generally appears to be a minority interest. Despite that, there is a common-sense fascination with the fact that 56.2 per cent in the Australian Values Study said they were 'religious', although that was not compared with the percentages who might say they are musical, artistic, talented, or even 'scientific'. While the Allport, Vernon, Lindzey Study of Values covered these and other values, it did so with ipsative scores so that if your are high on one you must be low on another. Back and Bourque's (1970) finding that what those in the working class identify as religious is called aesthetic by the middle classes, might not replicate in Australia because it is supposed to be an egalitarian and rather classless society. Great social distances can nevertheless be found there.

'Religiousness'.

Much social scientific work on religion assumes that the basic criterion for religiousness is a directly accepted and even concrete belief in God and in other conventional doctrines, rather than in the linkages between these beliefs and non-religious aspects of life or how religion becomes plausible. But what is prescribed (or expected) is not inevitably accepted and reconciled with other beliefs. Those who are outside a religion certainly view it quite differently from those deeply involved in a denomination, which in Australia, and elsewhere appears to be the most robust criterion of who is or is not a religious person. The importance of the perspective one adopts on religion was clearly recognised in Dittes' (1969) careful review, but it is often disregarded, as are the subtle distinctions that 'insiders' to religion make about their own beliefs and the beliefs of others.

In a recent study in North Queensland, Grichting (1985) asked people how they defined their own religiousness, and he found that of those who are 'quite' or 'very' religious, 29.4 per cent made reference to their own beliefs or to dogma while 45 per cent mentioned general ideological factors and 20.3 per cent referred to religious rituals. Of those who said they were not very or not at all religious, 34.4 per cent said that they rejected the rituals, and 30.6 per cent rejected religious ideologies. In the light of those results, to use Church attendance as a criterion of religiousness has little validity, in the sense that it is not generally thought to be important, except perhaps by those who are insiders to religion and who accept what is expected of them. But even that may be an unwarranted conclusion since Grichting also found that those who are religious account for their religiousness in experiential (48.7 per cent), ideological (28 per cent) or consequential and implicative terms (24 per cent). He also found that many Anglicans, Roman Catholics and other Christians said they were not 'religious' (73 per cent, 64 per cent and 62 per cent, respectively). Although fewer Anglicans identified themselves as 'religious', 9.8 per cent of those with no denominational affiliation said that they were religious. Such complexities about what it means to 'be religious' are disregarded in our conventional and usually direct questions about religion, where answers depend on what is asked, what one knows, and what can be said in ordinary conversations to match answers to the questions. Furthermore, the religious beliefs we reject may be as important to us as those we accept. What is doctrinally prescribed is not necessarily accepted by those with well formed beliefs.

To explore these features of belief, I have been asking students to write down some of the religious beliefs they hold and those they reject. Granted the difficulties of analysing the answers to such open-ended invitations, the beliefs accepted appear to be simple and direct, and fall into three main categories covering stories about Adam and Eve or the Fall, the Ten Commandments, and so on (26.6 per cent of the answers), statements about God's existence and characteristics (29.5 per cent), and about Jesus (15.0 per cent). But others rejected similar statements, often giving them a performative or active character, as in God or Jesus saves (31.9 per cent), and referring to specific Christian groups and traditions (like Catholicism) (15 per cent). These preliminary results suggest that what is accepted may be broader than what is rejected. A wide range of specific items were elicited in this material, and asking respondents to fit themselves into closed categories produces the kinds of findings we have come to expect from the outsiders to religion, for whom it is a homogeneous phenomenon. (That religion is differentiated by those who are closely involved with it may also apply to its investigators as much as it does to those we study.)

It is not clear who are the most appropriate people to ask for information for psychological analyses of religion or whether intensive or extensive investigations give the more useful data. If we are willing to accept generalisations about 'Australia' we get findings like those of the sociologists who align religions with social movements and ideologies that are not easily broken up. But a recent statement from the Church of England, Believing in the Church (1982), argues that it is not necessary for each individual who claims to be part of the Christian community to perform every role, but while it is important for deviations or

6

eccentricities to be permitted some authority and accepted structure for religion must be recognised. They also argue that 'a Christian concern about the place of the Bible, or about tradition or orthodoxy, has little or nothing to do with intellectual conformity as such'. There is little public debate about such matters in Australia.

Religious research.

The methods that psychologists typically use to calibrate religious belief ask about eternal life and whether 'God revealed himself to man in Jesus Christ', or about the frequency of Bible reading, and not about the parts of the Bible that are read most often, or how people practise what they believe. The items I have just cited are from a recent paper by Hilty and Morgan (1985) who have reworked King and Hunt's multi-component scale of religious orthodoxy. In an earlier paper, Hilty, Morgan, and Burns (1984) reviewed work on the dimensionality of religion and emphasised the instability of any solution while, perhaps inconsistently, producing one of their own with seven factors. Its specifically religious scales correlate between .59 and .23 (in their Table 3). By reordering that Table it becomes clear that their religious factors are intercorrelated and set against intolerance of ambiguity and a social conscience, in their homogeneous group of Mennonites. Another recent paper by Blachia (1985) reports a quite different set of measures which include as 'explanatory variables' localism, authoritarianism or dogmatism, civil liberalism, and theological and 'moral, political and economic' conservatism. It may be possible to find whatever one is looking for in religion and in religious data by putting the appropriate template over them, and Blanchia favours religious conservatism. If, like Milliken (1983), you stress the empty Churches in Australia and their traditional forms of worship you adopt a critical and observer perspective, rather than a participant's stance. But there is no ideal solution, although religious responses must cohere; in much the same way Guttman has repeatedly pointed out that Spearman showed in the 1920's that separate measures of intellectual and personality functioning must be inter-correlated, and Fowler (1981) has found support for this stage of developing faith.

Given the opportunity, religious believers can describe the less tangible aspects of their experience and the beliefs, and what they draw from the available doctrines to make their own religion specific. What they accept does not mirror what they will reject, not least because there is a mid-zone of neutrality and irrelevance. Expressing strong disbelief might conflict with an almost superstitious unwillingness to deny the existence of God, and an unwillingness to offend others by rejecting what they might sanction. That process could account for the fact that the great majority of funerals in Australia are still presided over by a clergyman. When I

7

enquired about this recently I found that in one Sydney crematorium on 29 May, 1985, only one of 29 cremations had no clergyman scheduled to conduct it, although the average time for these services has been reduced in the last 20 years from about 90 minutes to 30 (exept among the Orthodox Christians, who have retained long services).

Social constructions.

   Socially constructed roles for religion might be independent of whatever use individuals can find for it. The astonishing consistency in the values professed by those who identify themselves as Christians suggests a similar conclusion. When the eight separate questions about religion in the Australian Values Study were scaled, and divided into quartiles, Hughes (1984) found that those in the top quartile were predominantly female (63 per cent compared with 37 per cent of the men), with children (76 per cent), and older than 30.

They accepted their family as the dominant goal in life, respected authority, gave little stress to money, wanted work that would be useful to society, and said that divorce is too easy to get in Australia. They support the political Right, expressed negative attitudes to homosexuality, prostitution, and lying in one's own interest. This gives a clear picture of the 'typical', most religious Australians, who do not differ from those who are less religious in their sense of well-being, satisfaction with life, and meaning and fulness, or in other attitudes to the world and thoughts about death. They do not show an other-worldly perspective, despite the consistent and linear relationships between religion and a search for authority, maintaining the family and not disrupting society. The circularity in that conclusion should not be over-looked when explaining religion as a conservative process whether in political or psychological terms. Despite the fact that Gordon Allport drew attention to the way religion both makes and unmakes prejudice, many who are concerned with religion seem to disregard the possibility that it can also create conservatism and dependency, or release one from it. In the Australian Values Study, those in the least religious quartile were the ones who stressed their self-sufficiency and independence. The greatest consistencies in religion are, however, among the social rather than psychological variables, probably because religions are set within a secular order which defines and limits what it can do.

   Despite that, psychologists have in general been more concerned with the internal coherence and the structure of attitudes and beliefs than with what can be expressed through them in any social context. Perhaps we should have a moratorium on the use of survey methods to study religion, and on tests of contrasts between groups defined in terms of social and religious variables, while we find how religion is possible in psychological and social (rather than sociological) terms. That approach might show how religion (or rather Christianity) is different in Australia from elsewhere, since its tenets and practices are fixed by formal prescriptions and implemented against some cultural constraints.

When Argyle and Beit-Hallahmi (1975) summarised the social and psychological factors involved in religion they stressed that while there are differences in the character of religious activity between countries, 'religious participation is a means of affirming and maintaining both a culturally prescribed and sub-cultural identity' (p.29), so that religion serves a 'conservative function in the political life of both the USA and Great Britain' (p.110). That this is also true of Australia is shown by the Australian Values Study's results.

The Australian Census data support Price's (1981) conclusion that 'for many people religion is an important part of their ethnic identity', but especially for Polish, Italian and Irish Catholics, Orthodox Christians and those in the 'Anglo-Celtic' Churches which 'implicitly reinforce English-speaking culture' (Mol, 1985, p. 219). Those groups cover about two-thirds of Australia's population, although Price (1981) also emphasises that the 'small' religious categories now have a disproportionate influence in Australia. The numbers belonging to the 'ancient strands' of Christianity have grown from 55,000 in 1961 to nearly 200,000 in 1981, and there are now about 50,000 Muslims. These changes are largely a result of immigration, and it is not yet clear what impact they will have in the future, although the lowest proportion of those who state 'no religion' in the Census are 'from the traditional peasant societies with a strong Catholic, Orthodox or Islamic background' (Price, 1981). When Price concluded that the no religion figures show that 'Australians are thinking about their religious position and stating what it really is, instead of drifting along unthinkingly, content .to put on the Census schedule the long discarded religion of their childhood' he was referring to the fact that 'no religion', does not necessarily imply 'a lack of faith' or a move towards secularism.

Australian Christianity.

That denominational identifiers are close to our sense of self can be seen in their inclusion in the repeated answers to a simple question, 'Who am I?'. In my recent Australian data religion ranks after name, age, sex, and nationality, suggesting that some form of religious identification is still important there. This probably applies to the Aboriginals as well. They emphasise their 'dream-time', with its myths of creation, as the basis for their traditional identity which is closely in contact with nature. The indigenous Aboriginal religions (cf. Charlesworth, 1983) have, however, been obscured by the impact of Christian missionaries. With 80 per cent of Australia's population in five cities, and geographical and social mobility a fact of life, not many people stay in an area long enough to develop the roots that sustain an active parish, community, or Church-based involvement. Most Australians seem to accept their religion as a system into which one is born, and is seldom changed by it (except for the important minority of converts and strongly committed people, cf. Hunsberger and Brown, 1984).

The potentially divisive effects of religion are now protected under Australia's equal-opportunity and anti-discrimination legislation, while a recent High-Court decision has given Scientology protection as a religion, which the Rajneesh are also claiming.

Yet it is not clear how far religion is applied to the taken-for-granted realities everyday life, beyond its use in crisis and to order or understand life in nature, with a careful distance set between religion, science, and politics. Recent efforts have been made to produce an indigenous Australian Church, with an Australian Hymn Book, Prayer Books and a Lectionary that is shared by several separate Churches. The Uniting Church was formed in 1977 from some of the Presbyterian and Congregational Churches and the Methodist Church. In 1985 it removed the filoque clause from the Creed and opened its Communion to all believers. Sunday Schools have almost disappeared, but a great deal of social welfare is channeled through the Churches, which also own several radio stations, not to mention its property. Sunday is a day 'for the family', and most families, we are told, own a Bible, Cooking Book, Dictionary and Atlas.

While the Churches in Australia may seem conservative and beleaguered, they retain the strong support of about a quarter of the population, and implicit support from another half. Australia is still undoubtedly a Christian country, with its cultural origins in Europe. But there is no 'kangaroo' or indigenous theology, yet religion is not expected to be partisan in politics or in industrial and social disputes. Small, but vocal groups, including a Festival of Light, uphold the conservative and fundamentalist position that most lay people expect their clergy to proclaim. The failure of many of them to accept that is an important source of religious tension: for the majority, religion is a coherent but relatively isolated system that can be invoked when it is needed to mark social transitions, sustain family life, support morality, and ensure some kind of salvation. No one expects you to disclose what you believe, and if you do you are greeted with an embarrassed silence, unless you pick the right social context for it. Religion in Australia may therefore be like having a credit card: when you leave home you take it with you because it focusses on your denomination, sin and the Bible. This is different from the United States where it is un-American to say that you are not religious.

The pressures to conformity make Australian religion seem superficial to its outsiders, who find it easy to avoid making sense of it as a form of dependency than existentially. O'Farrell (1982, p. VIII) says that 'Australian Christianity is embattled, incompetent and in decline'. That historian's perspective desperately needs to be supplemented with good psychological data about what religion means to those who continue to be involved with it, and how it is used to do and explain things. Although Spilka et al (1985) say that 'In our culture (the U.S.), a naturalistic explanation is more available (than a religious explanation) and hence evaluated first', we have not yet established the limits of religious explanations although we know they conflict with other explanatory systems, including those we think of as being common-sense.

I must conclude that we know too little that is not superficial and intuitive about the psychology of religion in Australia because we have not done enough work to know how it fits with the rest of life. Only bold steps can resolve uncertainty about the directions that social and psychological research on religion could most profitably take in Australia.

Literature

Argyle, M. & Beit-Hallahmi, B. The social psychology of religion. London: Routledge and Kegan Paul, 1975.

Australian Bureau of Statistics. Social indicators, 1984, 4, 115.

Back, C.W. & Bourque, L.B. Can feelings be enumerated? Behavioural Science, 1970, 15, 487-496.

Black, A.W. The impact of theological orientation and of breadth of perspective on church members, attitudes and behaviours. Journal for the Scientific Study of Religion, 1985, 24(1), 87-100.

Black, A.W. & Glasner, P.E. Practice and belief: studies in the sociology of Australian religion. Sydney: Allen and Unwin, 1983.

Bouma, D. Australian religiosity: some trends since 1966. In: A.W. Black & Glasner, P.E., Practice and belief: Studies in the sociology of Australian religion, (15-24). Sydney: Allen Unwin, 1983.

Charlesworth, M. Religion in Aboriginal Australia: An anthology. St. Lucia: University of Queensland Press, 1984.

Deconchy, J.P. Orthodoxie religieuse et sciences humaines suivi de (Religious) orthodoxy, rationality and scientific knowledge. Paris, La Haye: Mouton, 1980.

Dempsey, K. Conflict and decline: Ministers and Laymen in an Australian country town.

Australia: Methuen, 1983.

Dittes, J.E. Psychology of religion. In: G. Lindzey & Aronson, E., _The handbook of social psychology_. Reading: Addison-Wesley, 1969, (second edition, _5_), 602-659.

Doctrine Commission of the Church of England. _Believing in the church: the corporate nature of faith: a report_, 1981.

Fowler, J.W. _Stages of faith: the psychology of human development and the quest for meaning_. San Francisco: Harper and Row.

Grichting, W.L. Dimensions of religiosity: Degree, domain and context, 1985. (unpublished article)

Harris, D., Hynd, D. & Millikan, D. _The shape of belief: Christianity in Australia today_. Homebush: Lancer, 1982.

Hilty, D.M. & Margon, R. Construct validation for the religious involvement inventory: Replication. _Journal for the Scientific Study of Religion_, 1985, _24_(1), 75-86.

Hilty, D.M., Morgan, R.L. & Burns, J.E. King and Hunt revisited: Dimensions of religious involvement. _Journal for the Scientific Study of Religion_, 1984, _23_, 252-266.

Hughes, P. _Religion and values_. Report from the Australian Values Study Survey. Canberra: Zadok Centre in the Institute for Christianity and Society, 1984.

Hunsberger, B. & Brown, L.B. Religious socialism, apostacy and the impact of family background. _Journal for the Scientific Study of Religion_, 1984, _23_(3), 239-251.

Hynd, D. Christianity in Australia: a bibliography. Harris, D., Hynd, D. & Millikan, D. _The shape of belief: Christianity in Australia today_. Homebush: Lancer, 1982, 201-228.

Lodge, D. _Small world: an academic romance_. Harmondworth: Penguin Books, 1985.

Malony, H.N. Psychology and faith: the Christian experience of eighteen psychologists. Washington, D.C.: University Press of America, 1978.

Mason, M. (Ed.) _Religion in Australian life: a bibliography of social research_. Bedford Park, South Australia: Australian Association for the Study of Religions and National Catholic Research Council. 1982.

Millikan, D. _The sunburnt soul: Christianity in search of an Australian identity_. Homebush West, NSW: Anzea, 1981.

Mol. J.J. _The faith of Australians_. Sydney: Allen and Unwin, 1985.

O'Farrell, P. _Foreword_. Harris, D., Hynd, D., & Millikan, D. _The shape of belief: Christianity in Australia today_. Homebush: Lancer, 1982, VII-IX.

Price, C. Religion and the Census. _St. Marks Review_, 1981, 2-7.

Rossiter, G.M. _Review of research related to religious education in schools_. Sydney: National Catholic Research Centre. 1984.

Spilka, B., Shaver, P. & Kirkpatrick, L.A. A general attribution theory for the psychology of religion. Journal for the Scientific Study of Religion, 1985, 24(1), 1-20.

Watson, R. & Purnell, H. Criminal law in New South Wales. Sydney: Law Book Company, 1981.

Wilson, B. Can God survive in Australia? Sutherland, NSW: Albatross, 1983.

Table 1: Religious Affiliation In Australia

	1971 %	1976 %	1981 %
Total Christian	86.2	78.6	76.4
Total Non-Christian religions	0.8	1.0	1.4
Not stated plus Indefinite	8.3	12.2	11.4
No religion	6.7	8.3	10.8
	100.0	100.0	100.0

Source: Australian Bureau of Statistics -1971 Census, 1976 Census, 1981 Census.

Psychiatry, mental health and religion.
H.C. Rümke as a case-study into the origins
of Dutch psychology of religion. (1)

J. A. van Belzen
A. J.R. Uleyn
Catholic University Nijmegen

Introduction

Generally speaking, one can say that, as in most countries, psychology in the Netherlands developed out of philosophy and psychiatry. The psychology of religion has a third important root: theology, in recent history especially pastoral theology. Purely psychological studies of religion are rare; most publications on subjects relating to the field of the psychology of religion are written by personally pious psychiatrists or interested theologians. Especially in the Netherlands, the psychology of religion is a very young science. A few books appeared before World War II, but these pertain more to pastoral psychology than to the psychology of religion, or else they review the psychology of religion abroad, especially the german efforts. One of the first books in the field of the psychology of religion that originated in the Netherlands is Rümke's <u>Karakter en aanleg in verband met het ongeloof</u> (Character and disposition related to unbelief). Rümke was also not a psychologist of religion in the strict sense, but a psychiatrist (although Rümke had for some years held a chair in developmental psychology, see Eisenga).

Born in 1893, Rümke has been well known in international psychiatry. A professor since 1933, he has occupied a leading position in the Netherlands, and many regard him to be the most important dutch psychiatrist of the century. He made important contributions to several areas, e.g. developmental psychology and psychogerontology, the study of neurosis and schizophrenia, phaenomenological psychiatry, etc. His ideas were spread to broad circles outside psychiatry and psychology. In 1939 he wrote <u>Karakter en aanleg</u>, and it became a classic. In the Netherlands it has been a bestseller, and it is still in demand. It has been translated and edited in english twice, and once in Spain. (The title of the english editions, which we will use here, was: <u>The psychology of unbelief</u>.) Psychologists of religion still refer to it, abroad as well as in the Netherlands. Also theologians still quote the book. (Heytink, Van der Ven) Many have welcomed the book, for whereas Freud strongly argued that belief is a neurosis, Rümke took the opposite stand and states that unbelief is a disturbance. <u>The psychology of unbelief</u> is a highly interesting book. In it Rümke presented the development of faith in 7 stages, which we will not elaborate on here, and indicated the hurdles that must be taken to reach a next stage. He thought that these hurdles, the problems one has to solve to reach a next stage may be regarded as determinants of unbelief.

Although interesting, The psychology of unbelief has not been the primary focus of our inquiry. (Faber has dealth with it in some depth, and we ourselves have published an article on its background and genesis elsewhere.) The result of our study help however, to understand, interpret and evaluate The Psychology of unbelief, as we shall see later. In accordance with one of the main lines of research of our department since Fortmann, and our interest to shed light on the psychology of religion by historical research, we decided to investigate what kind of contribution Rümke made to the theme 'religion and health'. For it seems reasonable to expect the author of The psychology of unbelief to have written more about religion that might be relevant for the psychology of religion. Secondly, for years Rümke has been the dutch authority with regard to mental health affairs: he wrote a great deal about it and he was very active in high positions in the international mental health world Rümke after World War II. We therefore initiated a longitudinal analysis of his complete works.

Mental health, diagnosis and religion
The theme 'mental health' indeed Look up a great part of Rümke's massive writings. When we look for his own theory on mental health, we find however, that there is none. Rümke's method was to compilate, to value and to compare the contributions of others, but he never made a real integration himself. His own contribution consisted in pointing out what, in his opinion, others had forgotten, or underexposed. Rümke didn't approve of closed theories and standarddefinitions, being convinced that we just are not able to tell what mental health really is (and he always blamed psychology for this; not enough research had been done in his view). He did not construct a definition of mental health, but rather tried to let his reader 'feel' what he meant by it. An example of such a circumscription: "We are now in a position to draw a supposition of some sort as to what health is: it is a question of creativity, of love, of form of lifel, of a current without stagnation, or a rhythm of opening and closing; it is a question of regulation, of adaptation and of 'tension psychologique'. Health is also a question of the distance between the experiencing ego and what has been experienced, as aspect studied little up to the present time." (Rümke, 1955) Rümke has most appreciated Soddy's description of the healthy person: "A healthy person's response to life is without strain; his

ambitions are within the scope of practical realisation; he has a shrewd appreciation of his own strength and weaknesses. He can be helpful but also accept aid; he is resilient in failure and level-headed in success; he is capable of friendship, and of aggressiveness when necessary. His pattern of behaviour has consistency so that he is 'true to him self', and no one about him will feel that he makes excessive demands on his surroundings; his private beliefs and personal values are a source of strength to him."

Above all, Rümke focused attention on two themes, which he considered to have been neglected by almost all colleagues. The first is the problem of the line between health and illness. Rümke held that flowing lines are supposed too easily. On the contrary, there is a great difference and a clear line between health and illness according to him. There is something wrong with an ill person, that is not so with a healthy one. Stated the other way round: an ill person lacks something that a healthy one does have. Unfortunately, we don't know what this something is, but it is exactly this that constitutes the essence of health. Rümke has stressed this theme in several places. His argument runs as follows:

Rümke quotes Jackson as stating: "the symptomatology of nervous diseases is a double condition, there is a negative and there is a positive element in every case". This implicates that in the case of disease, we are always dealing with two things: on the one hand the disease causes psychic functions to drop out, or to diminish; or disease alters them. This we don't observe directly, but we can deduce it from comparison with the normal. This reduction of functions is the so-called negative symptom. On the other hand we have the positive symptom. These phenomena strike us much more, and usually much more attention is given to them. But what is the positive symptom really? It is normal psychic life going on under the condition brought about by the dropping out of some function. (Rümke, 1950b) Take for example the delirium, what is that? It is the way in which man lives when certain higher integrations of psychic life fail. So, phenomena as hallucinations, confusions, are not the real symptom of the disease. The real symptom (= the negative symptom) is a disturbance of integrative activity of the patient. Positive symptoms as such cannot justify the conclusion 'disease', for positive symptoms every one can have, even the most healthy. Rümke often states that the "psychic disturbances of the healthy man" are many, e.g. amnesia, fluctuation of the affect, inhibition, depersonalisation, derealisation, anxiety, etc. Therefore such symptoms cannot lead to the judgment 'disease', although a) the duration of a phenomenon, and b) its relation to a psychopathological or neurotic personalitystructure might be an indication. Rümke's conclusion is that disease is not a problem of symptoms, of content, but rather of form. By this he means: "the way of living through". When a researcher can no longer feel his way into it, then pathology should be pronounced. In 1923 Rümke published a study on feelings of felicity. Here already we find this principle put into words: one might very well feel one's way into the feelings of felicity as described by the patients, the reason why the conclusion nevertheless should be 'psychopathology' is the way in which these feelings are lived through: it is impossible for the researcher to go through the experience genetically. The last and most important criterium is the form. To quote Rümke: "The fact that we not infrequently are able to diagnose the condition with certainty at a time when nothing at all is yet known concerning the patient's thoughts and feelings proves that this is true." (Rümke, 1960)

Rümke's second greater theme is: multiconditionality and diagnosis. Time and again Rümke advanced that psychiatry should leave causal thinking. For: the symptom, and its cause, are not the most important. What really matters, is what makes the symptom continue. In the diagnosis process, this has to be investigated. The task of the psychiatrist is to discover the conditions for a certain disease, and then to ask himself: 'on which of those can I exert a benevolent influence?' (Rümke, 1955) In investigating this, the clinical psychiater should take full account of all that has been fruitful in psychiatry up to now, and that can be considered as the foundations of psychiatry. As such Rümke names nine frames of reference. (See table 1; from: Rümke, 1961)

Table 1: <u>Rümke's frames of reference</u>
1. Physiology, anatomy, biochemistry, electrophysiology.
2. General objective psychopathology, doctrine of psychological constitution and characterology.
3. Driving forces, depth psychology, libido-energetic considerations.
4. Planes of development: dissolutions (Jackson), regression (Freud), unchaining of lower automatisms (Ey), the plane of thought development, phases of life.
5. Janet's "tension psychologique".
6. Subjective experience (phenomenology of Jaspers); comprehensible relations; the relation between the "ego" and the "self".
7. "Patterns of being" (anthropological psychiatry).
8. Interpersonal relations (Sullivan).
9. Union with the cosmos and with the transcendental-metaphysical- religious principle. Union with God.

Although he is reluctant to say so explicitly himself, we may conclude from the analysis of his total work, that this order also presents Rümke's hierarchy of the different systems. Rümke's opinion might be correctly summed up, when we say, that in the case of mental illness, factors stemming from the first two systems are always involved. In addition, factors from one or more of the other systems will be usually be influential. These can be decisive as to the course of and the recovery from the illness. (They might even be the only factors that can be dealt with in treatment.) Also with regard to the "psychic disturbances of the healthy man" Rümke expressed how important the first two systems are: "Psychic disturbances to the extremes of the normal and the pathological are due in large measure to the fact that man is not sufficiently equipped from the biological point of view to cope with his difficulties. Then appears the human conflict in its pathological form, then man is ill." (Rümke, 1954)

So far as psychiatry is concerned. It appears that in his thinking about health and pathology, Rümke remained an adherent to the so-called medical model. To Rümke psychiatry was a medical discipline, and it had to stay so. (This was and is of course still a point of discussion.) His psychiatric conception of health and pathology is after all a biological-somatic one: when someone is mentally really 'ill', then biologically and somatically something is out of order too. And when there is nothing wrong with biology and the body, then there is no disease. Then something else is the matter, e.g. a "psychic disturbance of the healthy".

Now we have to distinguish between Rümke's work as a psychiatrist in the university-clinic, and his private practice as a psychotherapist at home. Just because he was, after all, an adherent to the medical model, it is doubtful whether he used the systems 3-5, and especially 6-9, in his work as a psychiatrist. He knew about them, recognized them, had read a great deal about all these fields, but he never operationalized them to make them fruitful in his psychiatric practice. On the other hand we may be sure he paid attention to almost all of them when diagnosing, and in psychotherapy. But then we should be reminded that he regarded psychotherapy not as psychiatry, as treatment of the ill, but as care for the, in principle, healthy person. How he performed psychotherapy, we don't know, he never wrote about it. (Rümke (1965) does not really give insight in his practice.) Rümke was familiar with all of these systems, he had read the essential psychiatric literature since 1850, but he did not integrate it systematically and did not make a practically manageable tool or method out of it. In this respect he seems to have become the victim of his own erudition. His broad approach, taking into account all of great theories, quoting from world-literature and philosophy, made him a highly interesting lecturer and author. This approach, however, was too strictly tied up to his own style, age and experience. This approach proved to be intransmittable, and died with him in 1967.

Among all this the attention he gave to religion seems to have been rather minute, and we must conclude that with regard to substantial psychological theory on religion and health, he did not bring us much further. This lack of attention is more pronounced than expected. To verify the result, there are at least two possible tests: 1. a comparison with a quantitative measure of the attention to religion in his total works, and 2. find out what he did in practice by means of interviews. We did both, and had our result corroborated: also in other places in his work religion does not occupy a significant place. In his lecturing to students and his psychiatric clinic he did not spend any special attention to religion either. Neither did he , as we found out, in his private life; Rümke was far less religious than supposed.

Mental health work and values

To do justice to Rümke, just a few closing notes.

That as a psychiatrist he did not pay much attention to religion is consistent with his notion of health and pathology. The line he postulated between health and disease he consequently extended to the whole field of mental health work in general. He distinguishes here between mental hygiene and mental health work: Mental hygiene is the exclusive domain of the medical psychiater, dealing with the ill (in the sense just described). The goal here is: to heal, to re-store. Mental health workers on the contrary are dealing with the, in principle, healthy person: here a physician works together with psychologists, sociologists, philosophers of culture, theologians and others, with the goal to optimalize health. (Rümke, 1948)

Rümke also wrote a great deal about these topics, but always on a meta-theoretical level. In his many reflections on mental health and mental health care, in his textbook on personality and other such publications, occasionally some references to existential themes, and to religion can be found. It shows that Rümke had clear anthropological ideas, and was very modern with regard to theoretical science. So he drew attention to the fact that all scientific research is tied up to (mostly implicit) values. This applies equally to the notion of health one works with. (Rümke, 1951) (With these insights he was ahead of his time.) He pointed out that the goals proposed in care cannot be validated scientifically, but are based on pre-scientific choices. Within this framework he also stated that the attitude (of psychologists, psychiatrists, etc.) towards religion is not based on scientific

19

considerations, but on anthropological positions. He himself had made the choice to postulate in man a fundamental, irreducible tendency to commit oneself to supra-natural values. It belongs to full human development to "surrender"; remaining in some form of self-occupation or egoism might then be interpreted as unnatural, as a developmental disturbance. But Rümke points out, that this reasoning is the result of a pre-scientific choice. This commitment to supra-individual values can manifest itself in knowing that oneself obliged to adhere to abstract ethical notions, but also in religion. And in that sense, but only in that sense, one might say that not being religious, unbelief, is a developmental disturbance. This is the premises of his The psychology of unbelief, that therefore should not be regarded as a plea for religion, and certainly not as an apology for orthodox christianity (as many have interpreted it, and still do). We should add a final note concerning The psychology of unbelief: it is striking how Rümke's point of view resembles a modern theory on faith-development like Fowlers. In both the analysis is structural; it is concerned with the development towards an ethical goal; it is concerned with 'world-view' that might be religious belief. But whereas Fowler at least tried to empirically validate his theory, we find with Rümke the same disadvantage we discovered earlier: the whole thing remains intimately connected to his own experience. The psychology of unbelief is an excellent phenomenological analysis, based essentially on introspection. Rümke didn't make any attempt to validate the different stages he distinguished. This is highly regrettable, because now their generalizability must remain questionable, and it might be difficult to operationalize them in research or in pastoral care. (And as far as we know, this never has been done.)

For Rümke, psychology, and the other mental health disciplines (not psychiatry) can contribute to the opening of man's eyes to values, and the commitment of oneself to them. In the only place that Rümke mentions the psychology of religion in his work, he proposes consequently as one of its tasks: to investigate why some people are blind to values and do not reach surrender. (Rümke, 1954, p. 192-193) His Psychology of unbelief is an attempt to contribute to this part of the psychology of religion. But all of these scientific disciplines, and especially the practitioners, should also be modest: they should know that they themselves can neither constitute nor realize these values. They can only help an individual to recognize these values and to start moving towards them. As so often, Rümke expresses this eloquently in the next quotation, in which he reverts to the old, well-known moralityplay Everyman:

"Had this play been written in modern times there would be differences,

20

but the beginning and the end would remain the same. When abandoned by family, friends and possessions, instead of learning that neither 'Force', 'Wisdom' nor 'Beauty' could go with him on his last journey, Everyman would have had the sorrow of finding that 'Psychology', 'Sociology' and 'The Science of Human Relations', which had so expressly promised assistance, could not bring him to his ultimate aim and inner peace. Modern science can only fulfil its promises of help through awareness that it can never entirely meet the deepest need of man, a need met only by the humble surrender to the 'unknown'. Science can develop its full power only when imbued with religious consciousness in the widest sense." (Rümke, 1950)

These meta-theoretical reflections, his phenomenological and often almost literary style procured Rümke his great reputation. And deservedly, for he has something important to say about these subjects. His essays are still very worth reading by the representatives of the psychology of religion.

Literature

Belzen, J.A. van & Uleyn, A.J.R. Twee klassieke teksten uit de Nederlandse godsdienstpsychologie. In: Rümke, H.C. Karakter en aanleg en Psychologie van de twijfel. Kampen: Kok, 1985.

Eisenga, L.K.A. Geschiedenis van de Nederlandse psychologie. Deventer: Van Loghum Slaterus, 1978.

Faber, H. Psychology of religion. Philadelphia: Westminster Press, 1976.

Heytink, G. Pastoraat als hulpverlening. Kampen: Kok, 1984.

Rümke, H.C. Phaenomenologische en klinisch-psychiatrische studie over het geluksgevoel. Leiden: Eduard Ydo, 1923.

Rümke, H.C. Karakter en aanleg in verband met het ongeloof. Amsterdam: Ten Have, 1939.

Rümke, H.C. Samenvatting en opdracht (van het) Nationaal Congres voor de Geestelijke Volksgezondheid, (gehouden) 19-22 mei 1947 (te) Amsterdam. Dl. II. Zwolle: 1948, p. 131-138.

Rümke, H.C. Report of the chairman of the executive board. In: Annual Report 1948-1949 (of the) World Federation for Mental Health. London: 1950, p. 27-34.

Rümke, H.C. Problems in the fields of neurosis and psychotherapy. Folia psychiatria, neurologia et neurochirurgia neerlandica, 1950, 53, 839-846.

Rümke, H.C. Psychiatrie en maatschappij. Nederlands Tijdschrift voor de Psychologie, 1951, 6, 1-27.

Rümke, H.C. The psychology of unbelief. London: Rockliff Publ. Comp., 1952.

Rümke, H.C. Psychiatrie. I. Inleiding. Amsterdam: Scheltema & Holkema, 1954.

Rümke, H.C. Solved and unsolved problems in mental health. Mental Hygiene, 1955, 39, 178-195.

Rümke, H.C. Contradictions in the concept of schizophrenia. Comprehensive psychiatry, 1960, 1, 331-337.

Rümke, H.C. Nosology and classification. In: J. Zubin (ed.). Field studies in mental disorders. New York: 1961, p. 73-84.

Rümke, H.C. The psychology of unbelief. New York: Sheed & Ward, 1962.

Rümke, H.C. Over 'gesprekstherapie'. Huisarts en Wetenschap, 1965, 8, 127-131.

Soddy, K. Mental Health. International Health Bulletin (of the League of Red Cross Societies), 1950, 2(2), 8-13.

Ven, J.A. van der. Kritische godsdienstdidaktiek. Kampen: Kok, 1982.

(1) The investigations were supported in part by the Foundation for Research in the field of Theology and the science of Religions in the Netherlands which is subsidized by the Netherlands Organisation for the Advancement of Pure Research (Z.W.O.).

Psychological research on religion.
An international review.

K. Bergling
University of Uppsala

Introduction

In the family of psychological disciplines psychology of religion has become a recognized speciality, explored by both social scientists and theologians. Neither the size of international scolarship in this field, nor the trends of research activity is however previously explored.

For obvious reasons the total size of activity in such a field can never be revealed, because much research is hidden behind vernacular languages and never published in the internationally recognized scientific journals. An overview of the presumably top ten percent of all research, that passes reviewing, international publication and at the end reaches Psychological Abstracts, might however be of major interest to future research.

Important findings not seldomly produce increased activity in a particular branch of a science. Trend analyses of a 30-year-period may therefore reveal new insights into major changes of the discipline.

Problems

The purpose of this study was to explore:
1. What is the size of the international psychological research on religion?
2. What are the sizes of the major research areas of the discipline?
3. What do 30-year trends of the discipline show about major changes in the field

Method
Studies Reviewed

A sample of studies published 1951-80 and abstracted in Psychological Abstracts (PA) were reviewed.

The following criteria were fulfilled by these studies: (a) The object of investigation was "religion", which includs according to practice in some of the leading journals in the field not only religion in a narrow sence but also belief systems, ideology and morality. (b) Psychological investigation of "religion" as defined above was the main focus of the study – not just a background variable. (c) The year of publication was later than 1950 and not later than 1980 because of the often more than three year time lag between publication and inclusion in PA. (d) The study was published in an international language: English, French, or German. (e) The sampling unit of the studies were individuals, not groups or institutions, to separate psychology of religion from sociology of religion.

Classification

Each study was classified into one category. The categories were:
1. Developmental Psychology of Religion
   1.1 Religious and ideological development
   1.2 Moral development
2. Social Psychology of Religion
   2.1 Attitudes
   2.2 Religious Personel
   2.3 Religious Socialization
   2.4 Psycho-Biography
   2.5 Other
3. Research on Personality and Religion
4. Research on Religious Experience
   4.1 Mysticism
   4.2 Conversion studies
   4.3 Glossolalia
   4.4 Other
5. Educational Psychology of Religion
6. Research on Psychotherapy and Religion
7. Psychological Measurement of Religion
8. Reviews of Psychology of Religion.

Data Analysis

Graphic representation was chosen as the most appropriate method to summarize the findings. Frequencies for each year and each category were used as input to the computer program SAS/GRAPH.

The histograms were constructed by means of the SAS/GRAPH subprogram GCHART.

The polygons showing publication trends 1951–80 were constructed by means of the SAS/GRAPH subprogram GPLOT. All graphs were drawn in the same scale in order to facilitate comparisons between the graphs. The program had to be "fooled" to draw the graphs correctly. GPLOT draws the x-axis not according to the dominating convention, i.e. from origo, but from an arbitrary point below zero (at the scale chosen for these graphs the point was -3). This problem was overcome by overlaying a blank field from the base line of the graph to the x-axis starting at 0.

The three-dimensional graph summarizing all the data was constructed by means of the SAS/GRAPH subprogram G3D. The three variables used were: year of publication (x), category of publication (y), and frequency (z). The order of the categories were chosen so as to maximize the legibility of the graph. The graph was tilted about the y-axis at a 50-degree angle, and was rotated around the z-axis at 35 degrees.

Result
The Size of the International Research
"International" designates, that the research reviewed was published in an internationally recognized scientific publication that was abstracted in Psychological Abstracts. It was further written in one of the international languages: English, French, or German. Excluded from the study are the majority of all research that does not fulfill the quality criteria necessary to be included in Psychological Abstracts, as well as the few studies abstracted that were written in other languages (e.g. Russian, Japanese). The majority of all national research activity is selfexcluding from PA as it is not international in language and of unknown quality.

2 827 studies were found, that fulfilled the criteria mentioned in the Method section. The studies not published as monographs were found in 410 scientific journals or periodicals. As shown in Figure 1 Journal for the Scientific Study of Religion (JSSR) is the most influential in the field, with 234 articles, followed by Religious Education and Child Development, 67 each. Archiv für Religionspsychologie is ranking 22. (see figure 1)

As shown in Figure 2 developmental psychology of religion and social psychology of religion are the two largest categories, including together 50 percent of the sample.

Figure 2 shows the eight main categories in descending order. Research on personality is conventionally regarded as the third major category of general psychology. Research on personality and religion is however ranking 7. Minor categories are also the two more applied branches of research: educational psychology of religion (ranking 6) and psychotherapy and religion (ranking 8). The study of religious experience (e.g. mysticism, conversion, glossolalia) is often regarded as the focal area of the psychology of religion. Nevertheless this category is only ranking 4.

No less than 18 percent of the studies are classified as reviews, ranking 3 among the categories. (see figure 3)

The findings about each category will now be presented in descending order, beginning with the largest category: Developmental Psychology of Religion.

Developmental Psychology of Religion
The largest category was developmental psychology of religion, including 716 studies.

As shown in Figure 3 it was at the end of the 1950's that the research interest in developmental problems in religion started to grow. 15 studies each year were found in 1963 and 1964 and every year since 1969. A peak was reached at the middle of the 1970's with more than 55 studies each year 1974-77, with a top of 69 studies in 1976.

The two subcategories of the developmental problems are: (1) Research on religious and ideological development, and (2) Research on moral development. The two subcategories are of about equal size and show similar trends. (see figure 3)

Social Psychology of Religion

The second largest category was social psychology of religion, including 701 studies. Religion as a social phenomenon has been the focus of investigation in psychology of religion throughout the entire 30-year-period reviewed. The research interest increased linearly from the 1950's to the beginning of the 1970's, and reached its peak with 59 studies published in 1971.

After the peak that year the trend in research activity changed dramatically and only two years later the social psychology of religion had reached a plateau at a much lower level with about 15 studies a year from 1974 to the end of the period.

It seems as if the sociology of religions has taken over a large part of the previously more psychologically oriented investigation of religion as a social phenomenon during the last decade explored.

The recent dramatically increasing interest in developmental problems of religion may also have channelled research activity in a new direction. (see figure 4)

The studies included under the heading "social psychology of religion" are as compared to the developmental studies much more heterogeneous. Two distinct groups of studies have their background in practical problems in the religious denominations and the homes. For policy reasons much research is aimed at the study of religious personel (e.g. missionaries, priests/ministers, deacon/deaconesses, monks/nuns). A fourth of the studies belong to this subcategory. The other subcategory was studies of Religious Socialization, including about a fifth of the studies.

The largest subcategory includs Attitude studies, including a third of the reports. The distinction between attitude studies, studies of religious personel and studies of religious socialization is vague.

A fourth subcategory classified as social psychology included the 95 psycho-biographical studies found. It can be discussed whether these should have been classified as studies of "Personality and Religion". Theologians not seldom use the word "personality" in a common-sence mode designating the study of important persons, and not in the technical sense designating the study of the complex interrelation-ships of variables forming in a strict psychological sense the personality. Most psycho-biographical studies focus heavily on the social impact on the individual. That is the reason for the classification chosen here.

Research on Psychology of Religion – Reviews
As can be seen in Figure 2, the third category according to number of studies was "Reviews", including 497 studies. These cover three major areas of research:
(1) Research in the history of psychology of religion,
(2) Explorations in the theory of science applied to this discipline,
(3) Reviews of research in the field.
The fact, that almost a fifth of all research in psychology of religion belongs to this category shows, that there has been a constant effort at clarifying the identity of the discipline, its scientific prerequisites, possibilities, methods of research and results. (see figure 5)

As shown in Figure 5 the number of studies has been fairly constant over the 30-year period, never exceeding 20 per year. Roughly three periods can however be delineated:
(1) Before 1958, less than 7 studies each year,
(2) 1958-71 most years between 10 and 20 studies,
(3) After 1971, showing a fairly low activity as compared to the total volume of research.
It seems as if the breakthrough in psychological measurement of religion has diminished the need for reviewing by opening up new fields of unexplored possibilities for psychological investigation of religion.

Research on Religious Experience
The category ranked 4 includes 331 studies that in a narrow sence may be described as studies of religious experience. This category includes four quite distinct subcategories:
(1) Studies of mysticism, including 189 reports,
(2) Conversion studies, 61 documents,
(3) Studies of Glossolalia, and
(4) Other types of religious experience. (see figure 6)

The study of religious experience was popular in the 1960's and the beginning of the 1970 s with 15 to 20 studies almost every year.
From 1975 the research interest seems however to have been channelled into other areas of research. (see figure 7)

Psychometric Studies
Studies of research methodology in the psychology of religion is in general of two kinds:

(1) General studies of the philosophy of science applied to this discipline, which was classified under Subcategory 2 of the Category "Reviews",

(2) Psychological measurement of religion, an exclusive category for psychometry of religion.

This second distinctive category was found to include no less than 186 psychometric studies, which demonstrates the increasing social science orientation of the research. (see figure 8)

As shown in Figure 8 most of the psychometric literature on religion is of recent date, demonstrating a major change of the discipline starting around 1970 and being a characteristic feature of research throughout the last decade explored.

In the history of science major breakthroughs not seldom have a major impact by directing research activity into new fields. It is reasonable to believe, that the psychometric advances in the psychology of religion is to be seen as a major influence to the rapid growth; of research in developmental psychology of religion, social psychology of religion, and educational psychology of religion, which will be shown below. It seems however as if a corresponding influence on the study of personality and religion is still waiting, presumably because of the strong psycho-analytical orientation of much research in that field.

Educational Psychology of Religion

It is often argued that educational psychology of religion, often called Religious Education, would be of very recent date with its main influence from pioneering studies in the middle of the 1960's. The 144 studies found confirm that view. (see figure 9)

This category is heavily dependent upon the recent advances in the categories showing similar trends: developmental psychology of religion, social psychology of religion, and psychometric studies. It may, in fact, often arise difficulties in distinguishing e.g. studies of religious socialization from this category, as well as a majority of developmental studies have direct application to education. The main reason for not eliminating this category was however a wish to test the assumption that educational psychology would have such a late origin as a speciality within the psychology of religion.

Research on Personality and Religion

The category ranked 7 was personality and religion, with 138 studies.

The investigation of the religious personality in a strictly psychological sense, i.e. the complex interrelationships between various types of variables technically labeled personality, has been active throughout the

28

entire period explored. It has however never had any dominating position. During the 1970's this field has lost part of its relative position as a consequence of the increasing dominance of developmental and social psychological problems of research on religion.

As mentioned above, 96 psycho-biographical studies were classified as a subcategory of social psychology of religion. (see figure 10)

Psychotherapy and Religion

The smallest category, psychotherapy, has many names depending on the context of theology, psychology or medicine. Theologians talk about "pastoral care" or "pastoral counceling", whereas the terminology in psychology and medicine is psychotherapy, the term used here, and psychiatry.

As shown in Figure 11 there has been some research interest in this field throughout the entire period, but as measured in number of studies it has always been of marginal size. (see figure 11)

Three-Dimensional Representation of the Trends

Figure 12 presents a three-dimensional representation of the development of international psychological research in religion from 1951-80. (see figure 12)

Parallel to the x-axis that shows the years from 1951 to 1980 the eight profiles from Figures 3-11 can easily be recognized. The eight profiles taken together show the development of international research in this field.

The y-axis represents the eight categories of research, ordered so as to minimize the overlap of one profile over another. Starting from left to right the categories are: Developmental Psychology, Social Psychology, Religious Experience, Personality and Religion, Educational Psychology, Psychotherapy, Psychometry, and Reviews.

The z-axis showing the "hight of the mountain" presents the number of studies in each category published in one particular year.

From right to left the profile of each year can be followed. Comparisons over years show the changes in research profiles on the international scene. The dominating role of social psychology at the beginning of the 30-year period is dramatically changed at the beginning of the 1970's, when the new psychometric literature stimulates the study of developmental problems and educational psychology as well. The minor categories still remain down in the "valeys", partly covered by growing "mountains" of research reports from other fields.

Hopes for the Future

It is to be hoped, that research workers in psychology of religion in all countries would put priority into publishing the best of their research not only in vernacular languages but also in one of the international languages, so that this field as a whole can develop into an international standard with mutual exchange of views and results from numerous psychological and theological institutes joined in a common interest in the psychological study of religion.

Summary.

This study investigated trends in international research activity in the field of psychology of religion from 1951 to 1980. "International" designates here the following restrictions on the study: (1) Research reviewed was published in internationally recognized scientific publications and abstracted in Psychological Abstracts, (2) available in one of the languages English, French, or German. (3) The sampling unit of the reports was individuals, not groups or institutions. (4) In each study "religion", including belief system, ideology, and morality was the main interest, and not just a background factor. 2827 studies abstracted in PA were classified into one out of eight categories, according to their main objective. Ranking the categories according to number of studies showed: developmental studies 716, social psychology 701, reviews 497, religious experience 331, research methods 186, educational psychology 144, personality 138, psychotherapy 114. Dramatic increase in research activity was found in developmental studies, social psychology, research methods, and educational psychology. The other four categories remained similar in activity over the period. From about 1970 psychology of religion has increasingly gained a scientific orientation through the appearance of a specific literature on psychological measurement in psychology of religion.

Figure 1

Psychological Research on Religion
The 20 most frequent Scientific Journals

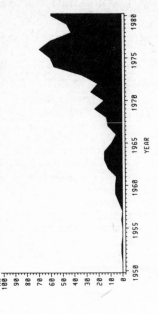

Figure 3

Developmental Psychology of Religion
716 psychological studies 1951–1980

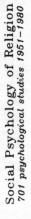

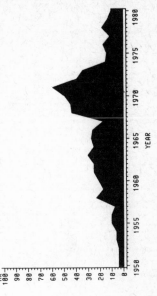

Figure 2

Research on Psychology of Religion
2827 studies
from Psychological Abstracts
in eight main categories

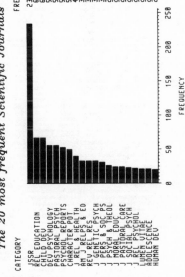

Figure 4

Social Psychology of Religion
701 psychological studies 1951–1980

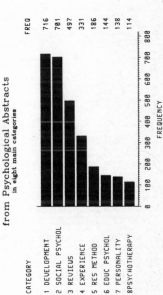

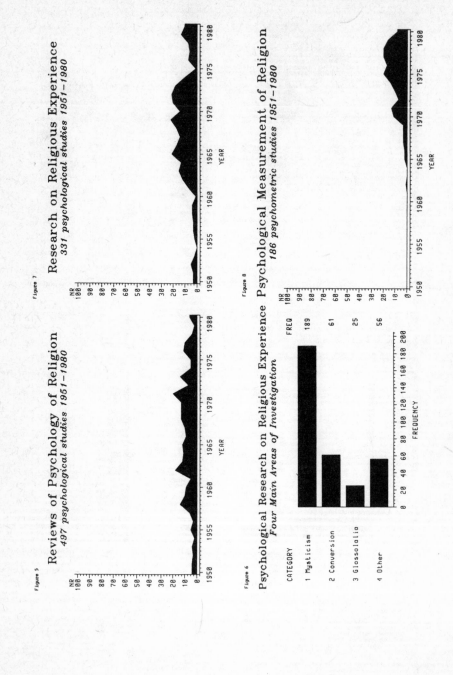

Figure 5

Reviews of Psychology of Religion
497 psychological studies 1951–1980

Figure 7

Research on Religious Experience
331 psychological studies 1951–1980

Figure 6

Figure 8

Psychological Research on Religious Experience
Four Main Areas of Investigation

Psychological Measurement of Religion
186 psychometric studies 1951–1980

Figure 9

Educational Psychology of Religion
144 psychological studies 1951–1980

Figure 11

Research on Psychotherapy and Religion
114 psychological studies 1951–1980

Figure 10

Research on Personality and Religion
138 psychological studies 1951–1980

Figure 12

Psychological Research on Religion
Trends in International Research 1951–1980

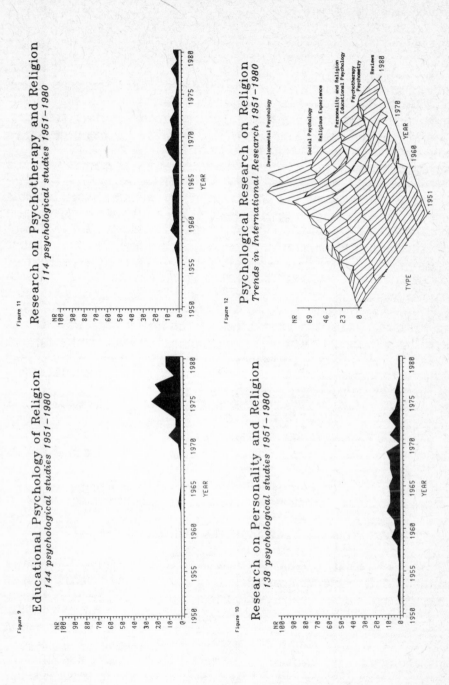

Clinical aspects of religiosity.

H. Grzymala - Moszczynska
Jagiellonski University, Cracow

While considering different approaches to the studies of religion one can differentiate between two main types: static and dynamic. The majority of studies rely on the first approach. They describe religious attitudes, religious preferences, values, personality dimensions and behavior at certain times and among certain group.

Statistical elaboration of the data from such research gives us information about correlation between particular variables but says little about causes of the given situation and hardly anything about possible changes in the future. In spite of the popularity of the above approach in most cases it is not possible to develop a diagnosis on its base or predict future developments. After all it remains mostly Judeo-Christian centric i.e. majority of research concern followers of Christianity as well as being applied to solving practical problems particular Church denominations.

The dynamic approach is less popular but seems to be more fruitful.

The main presupposition when studying religion in this way is that religion is not a single event or a collection of facts but that religion is process. More precisely it assumes that religion contains facts which constitute religious doctrine, cult and sentiment but these facts are continuously changing.

We can specify several kinds of changes in a given religious system
- changes within course of time
- changes between different geografic regions
- changes in the religiosity of different strata of the same society.

Another group of changes constitute those within an individual
- changes on its influence on the individual i.e. pathological or therapeutical,
- changes within course of human life i.e. in different life periods.

So, one can delineate between studies of external and internal dynamics of religion. External dynamics of religion remain a traditional field of interest in such disciplines as sociology of religion, comparative history of religion and geography of religion. Internal dynamics of religion studied by psycholgy of religion within scope of interest for developmental psychology of religion and clinical psychology of religion. Developmental psychology of religion studied changes within religion which are held in different periods of the individual life, religiosity of childhood, of adolescence, adulthood, it concentrates on stages of moral development, stages of development of religious concepts and its conditioning by the image of parental figures or specific role of the religiosity in particular age generated life situations.

The clinical approach to study of religion dominates psychoanalytical tradition. In fact psychoanalysis was the first recognized dynamic approach to the study of religion within psychology of religion. Since I would like to show connections between the clinical dynamic approach and external dynamic approach, I would like to return to the possibility of the external dynamic approach to analysis of religion.

Fig. 1: <u>approaches to the studies of religion</u>

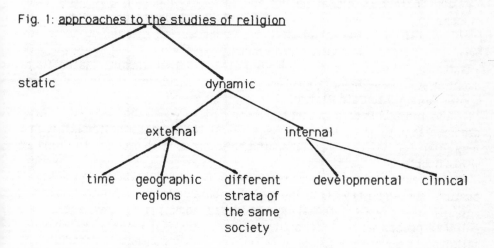

Let us consider first religion as an event changible within the course of time. As a very clear example we can take Buddhism and Islam as religious systems which have undergone many important changes since their beginning.

Buddhism changed from a philosophical and mystical doctrine which satisfied most consciences and devout followers, ascetic monks, but did not appeal to the broad social strata, into a real religion with a god of gods, i.e. Buddha, with countless less prominent deities, with rituals, symbols and iconography. The best example of dynamic change in a basic doctrine of a religious system can be found in tantric form of Buddhism, full of magic, demonology, rituals and orgiastic elements.

The same regularity concerns Islam. It started from an unified religious doctrine preached by Mohammed and in the process of evolution went trough different modifications resulting in the appearance of many new sects within Islam even some contradictory to original Mohammed teaching such as Sufi mysticism.

Over the years, both Buddhism and Islam went through processes of assimilating primary religious thoughts to meet the needs and expectations of the broad social groups. This dynamic also depends upon the assimilation by the new religion of the existing religious traditions in the given country. Example is that of Christianity in India and China in the XVIth and XVIIth centuries and Buddhism in Japan in the VIIIth century. This is an example for the second kind of external, dynamic changes.

In India, Catholicism met with Braministic tradition. Conversion to Catholicism was equal to becoming an outsider to one's own cast. This meant that Catholicism became the religion of the lowest out-cast people pariahs. To change this situation and to make it possible for the upper classes to become adherents to Catholicism the Jesuit priest Roberto de Nobili modified Catholicism in India by accepting bramin customs and permitted babtized Hindus to live according to previous cast roles.

The same process took place in China. Another Jesuit, Mateo Ricci adopted a Chinese name and started work on adopting and incorporating Confucianism into Catholicism.

He adopted a cult of ancestors and their pictures and introduced Chinese ceremonies into Catholic cult. As a result, Chinese Catholicism became less alien for native people than the religion usually brought to China by white people.

Another example of the same process are Buddhism in Japan in the VIIIth century, contemporary Christianity in Ethiopia or Islam in South Africa.

In all cases very interesting processes took place. New social and cultural processes and conditions forced old and already established religions to adopt new forms of ritual and a new content of doctrine. The situation made old religions change in ways appropriate for the intellectual capacity and emotional maturity of a new audience.

A third kind of external dynamic of religion might be described as a process of changes within the same religion in the same time and place while being the adoption of the religion by different social strata of the same society.

One example is the Roman Catholic religion in Poland in the XIXth century. Upper classes of Polish society accepted religion as a way of expressing opposition towards foreign powers which participated in the partition of Poland. It was a way of expressing national identity. At the same time it was a religiosity lacking authentic piety and was not a real acceptance of religious doctrine. Quite a contrasting picture was presented in the same period by so called folk religiosity. A very important aspect of this religiosity was constituted by special pietists attitudes based on a cult of local saints primarily connected with agriculture. Their religiosity created involved and much more real part their lives than the religiosity of the upper classes whose religiosity was mainly political.

All three aspects of the external dynamics of religion have not been taken under consideration by the psychology of religion. Because of this psychology of religion has been cut off from some very valuable sources of information dealing with the influence of religion on human lives as well as the influence of human beings on religion. Leaving examination of the external dynamics of religion for another subdiscipline Religionswissenschaft, psychology of religion makes it impossible to look for a more universal mechanism of functioning religiosity on the individual or on the social level.

In my opinion clinical studies of religiosity could gain a great deal of information by broadening its scope with an interreligious perspective, by seeing certain mechanisms of religiously originated pathologies and therapies in the light of external dynamics of religion. Initial attempts to enrich the perspective for the analysis of clinical phenomena was made by analysis of possessional and trance like states. Everyone would probably agree that we can learn much more about possession from Erica Bouguignon's or Felicitas Goodman's work than from separate case-studies of possession within one particular religion. This also concerns our knowledge of other human responses to life situations in the light of people's religious convictions. As an immediate field for such an analysis the role, mechanism and structure of religious conversion and experience in the light of external dynamics of religion could be examined.

Explicit declaration of internal dynamic approach to the clinical studies of religion is Pruyser's <u>A dynamic psychology of religion</u>. The same tendency concerns Fowler's <u>Stages of faith</u> in respect to developmental psychology of religion.

The clinical psychology of religion constitues a very rich and promising field of research but it might be more beneficial not only for psychology and psychiatry but also for other disciplines of 'Religionswissenschaft' while broadening its perspective to external dynamics of religion.

The development of symbols as key to developmental psychology of religion.

H. G. Heimbrock
University of Köln

I. Since the times of R. Goldman's famous study on the importance of Piaget's cognitive psychology to Religious Education (Goldman, 1964) the genetic perspective of the psychology of religion has called more and more attention to my colleagues and to me, who are working in the field of religious education. After a short period of psychoanalytic orientation at least in the german speaking countries the cognitive approach to religious development has become of predominant influence for contemporary curriculum construction. I will not investigate all the different reasons for this changing. One of it seems to me the more or less naive trust of several religious educators, that they have only to follow facts and datas in adapting the results of cognitive psychology wheras a reception of psychoanalytic models and experiences is still a rather obscure and doubtful business. Especially the works of L. Kohlberg and Fr. Oser have fed the illusion, that religious education is nothing than a strict follow-up to the cognitive development of the individual; educational intervention has only to provide some lift-up lessons in order to reach the next stage of development (Kohlberg/Turiel, 1978, 67; see also Oser, 1984, 263ff.) In this paper I will not deal with an educational criticism. Following the invitation to a symposion of psychologists of religion I certainly will be of more interest dealing with some psychological problems of the developmental concepts in the psychology of religion. As a matter of politeness I have to confess, that especially an article of A. Godin (Godin 1968) on the genetic development of the symbolic function inspired me to the following remarks.

II. The title of Godin's article already indicates precisely the main approach of cognitive psychology to the numerous phaenomena of human religion. In replacing other concepts like that of W. James (James, 1902) and R. Otto (Otto, 1917) it is almost familiar to our times, that modern psychology of religion is a secular scientific research. And its instruments and methods are directed to religion only as far as cognitive structures and mental representations are concerned. The status and quality of God himself or the theological question of thruth of religious symbols are excluded of psychological investigation.

The approach of cognitive psychology follows those decisions as far as it is interested predominantly in the developmental conditions that give individuals the possibility to deal mentally with religious symbols.

Since the famous research of Piaget on the development of the symbolic function in the child (Piaget 1959/1969) it is widely accepted that this development follows certain principles and goes on through four stages according the general development of human intelligence. I suppose, most of the audience is familiar to this. Therefore I will remember the central statements.

For Piaget the perspective of the details experienced in all his observations is correct formal operation with symbols as object representations. The extent to what an individual has the capacity to deal mentally with "reality" is the standard that decides the position on the developmental line. This line takes its beginning in a more or less chaotic status; all activities are directed by egocentric feelings. A very important step is reached, when the child is able to deal continually with mental objects; another one when it is able to take mental objects "as if" they represent other things that are not present. Mythic elements of biblical narratives hold in this theory of genetic development of the symbolic function only an intermediate position. They do not represent the fully developed sort of mental operations, because they do not belong to pure rational and objective thinking about reality. To end my rather uncomplete summary: the developmental perspective of cognitive psychology according to Piaget assumes a more or less continuing progress of the described mental operations in a lineal manner. Neglecting the various new results in several details, it seems to me that also other famous psychologists of religion as D. Elkind (Elkind,1971) or J.W. Fowler (Fowler,1976) took over the principal decisions of Piaget, as far as I have described it. Supposing that nobody of you will be astonished about that, let us have a look at a psychological theory that normally is judged to be far away from Piaget's mode. I am talking now about psychoanalysis in its Freudian fashion. And I must confess, that I was very puzzled to remark in Freud's work on symbols and especially in his criticism of religion the same basic assumptions about the normal human development of the possibility to deal with object representations. Although Freud is dealing with the emotional part of symbols and therefore neglects the cognitive peculiarities, he seems to be convinced of precisely the same developmental perspective from illusion to reality as Piaget stated it. Therefore his main argument against religion was, that its message would interrupt the normal development of thinking in the child (Freud,1927, 371). And his emphatic educational message came to the conclusion: the child must grow up and find out the hidden wishes in those illusions. And, in consequence man has to accept the necessities of the reality outside his inner and former desires - cut short: "Wo Es war, soll Ich werden".

III. In order to scatter your suspicion that the theologian allways has to reconcile and now even is trying to reconcile Freud and Piaget, I shall go one step further and notice some objections against both. Admitting the fruitful results in many details of the research, there still remain some questions concerning the fundamental assumptions of the described theories of human development of the symbolic function. Someone, who is forced by his own profession only to be an observer of the psychology of religion, as I am, first should draw his full attention to those questions, that are formulated by psychologists themselves.

I start with a discovery of a woman. C. Gilligan pointed out some deficits of cognitive developmental psychology as well as the psychoanalytic fashion (Gilligan,1982/1984).

After years of studying the developmental concepts of Erikson and of Kohlberg, she wondered whether both of them are authorized to talk about a complete structure of human development. And her argument against both, testet by research, is: in accordance to their scientific ancestors, they overlooked one half of mankind: that is the female part of the population. They identified, as Freud and Piaget did before, moral and cognitive and affective development of boys with childisch development in total.

The idea, that given developmental concepts do not fit to all groups of mankind, is a harsh criticism against the postulate of universal appropriation, which Piaget assumed and which Kohlberg explicitly demanded after his cross-cultural research.

Mrs. Gilligan's question stimulated me to look for similar methodical prejudice of the cognitive or of the psycho-dynamic sort of developmental concept. The crucial point of course is the "social construction" of what is called "reality" by Freud and by Piaget. Omitting the epistemological part of this problem to a symposion of psychologists with our philosophical colleagues, there still remains the suspicion: the assumed aim of Piaget's and of Freud's structural line of dealing with representations in the mind is not a result of God's eternal creation of human mental structures. At least in some respect, it reflects typical values of our modern western world.

In times, when we realize the dangerous boundaries of the belief in continuing progress of our technological behaviour with nature outside of mankind, we should pay attention to our behaviour with inner nature as well. This seems to me a question not only of moral quality but also a question concerning the fundamental principles of psychology and our special field in it.

To put the question in the frame of reference of religious phaenomena and of the development of religious experience: are our psychological models fitting to the object of our research, if we postulate symbols and illusions to be les mature and postulate pure language of logical symbols to be mature sort of thinking? To avoid misunderstanding, I should say, that this question does not only concern the propositions of Piaget and his students. It was a famous american psychoanalyst and a researcher of the psychology of religion, W.W. Meissner, who rolled up the problem in its psychoanalytical consequences. He pointed out at least one famous sort of religous experience, which is very difficult to assort genetically into the modell of psychoanalytic life-circle. "The problem can be stated in simplified form as follows: in terms of a developmental schema, are we to envision mystical states as embodiments of the highest, most differentiated, articulated, structuralized, and integrated attainments of an evolved religious capacity, or do they, on the contrary, represent regressive phenomena that reflect the most infantile levels of developmental fixation, if not aberration?" (Meissner,1984, 151). It seems obvious to me, that this is not only a special question concerning mysticism but also a general question concerning the social dependence of terms as "progression" and "regression".

To sum up all critical questions, let me emphasize two of them: the first is, to what extent do conventional models of the development of the symbolic function in cognitive and in psychoanalytic psychology fit to the object, that is researched? And the second: to what extend are they not following a given "reality" of human development, but an illusion of mature development, that is constructed in analogy to modern western faith in one special form of human progress?

IV. In my oppion the key to those problems is to find only, if we start to correct some fundamental errors in the treatment of human subjectivity in all our psychological approaches to the field of religion. To point out the solution in theological language would be quite easy; you only had to refer to P. Tillich's definition of religion as a matter of absolute personal concern.

This seems to be quite the contrary of Freud's and Piaget's judgements of human egocentrism. But the usefulness of speculative theological sentences to arrange psychological models of empirical value would of course not be accepted by everybody of you.

Fortunately, I am able to give some further hints to our questions refering to contemporary psychological research itself.

To start the discussion on the cognitive side of religious understanding, I should draw your attention to L.T. Howe. In his very stimulating article "Religious understanding from a Piagetian perspective (Howe 1978) he distinguishes between three qualities of understanding. The initial form is the things as individual given facts. The second one makes sense of things as representation for other things, obviously Piaget's "semiotic function".

But Howe now puts the question wether religious language is fully described in a system of symbols, in which there is existing a correspondance between a signifying expression and the reality signified. According to this author, we are forced to propose a third form of understanding if we are dealing with religious understanding in all its varieties. "Construal of experience and the world by means of some concept of the transcendent, then, involves considerably more than learning to signify a given in certain ways. It involves more than apprehending relationships. It is at once, and more genuinely, the constructing of both relationships and world in reference to a conceptualization of alternative possibilities to a conceptualization of alternative possibilities to the present." (Howe, 580) Following this argument of Howe, the psychology of religion should be very careful in dealing with Piaget's famous terms of adaption and assimilation.

A second hint, now in the language and system of psychodynamic sort of psychology. Changing our interest from Howe's stress of the activity of idealizing in treatment with symbols to psychoanalysis, you probabely would be surprised of a correction of Freud's former propositions. Exactly this has taken place by means of importing D. Winnicott's concept of the 'transitional object' into the psychology of religion (Winnicott,1953). Refering to this concept A.M. Rizzuto, in her excellent study about the development and the changings of individual images of the God representation (Rizzuto,1979) stated the helpfull function of religious illusions in the human treatment with reality. Following this way, she does not give up all need and possibility to talk of a pathological direction of this development, that might be possible. But the important point seems to be to me Rizzuto's disagreement with Freud: "Reality and illusion are not contradictory terms...Men cannot be men without illusions" (Rizzuto, 209).

I think, Howe and Rizzuto are pointing out the importance of personal fantasy in a succeeding development of dealing with symbols from two different points of view, but they come to at least an analogous result.

At this moment, there is no time to follow the various consequences of this new direction of looking at the development in the field of religious education.

But I think, the psychology of religion as a research of human development will take profit of the discussed corrections in several respect. To sum up my paper, I should indicate this shortly. First of all, scientific psychological study is able to look through the cultural boundaries of its underlying principles like 'reality' and 'progress', and therefore no longer is forced to follow them as an absolute scientific creed. Secondly, refering to the problem of our plenary debate, I think, the task of our discipline cannot be restricted to revelational systems, if the active human treatment with illusions and with the development of an idealizing understanding as a process in pointing out a central problem of the psychology of religion.

And finally, our discipline would gain a new quality concerning the field of the developmental research of various religious traditions. Measuring religious experiences by the level of formal operative qualities of thinking seems to me a rather imperialistic way of exporting our cultural and psychological standards to far eastern religions. If we decided to reformulate our models and methods corresponding to a less restrictive definition of 'reality', this would enable us to reach a real post-conventional level of research in our culture and in others as well.

Literature

Elkind, D. The development of religious understanding in children and adolescents. In: U.P. Stromen (Ed.), Research on religious development. New York: 1971.

Fowler, J.W. Stages in faith: the structural-developmental approach. In: Th.C. Hennessy (Ed.), Values and moral development. New York: 1976.

Freud, S. Die Zukunft einer Illusion. 1927, GW XIV, 321ff.

Godin, A. Genetic development of the symbolic function: meaning and limits of the works of R. Goldman. Religious Education, 1968, 439ff.

Gilligan, C. In a different voice. Cambridge Mass: 1982.

Goldman, R. Religious thinking from childhood to adolescence. London: 1964.

Howe, L.T. Religious understanding from a Piagetian perspective. Religious Education, 1978, 569ff.

James, W. The varieties of religious experience. 1902.

Kohlberg, L. & Turiel, E. Moralische Entwicklung und Moral-erziehung. In: G. Portele (Ed.), Sozialisation und Moral. Weinheim: 1978.

Meissner, W.W. Developmental aspects of religious experience. In: W.W. Meissner. Psychoanalysis and religious experience. New Haven, Londen: 1984,

Oser, Fr. & Gmünder, P. Der Mensch. Stufen seiner religiösen Entwicklung. Zürich: 1984.

Otto, R. Das Heilige. 1917.

Piaget, J. La representation du monde chez l'enfant. 1926

Piaget, J. La formation du symbole chez l'enfant. Neuchatel: 1959.

Use of the notion "Implicit Religion" in psychological study.
A discussion paper.

H.E. Lupton
Saint Martin's College, Lancaster

In recent years I have attended several conferences devoted to the social scientific study of religion, where some of the papers read by contributors seem to have had little or nothing to do with religion. I am not referring here to those papers concerned with such matters as the Christian experience of conversion, or the incidence of some religious practice such as public worship, or with the effects of a fundamentalist faith upon morality, or with the motivation of those who join a new religious movement. In all such cases, the religious nature of the phenomenon is explicit, and its religious nature will be acknowledged by all who can agree on a definition of the term Religion. I am referring rather to those papers to which a listener might respond, 'This is not Religion. Your research is concerned with an aspect of ordinary life in the modern world, and it is best understood in secular terms'.

Notice that I begin my own paper with a great assumption, which I will not argue here. I am assuming that it is possible to point to large areas of human behaviour and say, 'This is not Religious'. As we all know, there are those who insist that every behaviour is within the realm of Religion, just as there are political enthusiasts who insist that every action is a political action.

Let me give you some examples of the kind of conference paper to which I am referring:

Experience and meaning
Aspects of the transcendental experiences of adolescents
Articulation of the sense of the self and identity
The implicitly religious and the aesthetic
The religion of politics
Vegetarianism
Religion in the unfocussed majority
Diffused religion: theory and practice
Civil religious beliefs and American Presidential elections

These are the titles of some interesting and serious papers read to conferences in recent years where the general theme of the conference has been 'Implicit Religion'. The question I want to suggest to you this afternoon is this: When making a social scientific study of such phenomena, is the observer (the researcher) wise to adopt a religious frame of understanding? Would it not offer better insight and more productive research if the investigator were to conduct his study using frameworks developed in the mainstream of empirical social science? Does it constrain and limit psychological or sociological understanding of human behaviour to interpret in religious terms phenomena which are not explicitly religious, and events and interactions where the actors might themselves deny that their behaviour was religious behaviour? You will realise that my concern in this discussion-paper is with defining the borders that we should recognise as the limits of psychology of religion. Also in identifying the universe of ideas to which such research should owe prime allegiance. I am asking whether psychologists of religion should resist a temptation to impose upon behaviour which is not clearly and explicitly religious a religious interpretation and, whilst doing so, imagine that they are gaining scientific understanding of the phenomenon.

I will now explain what I understand by the term 'Implicit Religion', and here I am making use of some of the work done by my English colleague Edward Bailey, who has been energetic in the past ten years to persuade social scientists and others that the concept of Implicit Religion is a useful one. In contrast, I am suggesting that it is not a useful concept, and that if adopted as a frame of understanding, it may limit and mislead psychologists' understanding of human behaviour.

In his doctoral thesis, Edward Bailey (1976) does not give a precise definition of the term 'Implicit Religion'. Instead, he lists more than 50 synonyms, or equivalent expressions, which have been coined by social scientists to refer to the phenomena with which he is concerned. He argues that there could be no more eloquent testimony to the existence and significance of such an area of human experience, and to the need for its conceptualisation, than the many attempts which have been made to give it a name. Here are some examples of the terms adopted by those interested in what Bailey calls 'Implicit Religion'.

    basic religion
    common religion or civil religion
    diffused religion
    folk religion
    grass-roots religion
    invisible religion
    integrating foci
    lay religion

meaning systems
natural religion
para-religion
personal depths
popular religion
practical religion
pseudo-religion
quasi-religion
secondary religiosity
secular religion
unconscious religion
unofficial religion
ultimate concern
vernacular religion

I will not comment upon the various terms used, but notice in the list the term 'Invisible Religion', used by Thomas Luckman (1967); 'Natural Religion', used by the philosopher David Hume (1779); 'Secular Religion' and 'Civil Religion', terms used by R. N. Bellah and others in the 1960s; the expression 'Unconscious Religion', used by Mircea Eliade (1958); and Paul Tillich's (1959) expression, 'Ultimate Concern'. In addition to these well-known terms, there are various expressions that seem to mean, 'This is not quite Religion, but it is something like Religion'. In terms such as those we have on this list, Implicit Religion contrasts with Explicit Religion. Explicit Religion seems to require choice, and awareness, and the exercise of will, and self-labelling by the actor. In contrast, that which is Implicit Religion is so-named by the observer, and might be denied by the actor. The notion of Implicit Religion may thus be considered as an explanatory frame of understanding for a wide variety of human phenomena.

Let me give what I myself regard as an extreme example of the inappropriate use of religious frames of explanation being used to describe a secular phenomenon. The researcher gathered his data by participant observation when working for 400 hours behind the bar, serving drinks in an English pub. The general methodological procedures were drawn from anthropology. The researcher's description of the building and its furnishings reads like the description of a place of worship, with liturgical significance ascribed to the entrance, to the bar itself with its pumps and shelves of multi-coloured bottles, and to the door between two sections of the public bar. The priestly functions of the barman are considered as he greets customers, serves them with drinks, and at the end of the evening tells them to go to their homes. The pub is analysed as if it were an institution parallel to the Church, or as a rival to the Church. The commercial business of buying a drink of beer is described as a 'semi-sacrificial transaction'.

In order that I might emphasise the extent to which the notion of Implicit Religion is being used in a very broad and diffuse manner, it will be useful if I remind you of a writer who gives a much more restricted conceptualisation of Religion. In the first chapter of his book, The Scientific Study of Religion, J. Milton Yinger (1970) suggests that it is functional definitions of religion that are the most useful kinds of definition for social scientists. He does not think that individual systems of belief can be described as Religion, because he regards a complete religion as a social phenomenon. Yinger does not seem to be sure whether non-theistic systems of belief may be called Religion, although he indicates that something which is 'A Way of Life' may be studied as if it were a religion.

Yinger commends as an excellent functional definition of religion the list of defining features given by the anthropologist Clifford Geertz: "A religion is a system of symbols which act to establish powerful, pervasive, and long-lasting moods and motivations in men, by formulating conceptions of a general order of existence, and clothing these conceptions with such an aura of factuality that the moods and motivations seem uniquely realistic." (Clifford Geertz, in Banton, 1966:4)

Yinger then re-casts this rather abstract verbal definition of religion in the form of a four-cell matrix, and shows that various forms of religion, having different emphases, may be allocated amongst the various cells of the matrix. Clearly, this is a much more sophisticated conceptualisation of the term Religion than we find amongst those who are using in their research the notion of Implicit Religion or one of its synonyms. It is a conceptualisation which is much more likely to provide the researcher with limits and borders to the subject-matter of his investigations.

In advocating a more careful and close relation between Psychology of Religion research and concepts developed within general psychology, of course I have in mind such notions as those expounded by Yinger. Other relevant concepts from general psychology are the concept of the development of Self-Identity, which can be explored without any reference to the supernatural, and which may be considered wholly in terms of its functional effects. And other useful approaches could, I suppose be drawn from concepts used to study social perception; explanation of behaviour in terms of attitudes, or in terms of roles; or even attempts to find biological and neurological explanations of behaviour. What is in my mind, I suppose, is the larger question of whether Psychology of Religion has an independent existence or whether, for healthy growth, it must

47

acknowledge itself to be the branch of a tree: a tree on which it must depend for its sustainence.

I am suggesting that those who are at present using such frames of explanation as the notion of Implicit Religion are constraining their understanding of the phenomena. I am also suggesting that they are imposing upon the data an explanatory model which is necessarily rooted in a world-view which is itself religious, and specifically Christian. This is to root the psychological study of religion in a world-view which differs markedly from the general materialistic and deterministic assumptions of the mainstream of the scientific community at large, and of academic psychology. I see this as a serious problem for the Psychology of Religion.

Of course there is one kind of psychological study of religion which is indeed rooted in a religious world-view, namely Religious Psychology as it exists within some Christian churches. But Religious Psychology seems to be a branch of Pastoral Theology. It seems to be intended to be practical and useful for the great spiritual mission of the Church, and such a Religious Psychology must owe its prime allegiance to the universe of ideas we call Theology. In contrast, general Psychology as it has developed in universities during the past century owes its prime allegiance to a more free and dynamic universe of ideas current in the broad scientific community, and to philosophies which have now largely abandoned any notion of the supernatural. If I were to try to argue this assertion, I would extend the argument beyond science and psychology, and point out that the world-view of the vast majority of people in the developed western world is one which is shaped by the assumptions of industry and commerce in urban communities. The world-view of most westerners today, as inferred from their behaviour, is not rooted in theology, and it is not as it was in agricultural communities subject to the uncontrolable forces of nature and to the changing seasons. For today's world of industry and commerce, as for the scientific community, Religion is irrelevant. The great faith and belief of industry and commerce (as in the scientific community) is faith and belief in the possibility of prediction and control over the material world and over human life. In the present century, perhaps ordinary people now believe that they may be able to control their lives without supernatural aid. Thus Religion is separated from ordinary life.

Consider the example of a psychologist using the notion of Implicit Religion to study the daily life of people living in a typical urban community. He will assume that there must be there to be discovered an Invisible Religion, even though perhaps only ten percent of the population practice any form of Explicit Religion. He will assume that the people in his sample must have ultimate concerns, which direct their lives. It will be very difficult for the psychologist of Implicit Religion to accept a

48

possibility that modern urban men and women may be living their lives without an Invisible Religion, and without the direction given by Ultimate Concerns. That they may be living from day to day in a pragmatic manner. He will assume that if they have no Invisible Religion, then they will inevitably be burdened by a terrible Angst, by anxiety and remorse for what he himself perceives as the emptiness of their lives.

If such a psychologist approaches his research with frames of categorisation and analysis given by the notion of Implicit Religion, then he will be tempted to impose upon the data a particular world-view without acknowledging the possibility that this world-view might be falsified. In the general scientific community, in contrast, the assumptions and frames of understanding are acknowledged to be tentative and falsifiable, subject to later correction fundamentally. In making these remarks, I am echoing the theme opened to us by Professor Laurie Brown earlier this afternoon, when he emphasised the importance of theory in the Psychology of Religion, so neglected by much American psychometrics.

Here is an example of a categorisation of types of Religion devised by one group of sociological researchers in a large English city:

1 Official religon
2 Common religon
3 Invisible religion
4 Surrogate religion

In the first category of Official religion they placed conventional Christian church membership, with denominations, sects and organised cults. Also Civil religion (such features of life as might be seen in displays of patriotism), and Folk religion – by which they meant rites-of-passage and customs such as Mothering Sunday.

In the second category of Common religion they included superstitious practices connected with good luck and bad luck, as well as behaviour connected with the ideas of fate, providence, astrology, palmistry, ghosts, and déjà vu.

Their third category of Invisible religion was concerned with the various themes of central concern and central meaning to life, and here they used the ideas of Thomas Luckman.

Finally, their fourth category of Surrogate religion was a miscellaneous category which included things that were all-absorbing interests. For example, football of Marxism or psycho-analysis. The researchers said that they thought these four categories could include all forms of religiosity, at least in western culture.

At the time when this categorisation of Religion was made, in 1982, the researchers were concentrating on conceptual problems, and they had gathered no empirical data, although they were planning to study Religion in some 2000 adults, and conduct detailed interviews with 100 adults – so it was a substantial piece of work. The general aim of the research was to consider the social significance of Religion in the particular English city. When seeking manifestations of religiosity, the researchers had to devise some operational definition of Religion. Of course they included Explicit Religion (category 1), but they also included all beliefs, practice and experience having some supernatural reference. Thus the supernatural content became a crucial feature of their operational definition of Religion. A great problem for these researchers was that of deciding on the boundaries of their field of study. Where should it end? Should all life in the city be their interest? Eventually they decided to include some social phenomena that were obviously important to the lives of many people in the city – such as football. But (even in Britain) football has no supernatural reference, so it may only be regarded as Religion in a metaphorical sense. Their adoption of a supernatural content in their definition of Religion did provide them with a boundary to the subject-matter of their study, but this decision merely delayed the problem. Sociologists and anthropologists seem to have continual difficulty in defining the supernatural, as do psychologists.

I wonder whether it would have been better for these researchers to have taken a more narrow definition of Religion, one which excluded the notion of Implicit Religion. This would have brought advantages. They could then have focussed more clearly on testing hypotheses, such as those suggested by the advocates of a secularisation thesis (Bryan Wilson 1961, 1982, or Peter Berger, 1967.). For example, the hypothesis that those who adhere to an Explicit Religion have their daily lives influenced by that religion. Also the question to what extent their daily lives might be influenced by the world-view of the scientific community perculating down into the thought-patterns of ordinary people. Do ordinary people nowadays, and not only those who are trained scientists, expect empirical verification of beliefs? If they do, then they have a world-view very different from that of their ancestors.

The possibility that the pre-suppositions of most people's thinking in the western world have become materialistic and atheistic has important implications for the Psychology of Religion. For example, it must consider whether Religion is largely meaning-less for most western men and women today, so that they may use religious ways of thought only if they abandon temporarily their normal and habitual modes of thinking.

It may be that those psychologists who utilise the notion of Implicit Religion are attempting to do in Psychology what the various Death-of-God theologians attempted to do in the 1960s: writers such as Paul van Buren (1963), Harvey Cox (1965), William Hamilton and Thomas Altizer (1966). Those psychologists and social scientists who are using the notion of Implicit Religion seem to be unwilling to abandon Religion. They are not willing to explain human behaviour and relationships wholly by means of secular and scientific frames of understanding. Instead, they retain religious frames of understanding, and even explain what some might say is clearly not religious in such terms. A weakness of this procedure is that it limits understanding because its assumptions must be dictated by Theology.

The implication throughout this paper is that the Psychology of Religion will be most healthy, vigorous and productive if it is inseparably part of the broader scientific universe of ideas. Also that the broad scientific community utilises conceptual frameworks rather different from those within which traditional Christianity flourished. There seems to be little or no place for the concept of the supernatural (or rather, Divinity) in the scientific universe of ideas. As a scientific endevour, Religious Psychology – a sub-division of Pastoral Theology – is obsolete. Consider the phenomenon of meditation. In the past, studied and analysed and explained within a religious framework of ideas, today it might better be understood wholly in secular terms. 'Transcendental meditation', both as it developed as a form of therapy, and also as psychologists have studied the phenomenon, might provide a good example for this line of argument.

The suggestion that psychologists of Religion should abandon conceptualisations which use the notion of the supernatural is by no means revolutionary. The often-used categorisation of Religion proposed by Glock and Stark (1965) could be used without reference to the supernatural. Glock and Stark do refer to the supernatural, and they do use the term 'God' when they attempt to provide a definition of Religion. For these writers, "...some sense of contact with a supernatural agency" is a defining feature of religious experience. (1965:4) But if one reads further, it seems that their position is rather weak. They say that a behaviour or experience becomes religious if the actor claims it to be religious: "...events or feelings are only religious experiences if a person defines them as such.... Many of the events we shall be discussing are most often not given religious definitions by persons these days. We are not, then, concerned with such events in themselves, but only when someone attaches to them some sense of contact with the supernatural." (1965:42)

Now I will say something about Implicit Religion which is rather more positive and constructive. Since the publication of Thomas Luckman's book in 1967, there has been considerable interest amongst sociologists and others in his general aim of trying to make Invisible Religion visible. So many researchers have developed an interest in the matter that these terms must refer to some important feature of life in modern western society. The question is whether these features of society are most usefully conceptualised as relatively un-institutionalised and as private types of Religion or whether it would be better to describe such behaviour in other terms.

Those whose studies make use of such terms as 'Implicit Religion' commonly work from an assumption that in the modern world religion has not declined, but instead it has undergone radical change. Whereas in the past there was a close connection between personal response to religious symbols and the relevance of religious belief and symbols to everyday life; today, these two aspects of religion (vision, experience, the numinous, and practice) may be largely independent. One may see the disjunction whenever there is some great public controversy in which religion might have a place, such as argument about euthanasia, or abortion, or the level of taxation appropriate to provide for social services. In most such public controversy, one can see a clash of institutional positions, but little connection with the mystical roots of Religion, and with the individual and social experience of being religious.

A further example. Consider the hedonistic life-style or 'funseeking' practical philosophy which seems to be the ultimate concern of many young people on the west coast of the United States. One could say that Fun-seeking is not a New Religious Movement because it lacks institutional features. Those who are part of the Fun-seeking phenomenon are perhaps looking for secular 'peak experiences' comparable to the ecstatic experiences of some religions. One might explore the hypothesis that the disenchantement and alienation of modern urban life provide conditions for the emergence of a search for transcendental experiences. One might argue that it is such a desire for transcendance and for ecstacy that stimulates participation in many New Religious Movements, and also in the American Fun-seeking cult. One psychologist or social scientist might study such a Fun-seeking life-style in secular terms, using notions of Role or Self-Identity. But others clearly think that the phenomenon is best conceptualised in terms of some kind of Implicit or Invisible Religion. It follows from their general (unexamined) presupposition that radical change is taking place in the shape of religion that such a social phenomenon must be regarded as religious.

I am not sufficiently familiar with the experimental work that Jan van der Lans began here at Nijmegen in the 1970s on the function of meditation as a technique for inducing religious experiences, but perhaps these experiments would provide a further test of my argument. If a psychologist experiments with meditation techniques, why should he expect that the resulting experiences in his subjects will be religious? Is there good reason for labelling these experiences 'religious', and for using terminologies and categories of Religion rather than those of general Psychology to describe the results?

In a paper read to the Nijmegen conference in 1982, Antoine Vergote noted that Religion, and religious behaviour, are largely ignored by general psychologists, and he asked Why should there be such neglect? A good question. Psychology of Religion is, after all, one of the oldest fields of study in the whole history of Psychology. Dr. Verghote suggested that the personal unbeliefs and attitudes of many general psychologists may account for this lack of regard for the Psychology of Religion. He pointed out that there is something odd about the conventional scientific attitude to the Psychology of Religion, in that a stance of personal neutrality or abstinence is considered to be important on the part of the researcher. Yet when a psychologist researches into Art-experience or into Sexual Behaviour, his own private involvement in these activities is acknowledged and accepted, providing his methodology accords with scientific criteria.

Part of my criticism of those who use notions of Implicit Religion has been that they are carrying their personal religious committment and world-view into their scientific work. They might reply that General Psychology greatly neglects the study of experience of any kind. Many psychologists prefer to study the intellectual concommitants and consequences of experience – such as attitudes. The study of attitudes gives more precise results because attitudes are more static than is Religious Experience, which is a dynamic process and so one very difficult to measure or to describe. It may be that those who explain their researches in terms of Implicit Religion might argue well that it is from their personal committment to Religion, and from their religious world-view that they gain the insights that enable them to recognise new forms which religion is taking in modern western society. But such a reply from the advocates of Implicit Religion could be a very circular line of argument.

I will end this discussion-paper by mentioning what I see as both a commendable feature of the notion 'Implicit Religion', but also a feature which is a problem. Psychometric and behaviouristic approaches to the Psychology of Religion have tended to identify Religion with the verbal, with the intellectual, and with explicit religious behaviour of the sort found in the conventional Christian churches. It must be admitted that these psychologists reflect aspects of Religion which are undoubtedly important in Christianity, and particularly in Protestant Christianity. One might say that 'belief' is important in Christianity to an extent that it is not in other religions, where 'being religious' refers primarily to ritual and to action rather than to intellectual understanding and to cognition.

A commendable feature of the work of social scientists using such notions as that of 'Implicit Religion' is that it shifts the focus of interest from Belief to Action and to Experience. But I think that there is a very real danger that by the term 'Implicit Religion' they are conceptualising a kind of quasi-Christianity. So they will analyse whatever experience they identify as religious in terms that are Christian. Their psychology would perhaps be the stronger if they were to extend the notion of Implicit Religion to include implicit cosmologies wholly secular and atheistic, and completely without ritual. Perhaps they might acknowledge that the underlying phenomena of their studies are those fundamental assumptions in people's lives which direct their lives, yet which are very seldom made explicit, or formulated, or examined: the taken-for-granted elements of a world-view. But if so, then I myself would prefer them to abandon the world 'Religion' altogether.

It may be that those who favour the term 'Implicit Religion' have accepted without examination Thomas Luckman's hypothesis that Religion has not declined, but has merely changed in form. Yet even Luckman did not use the notion of 'Invisible Religion' in an unrestricted or loose manner. For example, when writing of conversion, he said ..."It is only within the religious community... that conversion can be maintained as plausible.... To have a conversion experience is nothing much. The real thing is to be able to keep on taking it seriously; to retain a sense of its plausibility. THIS is where the religious community comes in. It provides the indispensible plausibility structure for the new reality." (Berger and Luckman 1966:37)

In many of the studies of Implicit Religion, attention is given to a description of the so-called religious experience, but the plausibility-structure within which the experience gains meaning and continuing life is either ignored, or is imposed by the researcher.

Literature

Bailey, E. The Religion of a Secular Society. Unpublished Ph.D thesis. University of Bristol, 1976.

Banton, M. (Ed.). Anthropological approaches to the study of religion. New York: Frederick A. Praeger Inc., 1966.

Bellah, R.N. Beyond Belief: essays on religion in a post-traditional world. New York: Harper and Row, 1970.

Berger, P.L. The Sacred Canopy: elements of a sociological theory of religion. New York: Doubleday and Co. Inc., 1967.

Berger, P.L., & Luckman, T. The Social Construction of Reality. Baltimore Maryland: Penguin Books, 1966.

Buren, P. van. The secular meaning of the Gospel. New York: Macmillan, 1963.

Cox, H. The Secular City. London: Student Christian Movement Press, 1965.

Eliade, M. Patterns in comparative religion. London: Sheed and Ward, 1958.

Glock, C. Y., & Stark, R. Religion and society in tension. Chicago: Rand McNally, 1965.

Hamilton, W., & Altizer, T.J.J. Radical theology and the death of God. Indianaopolis: The Bobbs-Merrill Co., Inc., 1966.

Hume, D. Dialogues concerning natural religion. London: Fontana, (1779) 1963.

Luckman, T. The invisible religion. London: Collier-Macmillan, 1967.

Tillich, P. Theology of culture. New York: Oxford University Press, 1959.

Wilson, B. Religion in a secular society. London: Watts, 1966.

Wilson, B. Religion in sociological perspective. Oxford: Oxford University Press, 1982.

Yinger, J. M. The scientific study of religion. London: Collier-Macmillan, 1970.

The attitude towards tradition and religion – some psychological aspects of the process of identification.

J. Szmyd
Institute Nauk Spolecznyk, Cracow

I) The subject of the present paper belongs to the extended research area of psychology of religion. Within the said subject the author takes up certain aspects of the identification process taking place, on the one hand, in the attitude towards religion and a religious experience, and, on the other hand, in the attitude towards tradition and subjective experiencing of tradition. It is assumed that the comparative analysis of the attitude towards religion, taking into consideration the identification process within the structure of this phenomenon, as well as an analysis of the attitude towards tradition, open up additional, so far not fully utilized possibilities for a scientific clarification of several aspects of both religiousness and tradition per se.

Let me explain the meaning of basic concepts included into the present paper, namely the concepts of "tradition", and "identification", "attitude towards religion", and "attitude towards tradition".

Let us commence our clarification from the concept of "tradition". Following the accepted assumption that psychology of religion is interested in the place and role of tradition within the structure and functioning of a religious personality, in lives and behaviour of religiously inclined individuals and communities, including, among others, the correlation between the process of subjective experiencing of tradition and a religious experience, our main interest here will be focused upon such an understanding of the notion of tradition which treats it as a certain kind of a mental process, sees this phenomenon as it is reflected in an individual or collective psyche, takes into consideration above all the functional aspect of tradition, and relates it chiefly to the sphere of inherited values and life roles, norms and behavioral patterns, modes of reasoning and experiencing, models of perception and emotional reactions. Let us quote two examples of such an understanding of the term "tradition". One of them is the concept of the so-called "cultural heritage", formulated by Stanislaw Ossowski, Polish sociologist of the second quarter of the 20th century. The other is the notion of tradition as developed by a Swedish psychologist of religion, Hjalmar Sundén, and some of his followers.

S. Ossowki made his concept of "cultural heritage" include the patterns of behavior, feelings and reasoning with a varying degree of specificity. The notion encompasses, on the one hand, "certain tentative patterns of behavior in various situations, certain "style of living", ethic norms, general predilections, ways of reasoning". On the other hand, the cultural heritage" disposes us to have certain experiences, passing to us particular opinions, notions, images and sequences of images", or even "types of muscular or emotional reactions to particular gestures or words, or to particular psysical objects which are preserved by a given community" (1).

A characteristic property of the cultural heritage is the handing down of patterns of experiences with concrete contents which are positively evaluated and rendered objective in the lives of individuals and communities (2).

This handing down, as it has been emphasized by Max Scheler, and later by a famous theologian Yves Congar, occurs by way of nondiscursive communication means, i.e. by various symbols, models, behavior patterns, experiences, situations and existential facts, natural patterns of reasoning and feeling, etc., and the reception of the message is generally unconscious, automatic, and imitative (3).

H. Sundén, making a distinction between general and religious tradition, singles out the latter as a system of roles and situations determining specified interactions between a human being and a god. These roles fulfil an important function in the process of structuralization of perceptions of the reality in individuals accepting these perceptions, and in the process of shaping their life orientation. The religious tradition, expressed in the fullest way in holy texts, the Bible and other religious writings, also includes certain dogmas and moral norms. The above mentioned components of the religious tradition perform, as it has been demonstrated by Sundén (4) and confirmed by other Swedish scientists (5), an important function in the lives and personality changes of religious individuals, especially in the case of deeply religious people inclined towards mysticism, like, for example, Theresa of Avila, St.Birgitta, Augustine Aurelius, John Wesley, etc (6).

Let us proceed to the notion of an attitude.

The attitude towards tradition and religion is understood here as an emotional-appraising and intellectual approach to the object of an attitude, in the case of the attitude towards tradition to its specified content, for example to the values and roles handed down by the past; in the case of the attitude towards religion to its religious content, e.g. to God, or Church, as well as a readiness or predisposition to a specific behavior, determined by such an approach (7). This relatively broad definition of the concept of "attitude" also includes a narrower understanding of the term, i.e. as a relatively stable, acquired inclination to behave in a specific way towards certain individuals, objects, in certain situations, etc (8). We are selecting here the broader definition of the term, believing that it will be of greater avail in studies on tradition and religiousness, including the investigations of the process of identification with the domain of objects of tradition and religion.

Let me present the notion of identification as accepted in the present paper. Identification is a dynamic mental structure, expressed in a strong intellectual-emotional and intentional bond with a specified object, along with a high degree of oneness with the said object. This object can be personal, e.g. a particular person; social – e.g. a particular social group; cultural – as certain norms and patterns; institutional – e.g. selected social, political, religious organizations; ideological – e.g. certain values, ideals, etc. Identification, usually leading to a considerable degree of oneness with its object, is based upon numerous complex psychological processes and mechanisms, among others on the processes of internalization, acceptance as one's own of external values, opinions, behavioral patterns, norms, ideals, etc., irradiations of feelings and thoughts, transfer of emotional and cognitive attitudes from one object to another, introjection, incorporation of a picture of another individual or object into one's own "self", uncritical adoption of alien evaluations and interpretations and their treatment as one's own. Identification is also supported by such mechanisms as projection, unintentional subjectivization of external contents and signals; adscription to others of one's own feelings and motives, displaced to the subconsciousness, autoidentification, a sense and self-knowledge of one's own identity, an attitude of subordination, imitation, and numerous other mental processes and mechanisms (9).

The identification bond is usually related to an inclination towards emotional reactions to all the situations pertaining to the object with which the subject identifies himself. It also specifies a certain individual scope of choices, motivations and behaviors (10).

In truth, the identification process denotes a complex, social-psychological phenomenon the essence of which is not only, as it is commonly believed, an emotional phenomenon, but also cognitive and behavioral ones. In view of its structure, identification is related to the concept of an attitude, here the three-stratum structure plays a decisive role, but they are by no means identical. The difference between the two phenomena lies both in their semantic scope, the notion "attitude" is much broader in its scope in comparison to the concept of identification, and in their character and functions. Identification is present only in certain types of attitudes, in attitudes decisively positive. It complements certain elements of these attitudes, mostly their cognitive-emotional and behavioral components.

2) Let us present the characteristic features and properties of a typical attitude towards tradition, consisting in experiencing elements of the past which are positively evaluated and accepted in order to meet

specified inner needs. Such an attitude, considered here as a model, is generally characterized by the following:
- assignment of additional values to past events and objects, individuals and their achievements; adscription of the properties of goodness, beauty, and sublimity;
- specific hierarchization of elements of tradition wherein the priority is given to these which have been positively evaluated, and the ones that have not received such an evaluation are relegated to farther places;
- a tendency towards rendering traditional individuals mystical along with the adscription of the properties of extraordinariness, special importance and loftiness, charisma and holiness, (the so-called "sacredness of the past");
- an inclination towards idealization of people of the past and towards seeking in them examples for following;
-- an inclination towards identification with traditional models of behavior, roles and life situations;
- search for guidelines for solving contemporary moral and existential problems;
- a sense of respect, attachment, or even pietism towards all that the tradition encompasses; suggestive, emotional, and oftentimes non-reflective reception.

Furthermore, the attitude towards tradition is characterized by specific escapism, a flight from every-day troubles and burdens, from dangers and difficult problems of contemporary life, from the lack of sense and perspectives characteristic of the world as it has been found; a quasi-romantic inclination towards the idealized past, a specific "paradise lost", combined with a belief in the possibilities of finding the sought mainstay, support, and, at the same time, some instruction, advise, or, in other words, of discovering all that one lacks here and now, and what the future does not promise.

Numerous specified features and properties of the positive attitude towards tradition, the "traditionalistic" attitude, can be also adscribed, as it follows from empiric studies, to the religious attitude. However, here they gain, as it will be discussed later, a specific tinge and peculiarity.

Despite the differences in the objects of the two attitudes they demonstrate certain shared properties within their emotional, behavioral, and partly intellectual components. Briefly speaking, what is meant here is the common emotional dependence of the subject upon the object of the attitude. This dependence triggers certain susceptibility to suggestion on the part of the object's content; it facilitates the emergence of states of specific compliance and docility, a decrease in the level of criticism, soundness of judgement and evaluation. It releases the sense of pietism, and creates the possibilities for development of hasty beliefs in grandeur, magnificence and beauty of the specifically experienced values.

Such an experience is to a certain extent determined by the structure of the object of the two akin attitudes. Namely, both the objects include values most often originating in various historical periods and places, from diversified achievements and creative subjects. Yet these elements are placed in an extra-temporal and extra-spatial order, an order which is in a way universal and absolute. This extra-temporal and extra-spatial character, universality of the internally harmonious and distilled up to the point of its essence structure of the value which at the same time lies beyond any individual, triggers in the subject of the discussed attitudes among others a sense of their fulfilment, perfectness, dignity, or even sacredness. This, in turn, produces as a result the above mentioned specific emotional states.

The objects of the compared attitudes also reveal such properties which in a particular way influence the sphere of human behavior and thought. Especially important here is the fact that their contents include in a way crystallized data originating from various scientific disciplines and ancient wisdom, important situations and life roles, suggestive galleries of personal examples, personified ideals, principles and norms of behavior, well-tested archetypes of basic modes of feeling, practical reasoning and acting. Such a character of the two attitudes results in their operating as a system of life guideposts, moral examples, or as a "prefiguration" for the forms of actual thinking and feeling.

Our attention is drawn to the similarity of social-civilizational determinants of the processes influencing an increase and identification of interests in values originating from tradition and religion. There interests are generally intensified, what finds its confirmation among others in the most recent history of social relationships in Poland, in the face of a crisis in the priority order of values and basic regulatory mechanisms of the collective life, when the historically shaped ethos and custom are weakened, when the collective and individual existence are endangered. In such turning moments there usually emerges an intensified need for a flight both to tradition and to religion. This need rises most likely from the natural tendency of the man to preserve the continuity of the community he lives in, to maintain his individual identity, to ensure the individual existence and its subjective autonomy.

Let us proceed to the similarity between the psychological functions of the attitude towards tradition and the religious attitude. Both the attitudes meet a certain sphere of human existential needs. Their objects constitute a specific reference area for the man's aspirations and explorations, and sometimes also a place he escapes to from the reality. In a way, these subjects create a substitute for the real world. In particular, both the attitudes give similar, though not identical answers to the basic existentional problem, i.e. to the problem of finiteness. Within tradition and religion the man is able to find a specific continuation of his limitations in time; in tradition – in the retrospective, and in religion in the prospective directions. Both these fields provide a plane for intentional transcendention beyond the dimensions of time and space, beyond the boundaries of the present day and real possibilities. In tradition and religion the man can find a similar means for conquering his own time and human transience. In both fields he faces extra-temporal values, experiences his sense of belonging to and even certain identification with the world, which transgresses beyond the boundaries of time. Experiencing intensely these extra-temporal values, as, for example, during emotional participation in ceremonies and mysteries, or in religious mystic and ecstatic exaltations, the man has a subjective sense of crossing the boundaries of the realm of time and forming a specific union with the forces triumphing over the transience and death, thus fulfilling the so-called "yearning for the absolute" (11).

The afore, mentioned function of religion and tradition is related to further functions of the said phenomena. Both the fields can evoke in the man who experiences them a sense of specific rooting, dignity and festivity, characteristic sublimity and solemn bond with the object of the experience (12).

3) Let us pay attention to certain specific properties of the identification process as occurring in the attitude towards tradition in comparison to the specific character of this process in the religious attitude.
a) The object of the identification relation in the attitude towards tradition is chiefly constituted by homocentric contents in the form of particular human accomplishments, norms, examples, roles, etc. In the majority of cases, however, they are of an objective, depersonalized character, being in a way distilled from the subjective element. In consequence, the relation to these contents is quite often not of an interpersonal and closely intimate character. On the other hand, the identification relation in the religious attitude in numerous instances assumes an interpersonal character and individual tinge, since in this relation the main fiducial point is a personally understood god, let us disregard here religions that do not utilize the concept of a personalized god, and, in any case, what is meant here is a contact directed towards immanent and personal goals, i.e. the goal of life, personal immortality, etc. This is not an absolute difference, since in the attitude towards tradition there also appear moments of personal reference, and in the attitude towards religion there is also a place for extra-personal and intersubjective references. What is involved here is the difference in the

degree of intensity of the personal and subjective element in the two attitudes in question; in the attitude towards tradition the intensity of this element is usually lower in comparison to the religious attitude.

b) The consequence of the previously discussed peculiarity of the identification relations characteristic of the two attitudes is, in turn, certain specificity of the emotional and cognitive aspects of the identification bond occurring in these attitudes. In the emotional content of the identification relation when referred to the traditional content there prevail non-intense feelings, generally characterized by an introvert inclination, such as a sense of order, peace, harmony, filiation, spiritual affinity, a sense of continuation, etc. (13)   On the other hand, in the relation of identification with religious contents there dominate intense feelings, generally characterized by extrovert inclinations, as, for example, love, fear, humbleness, hope, pietism, surrender, trust, yearning, etc. Yet the role and place of these feelings depend within the two idenfification relations types upon diversified factors, including among others the scope of the identification object and the way it is understood. In the religious relation these feelings are among others dependent upon the understanding of "sacrum" and its domineering property. For example, if one regards "tremendum" as such a property, the relation will be characterized by fear, humbleness, etc. Should, on the other hand, the domineering property in the religious object be "fascinosum", such a relation will in turn reveal the feelings of trust, yearning, and above all of love (14).

Also within the identification relation in the attitude towards tradition, the structure and character of its emotional content is influenced among others by the mode of understanding of the indentification object, for instance in dependence of whether the prevailing elements in the object are of a normative-regulatory or personal-axiological character, and whether the formation of the identification object is undertaken from the standpoint of a pre-civilization mentality or of a mind shaped under the influence of a highly-developed scientific-technical civilization.

c) Certain peculiar properties of the identification relations occurring in the analyzed attitudes is also manifested in mechanisms governing the acceptance of the elements of the identification object. The elements of the object of tradition are generally accepted in a non-reflective way, on the basis of the sense of filiation, and invoking mostly the criterion of ancientness, or, in other words, of conviction that a given fact used to be accepted in the past as a relatively autonomous criterion, the criterion of ancientness most frequently includes elements of charisma, sacredness, authority, goodness, etc. In the motivation for the acceptance of the object very often an individual need for tradition is revealed (15).   On the religious plane, the acceptance of the identification object is generally related to certain reflectivity, and it takes place, what is supported by psychological literature dealing with the religious experience, on the basis of more complex criteria and slightly different needs of a human being.

d) The identification with given elements of tradition or religion is of a superior order in comparison to tradition or religion themselves, since they are both utilized here as means or media. This superior domain includes the sphere of human endeavors at controlling the reality or the existence, attempts at shrinking the distance to the world and at overcoming the sense of "solitude in the universe", efforts at grasping the sense and place of an individual existence in the world and at bridging the gap between the every-day life and "festivity", transcience and "eternity", etc. Nevertheless, one can observe certain differences in following this tendency in the attitude towards tradition in comparison to the religious attitude. In the former the prevailing element consists in practical reproduction or copying of certain models originating from tradition, whereas, in contrast to the religiously fulfilled union with the universe, the word, meditation and contemplation occupy lesser places. This phenomenon can be adequately exemplified by the type of the relation between an individual and the world that can be encountered in traditional cultures where the relation is fulfilled in a unverbal way and is defined during concrete activities of a more or less customary or ritual character, including also productive activities, e.g. harvesting.

e) Another characteristic property of the analyzed identification relations in tradition is in the most part directed towards the past, whereas the identification relation in religion or in the so-called mythologies of redemption or saving – predominantly to the future. The former occurs among others as a result of a need for an union with people of the past, for sharing opinions with those who in the ancient times experienced the same "mental states"; thus, it is directed retrospectively. The latter takes place as a result of dreams of a better life, conscious or unconscious attempts at a release from the limitations imposed by the present day, and is directed towards the future. Therefore, the religious relation displays numerous features characteristic of a bond with an object of an utopia, what follows from a connection of religion with utopia as such. And thus, utopia or its certain forms is an integral component of almost any religion, and especially of a religious consciousness. Various types of utopias are meant here, including specifically the so-called "escapist", "flight", or "heroic", "reconstruction" utopias with their division into "utopias of time", "utopias of place", and "utopias of eternal order". (16) There is a striking similarity in the genesis, internal mechanisms and functions of the afore mentioned utopias and religions. Both the utopias and the religious form of thought follow from similar needs and endeavors

63

of the man; they constitute similar orders and types of values, and jointly, though not in the same measure, fulfil similar goals, dreams, and yearnings of the man. To be more precise, they enable him to escape from the troubles of the real world, creating an independent substitute world where a human being finds a relief and peace; they constitute a peculiar sanctuary for the preservation of the loftiest ideals and values, a sanctuary situated in "utopian" time and "utopian" space. in other words, both utopias and religions make it possible to communicate with another world, better than the one the man has to live in; they also give a certain basis for dreams about such a world. They idealize the past and the future, dividing the stream of time into "good times" and "bad times", and projecting the man towards the "good times". Religions and utopias alike share also the fact that they constitute a specific method of crossing in time and space the borders of the reality, of transcending into the sphere of intentions, imagination, dreams and wishes. If one assumes that specific dreams of the man include the dream about starting his life anew, away from all that was and is, "the dream of wings", and the dream about happiness that can be achieved in the reality with no need to struggle for its transformation, "the dream of roots", then religions and utopias are just a way of fulfilling these dreams.

4) The above characterization has not exhausted, obviously, all the specific features of the identification relations in the attitudes towards tradition and religion. The properties that have been included into the analysis have been treated only in an introductory way. Our goal has not been, as it has been previously mentioned, to present a broad spectrum of these properties and to analyze them in a detailed way, but rather to give a sketchy presentation to some of them, selected for the review as examples and according to the criterion of being typical. This sketch of specific properties of the identification relation selected in such a way and compared in the present communication has been aimed at serving not only cognitive, but also heuristic and methodological purposes. Namely, its goal has been to show certain additional, so far not fully utilized, research area for psychology of religion and interdisciplinary empirical studies on religiousness, and also to make a preliminary evaluation of cognitive abilities of psychology of religion and other religion-related disciplines in this field. The aim, understood in such a way, has been accomplished. It has appeared that, firstly, the problem of identification belongs to significant for the cognitive viewpoint problems of sciences of religion and religiousness, including psychology of religion, and, secondly, the problem of identification by its very nature constitutes an integral element of social and psychological sciences, yet it has not been so far studied in a broader and more systematic way by these disciplines, what

is particularly apparent in psychological sciences. Thirdly, the problem of identification at the same time belongs to the subject matter of sciences of religions, but also here it has not been sufficiently probed into, as it might be expected. Among others, an acute need is perceived for studies on identification undertaken in the field of psycholgy of religion. As the fourth item one should say that identification, understood as a specific social-psychological process, is based upon several sociological and psychological mechanisms, and determined by a broad spectrum of social-historical, cultural and subjective factors which are distinctly visible and can be scientifically described in comparative studies on this process, e.g. in comparative studies on the identification relation in the attitude towards tradition, the preliminary attempt at which has been presented in this paper. And finally, the psychological analysis of the identification process in the attitude towards tradition and in the religious and other attitudes yields significant cognitive effects, both in regard to the very attitudes, and to much broader phenomena which the attitudes are included into, as, for example, with respect to the phenomenon of tradition and religiousness. To be more precise, the analysis makes, or can make, a contribution on the one hand to a better understanding of the specific character and structure of these attitudes, and, on the other hand, it allows for placing them on the level of a mechanism which is more extensive and subordinate in relation to the subjective functions of tradition and religion, i.e. on the level of the mechanism controlling fundamental, existential-metaphysical relation of the man to the existence, to the biological and socio-cultural reality. At the same time it allows for such a theoretical approach to the essence and basic function of tradition and religion, according to which these phenomena belong to specific instruments the man uses to adapt to the reality, instruments to which the man generally appeals when other means of broadly understood adaptation and homeostasis fail (17).

Literature

1. Ossowski, S. Wiez spoleczne i dziedzictwo krwi Social bond and blood_heritage. Warsaw: Dziele Collected Works (2 vols.). Warsaw: 1968.

2. Szacki, J.T. Przeglad problematyki Tradition. A review of problems. Warsaw: 1971.

3. Congar, Y. The Meaning of Tradition. New York, 27-29.

4. Sundén, H.J. Teresa fräu Avilla och religions psykoligien, Uppsala 1971e Den heliga Birgitta, Stockholm: 1973; Some remarks on St. Augustin's Confessioness IX, 4 in the light of role – psychology. In: Proceedings of the Colloquy of European psychologists of religion, Nijmegen: 1979.

5. Källstad, T.H. John Wesley and the Bible. A psychological study. Uppsala: 1976.

6. Szmyd, J. Psychologia religii Psychology of religion. Kraków: 1985.

7. Ekel, J., Jaroszynski, J., & Ostaszewska, J. Maly Slownik psychologiczny. A short dictionary of psychology. Warsaw: 1965.

8. Ekel, J., Jaroszynski, J., & Ostaszewska, J. Slownik psychologiczny Doctionary of psychology, (Ed.) Szewczuk, W. Warsaw, 106-215, and Maly Slownik psychologiczny A short dictionary of psychology, 45, 1079.

9. Marianski, J. Kosciól w apoleczenstwie przemyslowym The Church in the industrial society, Warsaw: 1983, chapter 2, "Formy przynaleznosci do Kosciola Forms of membership in the Church", par. 2, "Identyfikacja z Kosciolem w aspekcie psychologicznym Identification with the Church in the psychological aspect, 38-49.

10. Suchodolski, B. Kim Jest czlowiek Who is the man. Warsaw: 1980.

11. Goplan, S. Tradition: a social analysis. University of Madras, 1973.

12. Bloch, E. Vom Sinn der Tradition, (Ed.). Reinisch, L. Munich, 1970, Tradycja a nowoczesnosc Tradition and modernity, (Ed.). Kurczewska J., & Szacki, J.: Warsaw, 20-21, 1984.

13. Zdybicka, Z.J. Czlowiek i religia The man and religion. Lublin, 170-175, 1984.

14. Shils, E. Tradycja Tradition. Tradycja i nowowczesnosc Tradition and modernity, (Ed.). Kurczewska, J., & Szacki, J, 30-90.

15. Szacki, J. Spotkanie z utopia The meeting with Utopia, Warsaw: 48-99, 1980.

16. Cf. D. Elkind, The origins of religion in the child. Review of Religious Research, 1970, 1, 35-42. Dittes, J.E. Psychology of religion. In: The Handbook of Social Psychology. G. Londley and E. Aronson (eds). London: 1969. Maslow, A. Religious values and peak experiences. New York: 1970.

Two opposed viewpoints concerning the object of the psychology of religion. Introductory statements to the plenary debate.

Introduction by A. Vergote
Catholic University Leuven

I. Religion is not a worldview, even if there is an element of worldview in religion. The question as it is formulated contains a theoretical preconception which is falsified by the observation of religion.

I would first consider critically the formulation of the proposed question. The formulated opposition between "world-view-systems in general" and "restricted to..." brings religion within the general category of worldview. This is already a misleading interpretation. Admittedly there is a dimension of "worldview" in all religions, for they present a conception of the place of human being in this world and they set forward some ideas of the relation between the natural world and that which in some sense is a supernatural beyond the world. Historically religious representations are even the matrix of philosophy, of ethics and of today's worldviews.

But religions exceed the element worldview in them. They involve references to dynamic divine or, in any case, non natural and not human, somehow personal agencies who influence in some way the course of the world and of humanity. And religious behaviour corresponds to these conceptions in emotional relationships, in the symbolic actions of rituals, in prayers... If religion is encompassed within worldview-systems, it is restricted to only one of its dimensions. Religion in the strict sense is not a subspecies of worldviews in general.

The subsumption of religion under the general category of worldview is typical of the reductive modern western way of thinking. The rationalistic trend in our culture tends to make the rational mind (the logos) the core of the human being. W. Dilthey (1977) who forged the concept of worldview stresses the rational telos of this concept; a Weltanschauung tends to be conceived of in an abstract metaphysical form in order to be grounded and endowed with a general value. It is well known that, according to Hegel, religion is a system of "representational" knowledge that should be accomplished and surpassed in the system of "absolute", i.e. "conceptual" knowledge.

In the characterization of religion as a worldview there is a hidden theory of religion: the idea that religion has its origin in the speculative mind which asks questions about the world as totality. Or more flatly, in pseudo-scientific psychological concepts: that religion is born out of man's need for an all embracing, somehow systematic, knowledge of the world he is living in; a tourist-map for life. My contention is that we should refrain from including already an explanatory theory in the definition of the object of our discipline.

Freud elaborates a reductive interpretation of religion. But first he recognizes its specificity within the ensemble of cultural phenomena. He also explicitly states that it is the most complex one and that theoreticians of religion must not expect to be able to explain it by one factor. Discussing the concept of Weltanschauung, he thinks religion is a kind of it, but he admits that this interpretation does not allow an understanding of the connection between religion and ethical laws which are a constitutive dimension of it.

How then could prayer be brought within the category of a worldview? Nonetheless, on the basis of the factorial analysis of their results, the sociologists Glock and Stark (1965) conclude that "the ideological dimension" is the primary and, as has been shown, the most important and predicting dimension of religion, and they find this dimension typically expressed in prayer and devotion. "Ideology", which obviously is here synonymous with worldview, is actually an odd term for interpreting prayer! Man does not pray to ideas which are a more or less intellectual system established by human reason to organize its world. "Ideology" represents a typical logisization and neutralization of religious acts. In this line of thought, it could as well be said that love is an ideology. Indeed, love gives meaning to human existence and involves, consequently, a culturally variable content which is orientated and expressed by the idea people have of it. However, the theoretical terms of "meaningsystem", "worldview" or "ideology" do not grasp its existential specificity. By broadening its definition and applying the criticized categories the theorist would disregard the true nature of religion. The connection between meaning and religion is of course still more complex, as will be mentioned in statement 7.

II. The broadening of the object of psychology of religion is done for bad
   reasons and leads to absurdities.

A. There seem to be four reasons for the broadening of the definition of religion and consequently of the scope of psychology of religion.

1. While making a study of religion, the scientist is inclined to make the religious phenomenon congenial to his scientific mind. It is easier to construct rational theoretical concepts concerning religion, if it has first been reduced to the cognitive complex the individual is supposed to construct in order to interpret and to systematize his world. However, by its very nature psychology opposes the rationalistic reduction of human phenomena, for there is a psychology precisely because the human psyche

exceeds the _ratio_ in the strict sense.

2. A diffuse theological or philosophical preconception inclines some believing psychologists and - fewer - sociologists to consider man as a naturally religious being. A more or less conscious apologetic intention motivates their broadening of the definition of religion. They cannot accept that there are non-religious persons, and when they observe the fact, they think these persons have a hidden, an implicit or anonymous religion, which is ready to develop into an explicit religion if the religious message is freed from that which disfigures it. This fundamental postulate seems to me non justified.

3. Other people are convinced that the "traditional religions" are evanescing remainders of a cultural past and they interpret these religions as archaic forms of a general basic human disposition they then call religious in the broad sense. This preconception is also apologetic, be it that the intention goes in the opposite direction of the former group. The idea of secularization often involves a philosophy of history which imposes a necessary evolutionary law on humanity according to which the disappearance of "traditional religions" is equivalent to modernity. Short-term observations of the decline of religion in some areas seem to validate this philosophy of history and to justify consequently the broadening of the definition of religion. Sociologists are the leading figures in this way of thinking; as they employ statistics, their theory presents the face of empirical science. Unhappy psychologists of religion in particular let themselves be impressed by the apparently scientific prestige of this philosophy of history.

Some psychologists of religion indeed feel unhappy for two reasons. Firstly, in some settings their study of real religion catches only the interest of religious people; and when less people are religious, their psychology of religion is considered as outdated. Secondly, in a milieu which expects from psychology a contribution to efficacy and performance, the study of religion is less valued, but the magic words of worldview and meaning-systems still convey an ideological prestige.

4. In a pluralistic civilization, semi-official newsmedia develop a broad and confuse oecumenical language which places religion in the general category of worldview, next to non-religious worldviews. In a similar way they talk about religious and non-religious philosophy, whereas a philosophy is not a religion and a religion not a philosophy. This neutralizing language intends to show tolerance and respect for the different convictions. Unhappily this loose talk tends to form an official scientific tradition.

B. Two absurdities follow from the proposed broadening of the concept of religion.

1. One imposes religion on people who do not at all think their convictions and behaviour are religious, people who even feel betrayed by the religious interpretation of their conceptions. As Mr. Brown stated in his lecture, an external observer imposes on them the label of religion. I would add: he also denies them the right to be non-religious. Actually the observer who proceeds in this way is mostly a person who is himself not at ease with his departure from the religion of his own education. The observer can think he is right and understands the non-religious people better than they do themselves. But then he entangles himself the more in the second absurdity.

2. In the perspective of a broadened definition all is to be considered as religious, which means that nothing is. Just as when all expressions are called metaphorical there is no more a metaphor. We could apply to this broad conception of religion the mataphor of Pascal for God: a circle of which the center is everywhere and nowhere. If this paradoxical expression is a valuable metaphor for God, in science it is meaningless as an operational de-finition. The consequences Erich Fromm draws from his broadened definition of religion illustrates its absurdity: "Religion is any system of thought and action shared by a group which gives the individual a frame of orientation and an object of devotion" (1950:21). Fromm concludes forcefully, without humor, that each man is religious, for the devotion to sex, money, hygiene and cleanness falls under the given definition.

III Religion is not a mere psychological phenomenon. In defining religion psychology bases itself on a cultural tradition as is also testified by other disciplines studying religion.

In "psychology of religion" both elements designate a specific scientific discipline. As is the case for every science, we can only have a regulative idea of what is psychology. The progress of a science changes the conceptions of it. To call upon "general psychology" only displaces the problem, for "general psychology" results from psychological studies in different topics. Applying concepts elaborated in other psychologies, does not make psychology of religion an "applied" psychology, for every object of psychology reveals psychological processes and structures. And no object of psychology is merely psychological, for it belongs also to other disciplines. All that is human is psychic, but nothing is merely psychic. That makes the complexity of human sciences. Psychologists of religion often think that the main difficulty is in defining religion. However, it is still more difficult to define psychology! It is only by focusing our attention on specific objects, e.g. religion in the specific sense, that we progressively discover what is psychological in religion, language, art etc.

Of course religious categories such as prayer, cult, mysticism... are not congenial to the categories of general psychology. "Worldview" is even less! Indeed, all psychological categories identify some processes working within phenomena which can never be reduced to psychology alone. It is by focusing itself on religion that psychology of religion becomes psychology-oriented and does not lose itself in vague abstractions which are not to the point. Psychologists of religion in the christian area fear they may be considered as theologians if they study this particular religion. Do ethnopsychologists fear they will be seen as shamans if they study shamanism? And do psychologists of art fear they will make a work of art by studying art?

Since religion emerges with man, every element in religion is in some way psychological, but the whole of religion is not. Therefore there are other sciences of religion: history, philosophy, cultural anthropology, linguistic analysis... They restrict themselves to what a pre-given cultural consciousness considers as religion. Restriction in sciences is the negative pendant for the identification of a specific phenomenon.

Some sociologists and psychologists object that religions change, that "new religions" are born. Belonging to culture, religions indeed are historical phenomena. But the changing of religion is always an interpretation of a former religion. So are new religions, for example the "Moon-church". And most of today's "new religions" are vague and short-living syncretisms of elements borrowed from traditional religions (see the research of Glock on the "new religions" in California). Religions are neither eternal ideas nor physical facts. From a human viewpoint or within a scientific philosophical perspective religion can also be viewed as a mortal phenomenon. Suppose all religious symbols and beliefs have disappeared within a cultural area, then there will be no more empirical psychology of religion, but only historical psychology of religion as is practiced e.g. with respect to the ancient Greek religion.

IV. The formula "revelational systems" expresses correctly, if correctly understood, what is typical for religion and differentiates it accurately from "worldviews".

While considering the long cultural tradition of the religions themselves, I agree with the formula "revelational system", on two conditions.
1. That "system" is not understood as identical with worldview-system, but means: a structured ensemble of representations, discourse, iconic signs, symbolic actions, emotional experience, and consequential laws of conduct.
2. That by "revelational" is meant the specific religious consciousness the psychologist observes - as does the historian or cultural

71

anthropologist··, without involving himself in a belief commitment when he does his work as a psychologists. All religions are convinced that neither the knowledge and representations of the divine or supernatural entities, nor the rituals and the ethical laws are made by men, but are given to men by the supernatural agencies and their mediators. This universal religious consciousness typifies religion. For a historian all religions are revelational; the biblical religion being revelational in a specific form, in that it calls on historically dated and situated revelations.

This characteristic obviously differentiates religion from worldviews. As the expression itself reveals it, in a worldview, it is man who is the active center, who tries to organize the data of the world in a kind of totalizing perspective. The term is characteristic of the anthropocentric and theoretical mind. As I will explain further on, religious man, at least in the christian religion, appropriates personally and variably his religious system. But he does so in response to a religion which considers itself as revelational, not made by man as worldviews are.

We can understand that religions present themselves as revealed. The other dimension of the world, the supernatural agencies, precisely because they do not belong to the world, can only make themselves known by crossing the gap between their region and man's world. The revelational character of religion is coherent with its content. Sciences of religion elaborated theories to explain this phenomenon. Up till now, all theories are only fantasy conjectures. We may discuss whether future theories will be able to explain the origin and resources of religion better. An all-embracing theory, the possibility of which I doubt, does surely exceed the realm of psychology, for as an empirical science it cannot retrieve the remote origins of religion. Psychology must in any case take into account the bearing of the typical religious consciousness which constitutes the religious phenomena and which psychology studies from its specific viewpoint.

V. Psychology of religion should focus on the specificity of the studied revelational system and only on this condition will it bring about psychologically interesting data.

Psychology, while being an empirical science, studies general religious elements (experience, emotions, prayer, symbols...) as they occur in specific individuals and populations, related to a specific religion. The abstract and erroneous idea of the universal <u>homo religiosus</u> and the pseudo-scientific conception of a psychic automaton producing religion out of itself have been the major misguiding preconceptions. Religious man is largely the product of his culture and its religion. Different religions produce different possibilities of religious man. A religion which is at the same time universal and personal in its intention, as is the christian religion, brings even about very different religious personalities committed nonetheless to the same religious belief system. The whole history of christian culture and spirituality testifies to this diversity. By contrast, these psychologically most interesting subjective differences are not to be found in a religion whose intention and practice is bound up with the life of a group (clan-religion) and where the rituals are the core of the religion.

The interesting psychological questions are tied up with the peculiarity of the religion: symbols, rituals, metaphors, mysticism, the presence or absence of explicit belief commitment, the relation between religious beliefs and the non intrinsically religious domains. If psychology of religion within the christian area had been more attentive to its truly specific object, it would have made more really psychological observations and analyses of the complex dynamic processes involved in the belief-commitment and in the related religious doubts and conflicts. The poverty of psychological studies on rituals, compared with the richness of ethno-cultural observations and interpretations, is also striking; the reason lies obviously in the tendency of psychologists to work with abstract ideas instead of focusing, as do the anthropologists, on the way people perceive, interpret and practice their specific rituals. Psychologists seem to fear that while doing this they would be considered as psycho-theologians or as pastoral psychologists. This fear stems from the preconceptions mentioned above and from the consequent inability to distinguish the objective religious form and meaning of the rituals and the personal psychological processes which, on the one hand, are brought about by the rituals and by which, on the other hand, man responds to religious symbols.

VI. The delimitation of the guiding concept of religion allows the study of lived religion as a personal system.

One of the major tasks of psychological research related to religion is to study how individuals and types of populations integrate or fail to integrate the elements of their religion into a personal system. For example: what is their relative stress on the different dimensions of the proposed (christian) representation of God (the experiential dimension, the otherness of God, the dialogical or relational component). Another example: the personal connection between the representation of God, the personal interpretation of Jesus, the perception of the eucharist ritual. The correlation with personality tests or scales and the observation of the social, cultural, political milieu can enlighten to some extent the factors at work in the personal religious system. Without situating the subjects within the system of the religion they belong to, such studies cannot be adequately pursued.

VII. The delimitation of religion as a specific belief-system implies and makes possible the task of studying the connection between religion and the socio-cultural context of which the "worldview" is an aspect.

Because nothing in man is merely psychological, the psychological processes in religious man are codetermined by his cultural and social environment as well as by the objective religion he refers to. We cannot understand religious persons if we do not observe the harmonious and the conflicting influences they undergo. Psychology examines the interaction of man with the interacting cultural and religious factors. Becoming religious is a complex personal history which is an ongoing interactional process. Psychology of religion therefore, while focusing on religion, cannot elaborate valuable interpretations if it does not study also the bearing of life events and the influences the cultural environment exerts on their interpretation: death, health and illness; happiness, the striving for autonomy, sexuality and love; childhood and parenthood; the scientific worldview... In the perspective of this dynamic psychology religious belief and unbelief are connected topics, at least in western psychological observations today.

Religion is thus normally interwoven with all the domains of existence. It is so in various ways in different religions and cultures. It belongs also to psychology to analyse the manner in which individuals experience and perform the connections between their religious belief system and the human terrestrial values. This analysis has to be pursued with respect to various topics such as ethics, death, experience of nature... It is obvious e.g. that in one type of religious experience, the experience of the sacred, the perceptions of the world (or of art) are structured by the specific religious language and that in its turn this perception lends its content to religious language. Religion always has roots in non-religious phenomena. The logical fallacy of the broadening of the definition of religion consists in extending it to what is only a component of it. Psychology of religion then repeats the error of W. James (1958). As religion, according to James, is essentially personal experience, he identifies religion with emotion; but as no emotion is by itself religious, he had to accept that there is only religious experience when emotion is applied to "a religious object". The logical fallacy in the operational definition of religion leads psychology to a dead end.

74

Literature

Dilthey, W. Weltanschauungslehre: Abhandlungen zur Philosophie der Philosophie. Stuttgart: Teubner, 1977.

Fromm, E. Psychoanalysis and religion. New Haven: Yale University Press, 1950.

Glock, C., & Stark, R. Religion and society in tension. Chicago: Rand McNally, 1965.

James, W. The varieties of religious experience. New York: Mentor Books, 1958.

Introduction by J. M. van der Lans
Catholic University Nijmegen

To open a discussion on the demarcation of the domain of the psychology of religion might result in another debate on the conceptual definition of religion. For, as we know, the essential function of a conceptual definition is to delimitate the object of a scientific discipline.

In the psychology as well as in the sociology of religion a considerable number of reflections have been devoted to the issue of how to define religion. They have produced a conceptual scheme in which two approaches or options are clearly distinguished, usually indicated as the substantial and the functional definition. They are reviewed in the first chapter of every introductory textbook.

It is not my intention to re-open the discussion on the definition of religion. The literature provides us with theoretical clarity. In practise, however, the psychologist of religion, is often confronted with research-problems that lie beyond a simple choice between these two conceptual definitions.

Vergote, in his recent introductory book, titled Religion, Belief and Unbelief (1985), in a clear and convincing way has argued that a substantial definition of religion should limit the scope of our research. According to him the psychological study of religion should only regard human behavior that in our culture generally is associated with religion. Ideologies and value-orientations, that may have the function of substitutes of religion, are not the object of the psychology of religion.

For somebody, who in substance agrees with the position adopted by one he considers to be an excellent authority in our discipline, it is difficult to play the role of opponent. Nevertheless I will try to feed you with arguments in favour of another view.

I. Continuously the psychology of religion runs the risk of being too much religion-oriented and too little psychology-oriented.

It may be wondered whether in our discipline the definition of problems and their operationalisation is not too much influenced by the specific religious tradition the psychologist of religion knows intimately. What religious experience is, what religious behavior is, is usually defined in descriptive terms, in the language of the person of faith. For example Goodenough (1965) argues that the business of the psychology of religion is not to fit religious experiences into the categories of psychological theories but rather to see what the data of religious experiences themselves suggest" (quot. by Wulff, 1981,44).

Does this not mean that the field of vision of the psychologist of religion is confined to a specific set of content and forms which are tied to a given subcultural context instead of being determined by the categories of general psychology? Is it not inconsistent that, in setting bounds to the terrain of the psychology of religion, we use an external and non-psychological criterium, where-as when distinguishing mature and immature religion, we reject criteria derived from the religious field by arguing that psychology has its own criteria?

Perhaps the psychology of religion should take more distance from concrete, cultural-historical phenomena of religiosity and should define its object more in terms of general psychological structures and functions, of which concrete religious systems are the heterogeneous manifestations.

With approval I quote here two authorities. Paul Pruysser once wrote that "it entails serious risks to take as organising principles in a psychological work religious categories like prayer, mysticism, worship etc. The psychologist may lose his own ground if he employs religious categories since they are not germane to his psychological enterprise". (1968, 20). And according to James Dittes our understanding of what religion is will be impoverished until we can use the scientific constructs of psychology.

II. It may be wise to extend the domain of research in the psychology of religion to human behavior that has to do with a search for ultimate meaning.

Firstly I must state explicitly that this statement should not be interpreted as if I would abandon a substantial definition of religion in favour of a functional definition. It is only meant as an argument against those who say that the terrain of the psychology of religion should be confined to human behavior "that has reference to a supernatural being or to supernatural beings" (Vergote 1985, 16).

In our society a growing number of people has lost any connection with a religious-transcendental meaning system. Nevertheless they can be involved in questions, that are generally considered as the basic questions of life: What is the ultimate meaning of life ? How to give meaning to suffering and evil ? People involved in such questions are experiencing what Eliade (1952) has called "limit-situations". They are looking for an overall sense of wholeness. They are on the quest for "something more" in which to embed the reality of every-day. Some may find an answer in Humanism, some in a fatalistic world-view, some in science-fiction

III. A psychology of religion that will continue to confine itself to studying and investigating behavior that is connected with substantial religion, will be pushed off the scientific market.

In an excellent recent introduction into our discipline, I mean Raymond Paloutzian's Invitation to the Psychology of Religion, published in 1983, I found a quotation in which Joseph Havens tells how difficult it was still in 1959 during an APA-convention to get a group of psychologists together to discuss the relation between religion and psychology: "The difficulties confronting this undertaking were twofold: one, that we would be unable to find competent and thoughtful psychologists, with standing in their field, who would be interested; two, that such men, even if they participated, would decline for reasons of professional reputation, to come to grips solidly and imaginatively with the issues. If psychologists are personally religious, they tend to keep this fact aseptically separate from their professional work. If they are not, religious phenomena usually appear irrelevant to them."

With this quotation, Paloutzian illustrates the severe decline in the psychology of religion between 1930 and 1950.

In spite of the fact that now, 24 years later, the psychologists of religion are forming an accredited division of the APA and no longer need to meet secretly like in 1959, and in spite of the fact that the psychological study of religion has increased dramatically during the past 20 years, indicated by several journals, professional organisations and graduate programs, there are reasons to say that the future of our discipline is in danger again through the same two difficulties as Havens identified in those days. First, although a lot of competent and thoughtful psychologists with standing in their field are interested in the subject of religion now, I worry about the future now and then. Especially the psychologist of religion, who is working in a cultural setting where the process of unchurching spreads rapidly, is confronted more and more with the question of the relevancy of his discipline. For a lot of students in our faculty, the usual textbooks of the psychology of religion are describing the beliefs and ritual behavior of their grandparents, religious phenomena that they have never met in the environment in which they grew up. For them such a psychology of religion will be a fossil survival from the past with no utility for the present day. This is a bad conditon to recruit students who in the future ought to practise our discipline.

It might be so that restricting our attention to substantial religion, we will reinforce the tendency among academic colleagues in the social faculty to look upon the psychology of religion as a field unworthy of interest, an obvious victim in the retrenchment-policy of these days.

perhaps. They have in common that they are born and live in a cultural environment, where there is no longer a "plausibility-structure" (P. Berger) for a supernatural world-view.

If the psychologist of religion considers only those people to belong to the terrain of his discipline, who are seeking answers to basic questions in a sacred cosmos, to what other psychological discipline do we leave then the investigation of the remaining people's quest for wholeness ?

The proposal in the above thesis is analogous to what Dobbelaere (1982) has suggested for the sociology of religion, namely to expand the sociology of religion into a sociology of meaning systems. It is true that a psychologist doesn't study social systems but individual behavior. It would therefor be wrong to re-baptize the psychology of religion into the psychology of meaning-systems. The psychology of religion however should intend to study that part of human behavior that regards the search for ultimate meaning, whether religious or secular.

A good example of this kind of approach seems to be Yinger's investigations of what he called "non-doctrinal religion" but what was nothing else than the way and degree of people's search for answers to permanent problems of human experience. Another example might be Robert Wuthnow's research of some prevalent contemporary meaning systems and their correlates with attitudes, values and behavior.

Perhaps it is significant that both examples are sociological studies. Do we know psychological counterparts? I wonder whether Melvin Lerner's laboratory experiments in which he has investigated a general human tendency, identified as "belief in a just world" (1980), might be considered as an equivalent example in the psychology of religion. The belief in a just world is the sense of the necessity of a final order and structure. 'Lerner's experiments demonstrate that this belief is "too central a part in the organisation of human experience to be given up simply because the child learns that there is not an all-seeing, all-powerful adult figure who metes our punishments and rewards in direct response to how "good" or "bad" someone has been". (p. 26). Also adults appear to believe that the important events in people's lifes follow rules so that everything happens in the way it should. For some people the source of the belief in ultimate justice is found in a formal religious or other mythical system, but for others it can vary from situation to situation.

One could consider Lerner's experiments as a rare example of an investigation of the way, world-views are functioning in everyday-behavior. Do we agree that his study belongs to the psychology of religion ?

79

I admit that these are pragmatic arguments. But there is also an intrinsic argument. An extension of the research-field of the psychology of religion with the study of behavior that is connected with other symbolic universes of meaning than the traditional religions, might enhance the scientific level of our discipline. The essential nature of science is the process of developing general theories from particular observations. So the psychologist of religion begins with observations in the world of facts and then produces abstract concepts and theories, making inferences about common factors we think are operating through all those particular behavior events. If, from a social-scientific point of view, revelational systems and non-revelational world-views have key-aspects in common., they ought to be taken together on the level of concepts and theories which we use to make human behavior more understandable. To confine our attention to revelational systems only should mean to be content with a lower level of abstraction.

IV. The narrower the concept of religiousness that is operationalized, the less applicable our instruments of measurement will be.

This last statement doesn't need a long amplification. I will mention only two facts.

First, the majority of scales measuring religious beliefs and attitudes, start from the no longer valid assumption that the religious culture is homogeneous. Like medicine, our scales sometimes are provided with an information leaflet warning us that the scale can only be used for White American Protestants. The fact that scales in the psychology of religion are so tied to religious language, has always made it necessary to adapt the formulation of the scale's items to the religious idiom of the population to be studied. Not to mention the fact that a reformulation might nullify one of the major benefits of the quantitative approach, i.e. comparability of results, the task is becoming more and more difficult since the increase of religious pluriformity, even within denominations. Besides the familiar distinction between conservative and liberal Protestant denominations, we now also have to reckon with the differences between traditional and progressive Roman Catholics. Because of the impossibility to represent every theological position in pre-formulated items, a growing tendency can be noticed to drop scales in favour of unstructured interviews.

Secondly, it must be admitted that we have nothing to offer when colleagues from other psychological disciplines ask us for standardized instruments to investigate how, for instance, college students in our secular society are engaged in problems of ultimate meaning. They expect us to be specialists in these aspects of human behavior..

I have a feeling that we should be more honest and should indicate our discipline as the psychology of christian religion only.

Of course I know that not everywhere the psychologists of religion are suffering from such identity problems. In Western Europe it will be more the case than in Eastern and Southern Europe. And psychologists of religion, who work in social faculties, will be more confronted with it than their colleagues in theological faculties.

Nevertheless I have the idea, that by investing more energy in the conposition of scales that are sufficiently general to allow each respondent to indicate his or her personal faith, we will produce instruments that can be used inter-denominationally and cross-culturally and could so enhance the scientific relevancy of our research-work.

Literature

Dittes, J.E., Psychology of Religion. In G. Lindzey & E. Aronson (Eds.) The Handbook of Social Psychology (2nd ed.,vol.5). Reading, Mass.: Addison & Wesley, 1969, 602-659.

Dobbelaere, K. Godsdienst, Religie en Zingevingssystemen. Tijdschrift voor Sociologie, 1982, 3, 25-49.

Eliade, M. Images et Symboles. Essais sur le symbolisme magico-religieux. Paris: Gallimard, 1952.

Goodenough, E. R. The Psychology of Religious Experience. New York: Basic Books, 1965.

Lerner, M. J. The Belief in a Just World. New York: Plenum Press, 1980.

Paloutzian, R. Invitation to the Psychology of Religion. Glenview, III.: Scott, Foresman & Company, 1983.

Pruyser, P.W. A Dynamic Psychology of Religion. New York: Harper & Row, 1968.

Vergote, A. Religie, Geloof en Ongeloof. Kapellen: De Nederlandse Boekhandel, 1985.

Wulff, D. M. Psychological Approaches. In: F. Whaling (Ed.) Contemporary Approaches to the Study of Religion. The Hague: Mouton, 1984, 21-88.

Wuthnow, R. The Consciousness Reformation. Berkeley: University of Berkeley Press, 1976.

Yinger, Milton J. The Scientific Study of Religion. New York: MacMillan, 1970.

On contemplative psychology.

H.F. de Wit
Free University, Amsterdam

1. A definition of contemplative psychology.

Contemplative psychology is a psychology that forms an intrinsic part of the contemplative traditions of most world religions. The term 'contemplative psychology' therefore does not refer to academic psychological theory about contemplation, religion or religious behavior. It refers to the psychological insights and methods that are – often implicitly – present in the vision and practice of religions and that clarify and guide ones contemplative or religious development. So the term 'contemplative' is used here in the same broad sense as Thomas Merton (1953) uses it; it does not only refer to contemplation but it refers to all practices and perspectives that are part of contemplative traditions.

1.1. Does contemplative psychology exist?

Ever since the inception of the psychology of religion, psychologists (e.g. James, 1902; Jung, 1939; Clark, 1958; Leuba, 1972; Ornstein, 1972; Podvoll, 1982; Wilber, 1984) have been aware that contemplative traditions do contain psychological insights and knowledge about man and his spiritual development.

Of course the contemplative traditions themselves do not necessarily call these insights and knowledge 'psychological'. For the concept of 'psychology' is a rather recent notion. Nevertheless we can use this concept (also in retrospect) to delineate a paricular kind of knowledge. It is well known that the buddhist tradition contains one of the most explicit formulations of the psychological aspects of contemplative development (see e.g. Guenther, 1976; Lati Rinbochai, 1980). However in the other world-religions we also find psychological insights and approaches although they are less spelled out. Nevertheless they play a part in the spiritual training and guidance of the practitioners. Obviously the contemplative psychologies vary according to the contemplative traditions that they are embedded in, but as these psychologies are all about human beings, there seems to exist some common ground between all of them as well.

1.2. Is contemplative psychology a science?

Whether we consider contemplative psychology or science depends on our definition "science". I would like to restrict discussion of this vast issue here to two remarks. Firstly human intelligence might be broader than the intelligence of which scientific method is the formalized expression. That is human ways of acquiring knowledge and understanding might not yet be exhaustively captured and codified by our methodology of science. Secondly contemplative traditions are generally and fundamentally intelligent traditions as well. They do not only contain contemplative psychological theories of man (mind and behavior) but also various practices and methods by means of which the practitioner can examine and test the contemplative psychological theories involved. They contain a "contemplative methodology" as well.

This is not surprising for like any psychology contemplative psychology addresses the question of how we could intelligently approach and understand human life-experience. If we accept that the methods of contemplative traditions are valid ways to approach that question it would only be a matter of conceptual convention whether we would call contemplative psychology and its methodology 'scientific' or not.

1.3. The aim of research into contemplative psychology

Contemplative psychologies along with their particular methods contain, may be as yet in a rather implicit form, intelligent ways of understanding man. It is worthwhile then to formulate them explicitly and thereby clarify their psychological and methodological know how. That would not only contribute to our understanding of the epistemological, methodological and psychological value of contemplative traditions, but it might also broaden our perspective on and our practive of psychology of religion and of psychology in general. Moreover practical and pastoral theologists nowadays trust and lean more on the psychology of the scientific tradition, than on the psychology that we find in ' the contemplative traditions. Therefore they are bound by certain limitations that come with it. The implications of this shift in allegeance will be discussed below (4).

2. Contemplative traditions

Not only within the contemplative traditions themselves but also within the science of religion we find three more or less restrictive interpretations of what counts as a contemplative tradition. These interpretations obviously qualify the interpretation of its inherent psychology.

2.1. Contemplative tradition as monastic tradition

In a very strict sense the concept of 'contemplative tradition' refers to a context in which people devote their whole life to the practice of a religious discipline and to the spiritual exercises that are part of it. These people usually live together in what we call monasteries or cloisters of some sort: they study, pray, meditate and their daily life activities are permeated by a discipline that is supposed to develop and sustain religious or spiritual growth. In these cloisters the abbots are supposed to be trained in and to possess a practical knowledge of how to educate people in its religious vision and in the expression of that vision in word and deed. This know how is psychological and methodological in nature. It is contemplative psychology.

2.2. Contemplative tradition as a lay tradition

In a less strict sense the concept of a contemplative tradition is not limited to a monastic physical setup but it also covers religious disciplines that are practiced in the context of normal every day life. There seem to be two opinions here.

The first one being that religious discipline in every day life brings us closer to the vision or the perspective that is practiced in monasteries in its complete and purest form.

The second opinion is that ones every day life situation could be viewed as the "ultimate monastery". This refers to the possibility of a religious discipline that encompasses all aspects of human life in the same strict way as the religious discipline within the monastery encompasses all aspects of monastic life. Whether one views the lay contemplative as a prospective monk or nun or as the ultimate monk or nun there is a particular kind of knowledge and know how in lay contemplative traditions that is of a psychological nature, and that could be coined 'contemplative psychology' as well.

2.3. Contemplative tradition as a temporal (non religious) tradition

In an even broader sense, contemplative traditions could be 'non religious', that is without a connection with a particular religion. They nevertheless contain a discipline based on a particular kind of psychological knowledge, that guides its practioners towards the realization of the highest human values.

These traditions, like for instance confucianism, have in common with the religious contemplative traditions some normative anthropology, some notion of 'materialistic man' or 'fallen man' and the idea that human beings have the possibility to uplift themselves and others from their 'corrupted state' towards what is often called 'enlightenment'. Last but not least they contain practicable methods or disciplines that are conducive to bringing

84

about enlightenment.

Of course the notions of 'materialistic' or 'fallen man' and 'enlightenment' need to be qualified in order to understand what is meant here. In this short presentation I will use these notions more or less intuitively. For now we might say that 'fallen man' refers to our conventional, everyday life opinion about human beings.

3. Scientific psychology from a contemplative point of view

In our culture with its increasing secularization of human life, contemplative knowledge and disciplines seem to be on the way out. The discipline of contemplative practice itself is often no longer understood by lay people and monks alike as a means to religious development. Therefore discipline is often suspended or even rejected. On the one hand we see a narrowing down of contemplative discipline to the discipline of study of religious texts or to the discipline of social wellfare work. On the other hand we see that scientific psychology is filling the open place left by the gradual disappearance of contemplative psychology.

Scientific psychology being emancipated from religion explicitely states that it is not religiously bound. It wants to be religiously neutral and that is its strenght and its weakness at the same time. On the one hand its neutrality is a strenght because it is based on an image of man in which religion plays a very small part if it plays at all. Scientific psychology is up to date in that respect; it is primarily a psychology about 'fallen man'.

From the perspective of contemplative psychology, scientific psychology is therefore extremely worthwhile. For developing a clear and objective perspective on 'fallen man', is a necessary basis both for any contemplative psychology and for any contemplative development. On the other hand, scientific psychologists might become aware to what extent their 'neutral' theories about 'fallen man' are not particularly adequate when it comes to understanding man as a religious being. In that sense neutrality reflects a limitation. If we become aware of that and therefore are able to make this limitation explicit, its neutrality becomes a strength of psychology. If we are not aware of it, it becomes a weakness.

If we become aware of the limitations of conventional psychology and its outlook, we might wonder how contemplative psychology could complement conventional psychology. If we are not aware of it, we might fear that promoting contemplative psychology is a devious attempt to undermine and undo the independence of psychology as a religiously neutral scientific discipline.

4. Contemplative psychology and the psychology of religion

Let us turn to our last issue: is contemplative psychology a particular kind of psychology of religion? What is the relationship between these two psychologies? Let me start out with a remark on the meaning of the preposition 'of' in 'psychology of religion'.

If we would interpret the preposition 'of' in the possessive sense of 'belonging to', then contemplative psychology would definitly be a psychology of religion but conventional 'psychology of religion' would not. For the standard interpretation of the preposition 'of' in 'psychology of religion' is rather in the direction of 'about' than in the direction of 'belonging to'. And conventional psychology about religion is not and does not intend to be a psychology belonging to religion. This distinction between contemplative psychology and psychology of religion, has quite a few implications. I will discuss them briefly.

4.1. Third-person psychology and first-person psychology

Psychology of religion in the conventional sense of 'about', is closely aligned with what has been called third-person psychology, that is a psychology about other people; it has other people as its object of study. Third-person psychology and its methodology however tend to shun away from research into experience that is only available in the first-person sense. For the private character of first-person experience seems to exclude 'objectivity' as defined in third person methodology. Contemplative psychology however focuses rather strongly on experience as it happens to me or us. In that sense it is a first-person psychology that includes subjective or 'private' experience. It has its own notion of objectivity (see e.g. the 'acid test of truth' in Roberts, 1985: 171) which is somehow supposed to guarantee the trustworthiness of the contemplative approach. This touches upon an old issue of psychology as a science that we can only mention here; the issue whether the concepts of objectivity as they function in third-person psychology and first-person psychology could be special cases of a more general notion of trustworthiness.

4.2. The object of both types of psychology

A second implication that sets both types of psychology apart could be stated in terms of their object.

The object of contemplative psychology is the totality of human existence or human experience. The central question is: what is the place of all aspects of human life within the contemplative perspective and its development? How could one deal with all these aspects in a way that furthers one's contemplative development?

The object of scientific psychology of religion is religion viewed as one among the many non-religious aspects of human life. The central question here is: how could we gain a third-person psychological understanding of religious phenomena and how are these causally related to other non-religious phenomena.

4.3. Aim and method of both psychologies

Put briefly the aim of contemplative psychology is primarily a way of being, that is 'knowing' in the first-person sense of being wise, being free from confusion and ignorance. It is close to 'knowledge by acquaintance' (Russel, 1912). It has a quality of intimacy and directness, and it is closely connected with being completely aware of ones life-experience on the spot.

The aim of psychology of religion is scientific knowledge, that is true information about its object of study. This knowledge is primarily representational and indirect and as such distinct from (at a distance of) what it represents, roughly speaking. It is close to 'knowledge by description' (Russel, 1912).

The methods of contemplative psychologies consist of contemplative practices and disciplines (meditation, contemplation, prayer, a certain disciplined way of holding one's mind and conducting one's life) that bring about what the contemplative tradition views as its ultimate fruition or aim. Generally these methods could be characterized as 'awareness strategies' (see De Wit, 1985, 1986). For the starting point of fairly all main contemplative disciplines is the discipline of becoming aware on the spot of one's working basis, that is of the dynamics and patterns of one's fallen state of being.

The methods of psychology of religion consist of the empirical scientific method, which could be called a 'conceptual strategy' (De Wit, 1986) as it aims for the development of conceptual structures that represent human behavior (see 4.4.).

4.4. Relativity of image of man and language

The object of contemplative psychology being the totality of first person-experience is not a static but a dynamic totality. Therefore the image of man implicit in contemplative psychologies is not static but it is a developmental image of spiritual man. As one's way of being (wise or confused) changes in the course of one's spiritual development, the contemplative psychology that relates to one's way of being needs to change. That change is also reflected in a change of its terminology. Put differently contemplative psychologies often contain different levels of language that have their meaning relative to a particular state of being (see Wilber, 1984).

Psychology of religion however does not possess this kind of relativity. Fundamentally it works with (or strives for) one fixed image of "neutral" man, that would only change on the basis of research results. Along with that the language of psychology of religion is fixed to (preferably) one general level: the language of scientific psychology. Religion (whether it likes it or not) is then discussed in terms of this language.

All this reflects another difference, which has to do with the function of theories. Within contemplative psychologies, theories are fundamentally a posteriori means to convey or to point at a way of being. Language and theories are relative to human beings and in that sense they only contain relative truths. Through realizing (that is understanding experientially) the truth of a relative truth ones being is transformed. That transformation itself opens up a further perspective that involves awareness of the relativity of that relative truth, as well as awareness of the possibility to realize further (relative) truths. This is how theories are means or conceptual tools for the awareness strategies of the contemplative path.

Within scientific psychology of religion, theories fundamentally are an a priori means for conceptual strategies, that is for strategies of conceptualizing reality and to answer our selfconceived questions about reality. The theories both provide information and concepts by means of which we can state our questions. They structure our research and our experience in (preferably) one fixed way or paradigm, unless conflicting theories or counter-evidence prevent this. Theories articulate and clarify our conceptual representations or images of reality. They might obscure however awareness of these theories as theories. This obscuration involves confounding 'reality as we know it' with 'reality' or confounding the representation with the represented.

4.5. Role of the teacher

The last implication I would like to mention here refers to the teacher-student relationship. Within the contemplative traditions the teacher (director spiritualis, mentor, guru) relates to the totality of the students existence. Therefore this relationship is all encompassing and personal. In this relationship the teacher applies the contemplative psychology (whether he calls it such or not) of his tradition and thereby he guides the students.

Within the scientific tradition of psychology of religion the relationship between teacher and student is partial and possibly impersonal. For the teacher needs only relate to those aspects of the student's being that involve his being a student of psychology and of its methodology of research.

So much for this slightly black and white clarification of the differences between contemplative psychology and scientific psychology of religion. Nevertheless the black and white might point out the necessity of research in contemplative psychologies. However to bring that about psychologists and contemplatives need to work together intimately. Only by studying and practicing each others methods and disciplines, the scientific and the contemplative traditions of psychology could begin to enrich each other and thereby become of greater help to man as a religious being.

This paper introduces the concept of contemplative psychology, and reviews the concepts of contemplative traditions. It then discusses the difference between contemplative psychology and scientific psychology of religion. In view of the problematic state that pastoral psychology is in, the need for research into the often implicit psychologies of contemplative traditions is emphasized.

literature

Clark, W.H. The psychology of religion. New York: 1958.

Guenther, H.V. Philosophy and psychology in the Abhidharma. Berkeley & London: Shambhala, 1976.

James, W. The varieties of religious experience. Glasgow: Collins, (1902), 1977.

Jung, C.G. Psychology and Religion: West and East. Collected Works. New York: Pantheon, (1939), 1958.

Rinbochai, L. Mind in Tibetan Buddhism. Valois, New York: Gabriel/Snow Lion, 1980.

Leuba, J.H. The psychology of religious mysticism. London, Reprint: 1972.

Merton, Th. The sign of Jonas. London: Hollis & Carter, 1953.

Ornstein, R.J. The psychology of consciousness. San Francisco: Freeman, 1972.

Podvoll, E.M. The history of sanity and the history of neurosis. Naropa Institute Journal of psychology, 1982.

Roberts, B. The path to no self. Boston & London: Shambhala publ, 1985.

Russel, B. The problems of philosopy. London & New York: Oxford Univ. Press, 1912.

Wilber, K. A sociable God. Toward a new understanding of religion. Boulder & London: New Science Library, Shambhala, 1984.

Wit, H.F. de. Methodologie in contemplatief perspectief. In: L.K.A. Eisenga (e.d.). Over de grenzen van de psychologie. Amsterdam: Swetz & Zeitlinger, 1985.

Wit, H.F. de. The methodology of clarifying confusion. In: M.E. Hyland. Proceedings of the founding Conference of the International Society for Theoretical Psychology. Amsterdam: North Holland publ, 1986. (forthcoming).

The possessed man of Gerasa (Marc 5, 1-20).
A psychoanalytic interpretation of reader-reactions.

A.J.R. Uleyn
Catholic University Nijmegen

When asked about the effect Marc's story has on them, most people report rather negative feelings. At least the people I have interviewed last years.

Among the responses and reactions the following statements often return: I feel uneasy about it; I find it disturbing; highly embarrassing; it is a problematic story; rather unpleasant; it makes me feel uncomfortable, upset...

No doubt, the narrator, called Marc, shows to be a master in weaving into his story all sorts of elements which taken together produce a cumulative effect of uneasiness: something uncanny.

First there is his description of the demoniac: a savage madman, a mental patient exhibiting a very asocial and destructive behaviour, dangerous for him self as well as for other people. He is running around, producing harsh screams, tearing his clothes to pieces, wounding himself with stones. Equally threatening is the man's monstrous muscular strenght. Even if sturdy fellows succeed sometimes in capturing and binding him fast, again and again he proves to be the strongest by breaking his chains and freeing him self.

Second there is the appearance of a still stronger superman, called Jesus. For his superior Power even a whole legion of Roman soldiers and demons is no match. They take to flight and their panic takes possession of a herd of pigs which results in a gruesome collective suicide. No wonder the local population reacts with consternation and alarm. They distrust the unexpected benefactor-wonderworker and urgently request him to leave them in peace. For the tremendous destructive power he has at his disposal is menacing and ominous.

A comparative examination of different cultures shows that humans experience uncanny feelings when faced with two categories of persons. First in the case of mental patients who are very disturbed and psychotic, epileptic or possessed. Second in the case of people who dispose of superhuman capacities: wonderworkers, sorcerers, magicians, wizards, enchanters, hays, witches, shamans.

An uncanny feeling takes possession of us because both classes are associated with dangerous impulses and forbidden wishes; with dark forces, with unadmissible and bad actions. In short with everything personified by the devil and the demons.

The mentally handicaped is in a passive way connected to the evil because he or she got unwillingly into the power of Satan; the sorcerer and witch on the other hand are actively associated with the evil One through a pact and they share in his destructive powers.

In other words Marc's story about the Gerasene madman contains already at its manifest level a certain number of elements amply sufficient to evoke an uncanny atmosphere.

But a psychoanalytic intepretation is going one step further searching for something deeper. The assumption is that in addition to the already mentioned conscious factors (the so called surface structure of the narrative) we have to reckon with unconscious or latent reactions. Freud has demonstrated that we are unaware of much that is going on in our minds. That the reach of our experience in always going further than the grasp of our clear consciousness.

As a technical term, in the psychoanalytic sense, the Uncanny (das Unheimliche; literally the Unhomely) is a feeling of being upset and scared by something that appears as strange, disturbing or even as horrific, whereas it is in fact something that long ago has been very familiar and near. (1)

A reality we have known for some time as belonging intimately to ourselves has only later on become something strange, upsetting and alarming because it has been estranged from us; we have dismissed it and disowned it. Under the compelling influence of our educators we have been socialized: we have learned to give up what formerly was ours. We have renounced it, pushed it away, repressed it. Why? Because the "familiar things" we are dealing with proved to be at variance with the reality principle, with parental authority, with the prevailling standards of behaviour, with rational thinking. A severe interdiction, a taboo, has come into force. The once familiar thing became burdened with feelings of shame and guilt and it was banished from our consciousness.

A person who is getting an uncanny feeling is experiencing an anxiety signal, a warning of some danger. Look out, it says, you are on a dangerous declivity. If you do not stop you will irresistibly be carried away. Why? Because an urge which you thought to have definitely overcome and stamped out once and for all, many years ago, proves at this moment that it still is present and very active. The inadmissible impulse has not been exterminated at all. It is waking up, raising its head again. That gives you a fright. it makes you fearful. You feel uneasy, unsafe. For you realize it was a mistake when you thought to be sure that it would not happen to you any more.

Now you have the sensation of falling back, of being on the verge of regression. You got the proof that your former belief was only an illusion. The farewell has obviously not been wholehearted...

The uncanny according to Freud, Reik and other psychoanalysts is that class of the terrifying which leads back to something long known to us, once very familiar. But these familiar things have become unfamiliar and terrifying because they have undergone estrangement and distortion through repression.

The uncanny experience occurs when the repressed is coming back; when the wish or belief we had surmounted seems once more to be confirmed. This return of the repressed is the intrusion of something from which we had dissociated ourselves. But nevertheless it is asserting itself again as persistently present and powerful.`

When we dimly realize that we are fascinated by the "abomination" we are having a very disturbing sensation: an uncanny feeling.

Further analysis shows that all uncanny things are in some way related to irrational beliefs, to magic thinking and to the narcissistic feeling of omnipotence. It has to do with the deeply rooted conviction of His Majesty the Baby to be the center of the universe, the most important being, invulnerable and immortal, having at his disposal parents and other people to gratify all his wishes and needs.

But why, could we ask, does the return of this infantile feeling of omnipotence provoke anxiety? Why should the cherished belief of our childhood become so terrifying on its reappearance?

The answer to this question is to be found in the conflicts provoked by the long and painful process of education and socialization. In the course of becoming an adult the original sense of omnipotence, the primary narcissism has taken on the meaning of overstepping one's bounds and limits. It becomes the frightening act of penetrating into a severely forbidden domain: a behaviour arousing such terrific things as presumption and hubris. The certainty that transgression of this taboo will mercilessly be punished. The dread of being mutilated, castrated of even killed. This is the reason why at the return of the repressed what re-emerges is not the reminiscence of the once pleasurable feeling of omnipotence but the dark menace of abandonment, rejection, castration and death.

In other words in our experience the wish to be omnipotent is inseparably connected with disobledience and forbidden agression. To indulge in narcissistic grandeur and selfsufficiency becomes the same thing as insurrection and revolt against parental, especially paternal, authority.

The essence of the psychoanalytic explanation lies in the fact that our narcissistic sense of omnipotence is intimately connected with the oedipal complex. We have learned to experience and to interpret the external reality in its frustrating aspects as the manifestation of the punishing Father. On this line of our emotional development the hostile world appears to us as the personification of Evil, as the negative paternal

Power, as the Devil. The opposite of friendly reality, the positive Parent, the loving God.

Under so called normal circumstances our sane and solid sense of reality is strong enough and our socialization sufficient to hold in check our inadmissable urges. But indirectly and without noticing it clearly, our narcissistic and oedipal wishes are activated by the pleasure we experience in identifying with hero's who dare to indulge in forbidden impulses and behaviour.

Psychoanalytically speaking this is one of the main ingredients warranting the worldwide success of literature, theater and movies.

The mechanism at work in this process can be explained as follows. As a reader, listener or spectator we accomplish in our imagination the same grandiose achievements as the hero does. He is acting as our substitute. It is important to notice that during the first stage of this identification process we are not bothered by any feelings of anxiety, shame or guilt. In spite of the fact that the hero-superman is acting out all sort of forbidden impulses which interfere with commonsense and with our interests; wishes which are asocial, punishable or sacrilegious. What is coming to the fore in our experience is a feeling of solidarity with the hero; usually a sympathetic, young, intrepid and intelligent person struggling bravely with the negative father figure. Our longing for transgression of limits, for superhuman power, for oedipal emancipation are all deeply gratified by the hero's performances. But this satisfaction is taking place outside the realm of consciousness. The alarmbell of our superego, the voice of conscience does not yet ring. Among other reasons because the Father has sufficiently been made unrecognizable. The attack is not brutally straight at him. Revolt and agression are directed against malicious authorities, foreign occupiers, corrupt administrators, unjust laws and institutions, demons and devils.

However, sooner or later, our identification with the hero is getting problematic. The absorption in his grandiose enterprise gets disturbed by secretly growing uneasiness. In stead of gratifying it becomes uncanny. The warning that to give way to regression and to permit the repressed to return is dangerous. The message: to indulge one's feelings of omnipotence and to yield oedipal agression is not allowed ! This surely will avenge itself !

In most of the cases the emergence of anxiety and guiltfeelings during a second stage of the identification process is caused by the tragic fate the hero has to face. His destiny appears as ominous.

After his first successes, sooner or later, he has to suffer dire affliction. His courage is not appreciated; his daring attempts are abortive. The struggle against injustice and evil proves to be not that simple. The overall impresion made by the complete story seems to be that the heroic style of life is doomed to failure and that revolt gets inexorably punished. In other words, the uncanny feeling makes our former identification with the hero change into keeping our distance. Till at the end we finish by disapproving his defiant performance as not realistic...

Back to Marc's Gerasa-story.
    Thusfar some general considerations on the uncanny and on the role stories may have in the emergence of this important experience.
In his narrative Marc is giving central importance to Jesus' victory over Satan and he is emphasising the destruction of the demonic hordes. The fact that the tormented madman is liberated from his rage comes in a certain sense only at the second place. What Marc has in his mind is to show most clearly that we humans when faced with Evil, are completely defenceless and that we have to recognize the superiority of its brutal forces. Bur Marc also wants to make clear that we can depend upon Jesus, that we can rely on him. That the solution for our predicament consists in feeling one with Him who is demonstrating a still greater, a supreme power. Indeed, the Jesus Marc is putting on the scene is "the only one who is able to break into the strong man's house and make off with his goods because he has first tied the strong man up" (3,27). This strong man is of course Satan, the personification of Evil.
    It is important not to loose sight of the context in which the Gerasene story appears. It is only a part of a longer narrative describing four spectacular miracles of Jesus who shows his colossal and unquestionable superiority by performing prodigies. Marc's purpose is to prove that evil and suffering have indeed found their master in him. For he stands up against the hurricane when the boat of his followers is nearly destroyed; he heals a woman suffering from haemorrhage for twelve years who had spent all her money on doctors without any improvement; he calls back to life a dead girl...
Jesus, says Marc, triumphs over the hostile cosmic elements wind and water, over terror and suffering. He proves to be the Master of life and death. In short he is able to overcome all sort of human limitations. In this series belongs also the unclean spririt of Gerasa, the so called unvincible One, possessing the strenght of a whole Roman legion.
By making disappear the demonic legion into the abyss of the lake, Jesus eliminates the enemy of mankind: the harsh and frustrating reality of Evil. All human misery, suffering and death are swept away from the surface of the earth. The monstrous negative fatherfigure, Satan, is liquidated and burried. Dumped into the depth of the see... Or has he only be repressed and denied?...
For in the second part of his story Marc becomes dampening and

sound-deadening. The triumphant feeling of being invulnerable and almighty has gone. The superior Jesus himself has to take a failure. The people of Gerasa sends him away. In this manner the narrator insinuates that the intoxication of omnipotence is followed by disenchantment. The belief to be above hostile reality appears to be a dangerous illusion; a sort of hubris or megalomania.

In other words the atmosphere is getting "uncanny".

The feeling creeps upon us that if we shut our eyes to the power of Evil or if we try to deny the existence of destructive forces we surely will be punished. Sooner or later. For all we are doing then is to imagine away our feableness and to forget that humans are incurably limited in their possibilities.

Marc's story has an uncanny effect because it makes possible for unconscious material, forbidden and therefore repressed, to escape the censor. Unconscious material composed of infantile fantasies about narcissistic an agressive wishes and the punishment that inexorably will follow. It is the return of the repressed sense of omnipotence that makes the story uncanny. It is disturbing our sense of ourselves and our normal orientation in the world.

Jesus appears as an uncanny figure who is doing what we as adults cannot do. He indulges unrepressed, infantile, immoral desires through rebellious acts which are essentially denials of the rational.

Considering the narrative structure of Marc's Gospel taken as a whole, the Gerasa-story seems to function as a fore-warning. After having portrayed Jesus as the invulnerable Saviour, Marc makes an abrupt transition in 8,31. From then on Jesus appears no longer more as a powerful wonderworker. The opposition and influence of his adversaries gets stronger and stronger till Jesus ends completely powerless, hanging executed on a cross. Marc's purpose is first to evoke the illusion of omnipotence and then to undermine it. In this dramatic narrative process the Gerasa scene comes as a first red light signal; an anticipation of the later total disenchantment. (2)

A final remark.

The interpretation proposed in this study is typically male. This one-sided masculinity is due to the simple fact that all the persons involved are men: the madman; Jesus the wonderworker; the people interviewed about their reactions; the author and analyst. And last not least Freud, the man who developed the theory about repression, oedipal problems and the uncanny.

Summary

The article tries to demonstrate that the disturbing impression Marc's story makes on some readers is in fact the uncanny feeling such as it has been described by Freud and other psychoanalysts.

An extended version of this article can be found in: Uleyn, A., Psychoanalytisch lezen in de bijbel. Hilversum: Gooi & Sticht, 1985.

Literature

1. Freud, S., Das Unheimliche, 1920. G.W. XII, 229-261.
   Reik, T., Der eigene und der fremde Gott. Wien 1923.
   Bergler, E., The psychoanalysis of the uncanny. International Journal of Psychoanalysis, 1934, 15, 215-244.
   Bach, S., Narcissism, continuity and the uncanny. International Journal of Psychoanalysis, 1975, 35, 77-86.

2. Uleyn, A., A psychoanalytic approach to Marc's Gospel. Lumen Vitae, 1977, 32, 479-496.

Martin Luther's personality and works from the point of view of the role theory.

J. Wedzel
Jagiellonski Uviversity, Cracow

This paper contains a general analysis of the formation of M. Luther's personality and religious attitudes.

As a starting point for the analysis the role theory of Hjalmar Sundén, as described in his book Religionen och rollerna (1959), was chosen. This theory is also elaborated in many other books and papers. However only some of them are developed from a strict interpretation of Sundén's original work (Unger 1976; Grzymala-Moszczynska 1979; Capps 1982). Sometimes interpreters have gone far beyond the boundaries of Sundén's theory causing the theory to loose its autonomous status and so it becomes one of the elements of the compilatory excerpts which construct it (Källstad, 1974).

When starting an analysis of the personality and religious works of Luther from the point of view of role theory, three points seem to be of crucial importance. 1/ Evolution and Luther's understanding of God's and man's role within the course of time, 2/ the period covering Luther's internal struggle with the feeling of his own sinfulness and his external struggle with the institutional Church which was resolved in his denying salvation by works to claim salvation by grace, 3/ the process of Luther taking a Biblical role and adopting God's will for the situation.

Luther's understanding of the role which God plays towards human beings was determined by two factors: the religious atmosphere of his family home and by the highly commercialized and awe inspiring religiosity of the Middle Ages. Initially Luther understood God and man according to contemporary religious thinking. He saw the contrast between the concepts of an avenging might and man as a mere nothing in opposition to a God of Justice and Law and human beings.

All the changes in his concept of God as well as his understanding of man started when he started studying the Bibel, especially Saint Paul's letters. This occurred when he started to lecture in Wittenberg. Changes in his perception of God brought him to changes in his anthropological conceptions.

His concepts of God and man became for him the key problems which had to be solved before he could establish his theology. Based on the New Testament. Luther felt God was distant and attributed to him the possibility of forgiveness and mercy. He felt man was fallen in sin and had the hope of salvation through faith. Between God and man was lying the martyrdom-cross which is the hope that man will reach God. And what about Luther's internal struggle with the feeling of his own sinfulness from the point of view of Sundén's role theory?

According to the medieval religious convictions Luther perceived himself as a nothingness towards an omnipotent and severe God. He, as well as other people, were sentenced to damnation. At the same time God was perceived by Luther as being a ruthless and avenging Judge. This perception resulted from the fact that Luther's contact with God was full of awe and simultaneously full of intense exertions to gain his own salvation through good works.

After revaluating his understanding of God, which resulted in changes in his understanding of the human being Luther came to a clear individualization of the interaction between God and Luther. God appears as a kindhearted and forgiving father and became for Luther a partner in mutual, personal contact. It is Luther himself who fills up the abyss between God and man in order to bring closer these two beings. This act grants to Luther a feature of certain individualization and even sui generis priority in structuring the God-man relationship. It can probably be seen as a special mission which Luther undertook and which made him in his own eyes a chosen person in personal interaction with God. The interaction between man and God assumes, according Sundén's conception, a process of role taking and role adopting. As a necessary conditon for such s process Sundén specifies that a person must experience a sufficiently difficult situation which can not be solved by "technical" or secular means. In "Luther's case" it is clearly a situation which could not be handled by methods offered by the secular world or by contemporary religiosity.

At the same time Luther had at his disposal assimilated religious tradition, which according to Sundén is supposed to be a necessary condition for the process of role raking and role adopting. Acquired religious tradition became for Luther the solution to his complicated situation. Discarding theological trends of the contemporary church Luther used his own knowledge of theology based on the Bible. His studies on the Bible became more thorough and concerned especially Saint Paul's letters. These letters reveal to Luther a new way which could help him resolve his difficult situation.

Luther's external struggle with the institutional church can also be explained in terms of the role theory.

Awareness of an external threat from powerful Rome together with his very difficult internal situation became the very reason that he was so adamant in confirming his own new convictions by way of identification with a chosen Biblical personage. This is turn implies that Luther expects

God to assume a similar role with him i.e. God will let Luther realize his powerful and effective care.

Who is the Biblical personage that Luther chose in order to take his role towards God and towards syrrounding reality? The fact that Luther very often quotes Saint Paul's letters as well as some similarities between both characters in how they approach problems of God and man seems to prove that Luther takes the role of the apostle Paul and as result has a way of understanding God the same as that which appears in Saint Paul's writings.

Luther's basic theological assumptions are: man is not justified by good works but by faith. This comes directly from Paul's letters: "The righteous will live by faith" (Rom. I, 17). Good deeds prescribed by the law as the only way to achieve salvation proved in Paul's reasoning to be an insufficient "ticket to Heaven", because according to Paul "by observing the law no one will be justified" (Gal. 2, 17).

Let us look now at the analogous events and situations in the lives of both Saint Paul and Luther. The conversions of both men were dramatic, awe inspiring eventos, which directed them on the way "to the Truth". Christ revealed himself to Saul near Damascus, blinds him with his brightness, and throws him on his knees. After that the man who formerly persecuted Christians became a faithful follower of Christ. Similarly, Luther, thrown to the ground by a heavy storm near Erfurt, took a vow to take the habit. There is a similarity in both cases: Paul as well as Luther were converted under the influence of unusual, forceful and terrible circumstances. Furthermore Paul's conflicts with Roman authority and his imprisonment reminds us of Luther's clash with the Pope and the Emperor.

Paul's perception of God was also influenced by external events. The unremitting persecutions he was submitted to caused his perception of God to agree with the actual situation. The miraculous saving of Saint Paul from a Roman jail proved unquestionably God's protection of the apostle.

The concept of God as an omnipotent protector of his followers, especially his "warriors of faith" in part removed the feeling of external threat and gave sense to preaching the Gospel. Let us look in a global way at Luther's process of taking and adopting Biblical roles.

Luther's actions were stimulated mainly by his fear of his own salvation together with a conviction of his own sinfulness. Since it was impossible to solve his own complicated internal situation Luther found in Saint Paul letters the answer to his own problems. He accepts Paul's theology which perfectly answers all Luther's torturing questions and doubts. The problem of evil which puts Luther in a desperate internal struggle finds its solution in Paul's teachings. It does not disappear, but finds a counterbalance in good radiating from the New Testament. Luther had to find biographical similarities between himself and Paul and therefore Luther identifies himself with Paul's person and expects God to deal with him in a way analogous to the way God dealt with Saint Paul. So, we have the process of Luther taking the role of Saint Paul and at the same time adopting the role of God according to the situation he perceived as being similar to Saint Paul's situation, i.e. expecting God to solve his problem in the same way he solved Paul's problems. When Luther starts role taking he experiences a special readiness to accept God's every "instruction" and expects that God will treat him similary to his predecessor in the Biblical myth. Thus in Luther there are three necessary elements for the process of role taking and role adopting i.e. situation, interaction and expectations.

The process of role adoption also creates a special perception of failures. "Normal" failures are perceived as having special intention such as the intervention of God, which contains some special purpose and meaning. This perception of failures may be treated as a process of special importance. It allows Luther to cling relentlessly to his position, since he is certain that every misfortune occurs according to God's will. Furthermore he is conscious of the fact that God will not abandon him even in the most difficult moments just as he did not abandon Saint Paul in various dangerous situations (at court or in the Roman prison).

So, it seems that the hypothesis concerning Luther role playing St. Paul is demonstrated. At the same time Luther adopted the role of God in expecting him to act similarly as he acted towards St. Paul.

In recapitulation we might state that Hjalmar Sundén's theory based on social psychology sufficiently explains the formation of religious attitudes in an individual. Of course the role theory is not the only possible method of researching religious experience. However within the scheme of reference presented by social psychology the theory fully answers questions concerning the way of shaping religious personality. The theory does not require the compilation of other psychological theories in order to perform its purpose. So, for example Källstad's study seems to be to distant from original Sundén's conception.

There are of course many other problems which might be analyzed from the point of view of the role theory i.e. analysis of the influences on Luther's religiosity his perception of the roles of his mother, father, the Church and the Devil. Such an analysis of course must be based on a broader scope of Luther's works.

The presented paper is only an attempt to show that Hjalmar Sundén's theory is an autonomous conception, which explains the process of forming religious attitudes from the point of view of social psychology.

Literature

Capps, D. Sundén's Role-Taking Theory: The Case of John Henry Newman and His Mentors. Journal for the Scientific Study of Religion, 1982, 1, 58-70.

Febvre, L. Un destin: Martin Luther. Paris: 1952.

Grzymala-Moszczynska, H. Teoria roli Hjalmara Sundéna. Studia Religiologica, 1979, 4, 149-159.

Källstad, T. John Wesley and the Bible. A Psychological Study. Uppsala: 1974.

Källstad, T. (Ed.). Psychological Studies of Religious Man. (To the honour of Hjalmar Sundén). Uppsala, 1978.

Landgraf, W. Martin Luther. Reformator und Rebell. Berlin: 1981.

Lau, F. Marcin Luther. Warszawa: 1966.

Luther, M. Martin Luther Werke. Kritische Gesamtausgabe. Weimar: 1883.

Sundén, H. Die Religion und die Rollen. Ein psychologische Untersuchung der Frömmigkeit. Berlin: 1966.

Sundén, H. Some Remarks on St. Augustine's Confessions IX, 4 in the light of role-psychology. Proceedings of the Colloquy of European Psychologists of Religion, Nijmegen: 1979.

Sundén, H. Exegesis and the psychology of religion: Some remarks on the interpretation of the parables of the kingdom. Temenos, 1975, 11, 148-162.

Sundén, H. Luthers Vorrede auf den Psalter von 1545 als religionspsychologisches Dokument. Einige Bemerkungen. Archiv für Religionspychologie, 1983, 36-44.

Sciegienny, A. Luther. Warszawa: 1967.

Unger, J. On religious experience. A psychological study. Uppsala: 1976.

Wantula, A., & Niemczyk, W. Wybrane Ksiegi Symboliczne Kosciola Ewangelicko-Augsburskiego. Warszawa: 1980.

William James' model of mysticism

J. H. Clark
University of Manchester

1. Introduction

In his classic book The Varieties of Religious Experience, William James (1902) places mysticism at the heart of religion. He clearly regards it as a key topic. He proposes a set of four 'marks', or criteria, by which mystical experiences may be recognised. He then goes on to provide a set of 'typical examples' of mystical experiences. These examples were listed in Table 1 of my paper at the Second Symposium (Clark, 1982), where they were each given, by me, a serial number.

Since James says that he has arranged his examples in order of increasing 'religious significance' he seems to lead one to expect that his four 'marks' would occur more frequently towards the latter end of his series of examples than towards the beginning.

One examining the examples however (Clark, 1982), I discovered to my surprise that the reverse was the case.

In the present paper I wish to explore this discrepancy in greater detail and to propose a possible explanation for it. In particular, I wish to propose a modification of William James' model of mysticism, based on my map of mental states (Clark, 1983).

2. William James' model of mysticism

William James' model of mysticism is not set down explicitly in his book (1902). However, he makes a number of statements about mysticism and we can assemble a rough model by collecting them together.

2.1. His model of religion

To begin with, he sets his discussion of mysticism within a more general model, of religion. He defines religion as follows: "Religion, therefore, as I now ask you arbitrarily to take it, shall mean for us the feelings, acts, and experiences of individual men in their solitude, so far as they apprehend themselves to stand in relation to whatever they may consider the divine".

I have briefly displayed his further discussion of religion, in Figure 1. This shows mysticism to be one kind of 'personal religion'.

<u>Figure 1</u>. William James' model of religion.

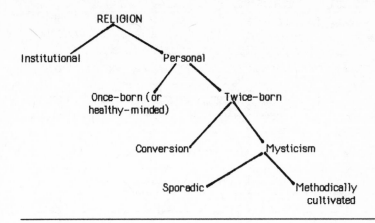

James gives his two lectures on mysticism a place of honour within his book (1902) and says: "One may say truly, I think, that personal religious experience has its root and centre in mystical states of consciousness;....."

2.2. <u>His four 'Marks' or Criteria</u>
Then, in order to be clear as to his own use of the word mystical, he proposes: ".... four marks which, when an experience has them, may justify us in calling it mystical for the purpose of the present lectures."

These 'marks', or criteria, are well-known and I will only give very abbreviated versions of them here:

1. <u>Ineffability</u>: i.e. inexpressibility in words; things that cannot be spoken.
2. <u>Noetic quality</u>: i.e. states of knowledge, of truth, of significance.
3. <u>Transiency</u>: i.e. these states rarely last for more than half an hour.
4. <u>Passivity</u>: i.e. feelings such as being grasped and held by a superior power.

About the first two 'marks', Ineffability and Noetic quality, he says: "These two characters will entitle any state to be called mystical, in the sense in which I use the word."

The other two 'marks', Transiency and Passivity, he says: "are less sharply marked, but are usually found."

2.3. His forty-three 'Typical Examples'

I have been able to identify forty-three separate 'typical examples' of mystical experience in the text and footnotes of James' lectures XVI and XVII. In my previous paper, to the Second Symposium (Clark, 1982), I gave each of these 'typical examples' a serial number and a page reference, and quoted their opening and closing words.

(Please note that, in this present paper, I do not discuss the five or so drug-induced states also included by James in his lectures on mysticism.)

3. Method

3.1. Occurrence of the 'Marks' in each 'Typical Example'

I examined the forty-three examples several times and recorded the definite presence of a 'mark' by the firgure 1 and its definite absence by the figure 0. In doubtful cases I chose 1/2.

Tables 1.1, 1.2 and 1.3 show my latest version of these judgements. It is based, informally, on my several previous versions, including the one recorded in my previous paper (Clark, 1982).

I have also studied and discussed versions by two other people (C.H. and A.H.) who applied the same method, independently, but were, however, both familiar with the above-mentioned paper.

3.2. Classification of the 'Typical Examples' by the Furthest Mental State Reached

I have classified the forty-three 'typical examples' by the furthest mental state reached in the set of mental states which occur along the variable, Intensity of Mood, described in my book 'A Map of Mental States' (Clark, 1983). These mental states, together with the letters of the alphabet used as abbreviations of them, are as follows:

A	Average state (of everyday life)
P	Peak experience
M	Mystical state proper
V	The Void (or Nirvana)
O	The Origin (of the map)
Z	Zero state
Ee	Eerie state
A*	Enlightened Average state

These states are all described, with illustrative examples, in my book (Clark, 1983). They can be set out as a network, or 'directed graph', as follows:

$$A \rightleftharpoons P \rightleftharpoons M \longrightarrow V \longrightarrow O \rightleftharpoons Z \rightleftharpoons Ee \rightleftharpoons A*$$

I have performed the classification of the forty-three examples by comparing them with the examples of the different types of mental state given in my book (Clark, 1983). I realise this method is very subjective. Moreover, I have been influenced, especially where James' examples are very short, by the place occupied by them in James' own series.

4. Results

The results of my scrutiny of the 'typical examples', for the occurrence of 'marks', are shown in Tables 1.1, 1.2 and 1.3.

Table 1.1 The occurrence scores of each of the four 'marks' in the 'typical examples' of mystical experience, serial numbers 1 to 17. (The presence of a 'mark' is shown by the figure 0 and a doubtful case by 1/2.)

Serial Number	'Marks'				
	1	2	3	4	all
1	0	1	0	0	1
2	0	1	0	0	1
3	1	1/2	1/2	0	2
4	1	1	0	1/2	21/2
5	1	1	1	0	3
6	1	1	1	1	4
7	0	1	1	1	3
8	0	1	0	0	1
9	1	0	1	1	3
10	0	1	1	1	3
11	0	1	0	1	2
12	1	1	0	0	2
13	1	1	1	1/2	31/2
14	0	1	0	0	1
15	0	1	1	1	3
16	1	1	0	0	2
17	1	1	1	1	4
Total:	9	151/2	81/2	8	41
% (n=17)	53	91	50	47	60 (n=17 x 4 = 68)

Table 1.2 The occurrence scores of each of the four 'marks' in the 'typical examples' of mystical experience, serial numbers 18 to 26. (The presence of a 'mark' is shown my the figure 1, its absence by the figure 0 and a doubtful case by 1/2.)

Serial Number	'Marks' 1	2	3	4	All
18	0	1	0	0	1
19	1	1	1	0	3
20	1	1	0	0	2
21	0	1	1	1	3
22	0	1	1	1	3
23	1	1	1	1/2	31/2
24	0	2	0	1/2	11/2
25	1/2	1	1	1/2	3
26	1	1	0	1/2	21/2
Total:	41/2	9	5	4	221/2
% (n=9)	50	100	56	44	63 (n = 9 x 4 = 36)

Table 1.3 The occurrence scores each of the four 'marks' in the 'typical examples' of mystical experience, serial numbers 27 to 43. (The presence of a 'mark' is shown by the figure 1, its absence by the figure 0 and a doubtful case by 1/2.)

Serial Numbers	'Marks' 1	2	3	4	All
27	1/2	0	0	0	1/2
28	0	0	0	0	0
29	0	1	0	0	1
30	1/2	0	0	0	1/2
31	0	0	0	0	0
32	1	1/2	0	0	11/2
33	1	0	0	0	1
34	0	0	0	1	1
35	0	0	0	0	0
36	0	1	0	0	1
37	0	1	0	0	1
38	0	0	0	0	0
39	0	1/2	0	0	1/2
40	0	0	0	0	0
41	0	1	0	0	1
42	0	1/2	0	0	1/2
43	0	0	0	1/2	1/2
Total:	3	51/2	0	11/2	10
% (n=17)	18	32	0	9	15 (n =17 x 4 = 68)

106

The contents of Tables 1.1, 1.2 and 1.3 are further analysed in Tables 2.1, 2.2 and 2.3.

Table 2.1: Total Occurrence Scores of each 'mark' for the 'typical examples': serial numbers 1 to 17, 18 to 26 and 27 to 43. (Note that the % scores for the first two sets are similar, and greater than those of the third set.)

Total Occurrence Scores of the 'Marks'

Serial Numbers	1. Ineff.		2. Noet.		3. Trans.		4. Pass.		ALL	
	Score	%	Score	%	Score	%	Score	%	Score	%
1 to 17 (n = 17)	9	53	151/2	91	81/2	50	8	47	41 (n=17 x 4 = 68)	60
18 to 26 (n = 9)	41/2	50	9	100	5	56	4	44	221/2 (n=9 x 4 = 36)	63
27 to 43 (n = 17)	3	18	51/2	32	0	0	11/1	9	10 (n=17 x 4 = 68)	15

Table 2.2 Total Occurrence Scores of each 'mark' for the 'typical examples': serial numbers 1 to 26 and 27 to 43. (Note the drop in the % scores in the second set as compared with the first.)

Total Occurrence Scores of the 'Marks'

Serial Numbers	1. Ineff.		2. Noet.		3. Trans.		4. Pass.		ALL	
	score	%	score	%	score	%	score	%	score	%
1 to 26 (n=26)	131/2	52	241/2	94	131/2	52	12	46	631/2 (n= 26 x 4 = 104)	61
27 to 43	3	18	51/2	32	0	0	11/2	9	10 (n= 17 x 4 = 68)	15

Table 2.3 Total Occurrence Scores of each 'mark' for all the 'typical examples': serial numbers 1 to 43. (Note that the second 'mark', Noetic quality, ranks higher than the first, Ineffability.)

Total Occurrence Scores of the 'Marks'

Serial Numbers	1. Ineff.		2. Noet.		3. Trans.		4. Pass.		ALL	
	Score	%	Score	%	Score	%	Score	%	Score	%
1 to 43 (n = 43)	161/2	38	30	70	131/2	31	131/2	31	731/2 (n=43 x 4 = 172)	43
Rank	2		1		3		3			

My classification of the 'typical examples' by the furthest mental state reached, along my variable Intensity of Mood (Clark, 1983) is shown in the right-hand side of Figure 2.

I have grouped serial numbers 1 to 17, 18 to 26, and 27 to 43, into three sets. The first is James' set of "sporadic" examples. The remainder are his "systematically cultivated" examples. These 9 have subdivided after 26 because of the drop in occurrence scores, seen in Figure 2.

5. Discussion

In five 'typical examples', those with serial numbers 28, 31, 35, 38 and 40, no 'marks' were found at all. In another five, with serial numbers 27, 30, 39, 42 and 43, the score was only 1/2, i.e. 'doubtfully present'.

In seven 'typical examples' neither of the first two 'marks' were found: numbers 28, 31, 34, 35, 38, 40 and 43. In another four, 27, 30, 39 and 42, the score was only 1/2 for the first two 'marks'.

William James' forty-three 'typical examples' of mystical experience do not, therefore, exhibit his criteria or 'marks' as fully as would have been expected.

Moreover, although the second two 'marks' are indeed 'less sharply marked' than the first two (see Table 2.3), nevertheless the second 'mark', 'Noetic quality' occurs more than the first, 'Ineffability', thus reversing the order in which James presented them.

The most striking finding is, however, the drop in the occurrence of the 'marks' after serial number 26. (See Figure 2.)

108

Having attempted to classify the 'typical examples' by the mental states, on my map of mental states (Clark, 1983), as shown in Figure 2, I have formed the opinion that the above-mentioned drop in occurrence of the 'marks' can, perhaps, be explained by the idea that, at about serial number 26, the series of 'typical examples' goes through a limit, the maximum Intensity of Mood on my map, at V (The Void). After this the series returns to A* (the Enlightened Average state).

I would suggest that, up to serial number 26 the four 'marks' put forward by James apply well but that, after that, the mystics are more concerned with other aspects of their experience.

Thus, when describing V (The Void) they, in fact, interpret it as 'The Truth', 'The Godhead', 'The ONE' and so on; and when describing A* (The Enlightened Average state) they are mainly concerned with the extra-ordinary transformation that has occurred to their 'ordinary life'. In particular they discuss their sense of 'perfect freedom'.

If James' model of mysticism is modified, by taking into account the idea that his dimension of 'religious significance' is interrupted by a limiting state, then the discrepancy in the occurrence of his four 'marks' is, perhaps, explained.

Acknowledgements
I worked on this paper and my previous paper (Clark, 1982) during two visits to Professor Nils G. Holm, at the Institute for the History of Religion at Åbo Akademi, Åbo, Finland, in August 1980 and August 1984. I have also benefitted greatly from discussions with Christine Hubbert and Angela Hawkins about detecting the occurrence of the four 'marks'.

Summary
William James' series of forty-three 'typical examples' of mystical experiences in his lectures XVI and XVII, on Mysticism, in his classic book The Varieties of Religious Experience (1902), were examined to see whether his four 'marks' or criteria for mystical experiences were exhibited by them, as would be expected.
In five examples (12%) no 'marks' at all could be found and, in another five only one 'mark' each; and they were doubtfully present. Moreover, the total occurrence of 'marks' per example, with a possible maximum of four, was found to drop sharply in the examples following the example with the serial number 26. (These serial numbers were given to the examples by myself (Clark, 1982).)
Thus, this fall-off in 'marks' occurred late-on in the series of forty-three 'typical examples'. This was a paradoxical discrepancy, since James seems to lead one to expect that the 'marks' would occur more frequently as the series progressed along his dimension of 'religious significance', not less.
When each example was classified by noting the furthest mental state reached within it, using the series of mental states described by myself (Clark, 1983), then the later members of the series of examples were seen, generally, to be further along the series of mental states. These mental states are shown, in the present paper, as being ranged along the variable of Intensity of Mood, from A, P and M to V and A*, where these letters stand for Average state, Peak experience, Mystical state proper, The Void and Enlightened Average state.
I go on to suggest that the paradoxical discrepancy, mentioned above, is due to James' dimension, of 'religious significance', containing a limit. This would correspond to The Void, V,

in the above set of mental states. Those 'typical examples' classified by myself as having reached the states V and A* no longer show the 'marks' to any extent, apart from serial numbers 19 and 20.

This finding leads, in turn, to a consideration of the need for different sets of 'marks' or criteria, for different sections of the mystical path. Thus, although James' four 'marks' apply well to examples classified as reaching mental states P and M, after that they are no longer suitable as criteria for mystical experiences.

Literature

Clark, J.H. "Plotting the mystical path: a re-examination of William James' four criteria." Proceedings of the second symposium of European psychologists of religion, Nijmegen, 1982.

Clark, J.H. A map of mental states. London: Routledge and Kegan Paul, 1983.

James, W. Varieties of religious experience. Harmondsworth: Penguin, 1982 (1902).

Classification of Mental State

Serial Numbers	Sum of the Occurrence Scores for ALL 'Marks' (½ 1 1½ 2 2½ 3 3½ 4)	Z	Ee	A	P	M	V	0	Z	Ee	A*
		Intensity of Mood → MIN. LOW AV. HIGH MAX. Mental State						Int. of Mood → MIN. LOW AV. Mental State			
1	* *			x							
2	* *				x						
3	* * * *				x						
4	* * * * *					x					
5	* * * * * *			x							
6	* * * * * * * * *					x					
7	* * * * * * *					x					
8	* *					x					
9	* * * * * *					x					
10	* * * * * *					x					
11	* * * *					x					
12	* * * *					x					
13	* * * * * * *					x					
14	* *					x					
15	* * * * * *					x					
16	* * * *					x					
17	* * * * * * * *					x					
18	* *					x					
19	* * * * * *						x				
20	* * * *						x				
21	* * * * * *					x					
22	* * * * * *					x					
23	* * * * * * *					x					
24	* * *					x					
25	* * * * * *					x					
26	* * * * *					x					
27	*						x				
28	* *					x					
29	* *										x
30	*						x				
31							x				
32	* * *						x				
33	* *						x				
34	* *										x
35											x
36	* *										x
37	* *										x
38							x				
39	*						x				
40							x				
41	* *						x				
42	*				x						
43	*										x

Figure 2. Histogram of the Sum of Occurrence Scores for ALL 'Marks'; and a Classification of the Furthest Mental State described in each 'Typical Example', using an 'Intensity of Mood' variable from A Map of Mental States (Clark, 1983).

Bibliodrama about Job: some preliminary notes

A. Gerritsen
Catholic University Nijmegen

Studying Sundèns (1966) role theory I came to the conclusion that there is a remarkable affinity between this theory and the practice of bibliodrama. My guess is that the so called "Phasenwechsel" from usual daily experience to religious experience can be studied in vivo in a bibliodrama. It is as if bibliodrama is a straightforward methodological deduction from Sundèns theory. In this paper I will investigate the relation between Sundèns theory and the practice of bibliodrama. To do so I will first briefly review Sundèns theory (A) and second I will summarize the practice of bibliodrama (B). I will conclude this paper with a specific Bible drama: the Book of Job (C).

A) Sundèns theory of religious experience

1. Frame of reference

Sundèns thesis is that knowledge of the religious myths and stories (for instance a Bible story) is a necessary precondition for religious experience. He mentions social acceptance and personal attitude as the two other facilitating factors enhancing a religious experience of reality. In the construction of our reality we are constantly interpreting our life events according to our previously learned frames of reference. In these frames of reference roles are of the utmost importance. Sundèn points to the fact that by taking the role of another we can feel, think and behave like him or her. By taking the role of for instance a person in the Bible we can even see and behave like this person unto the divine partner. Thus, identifying with a person or theme drawn from religious tradition conditions religious experience. The shift from a mundane interpretation of our reality to a religious one he calls "Phasenwechsel".

2. Interactionism

I will now go into the anthropological premises of the theory. Sundèns theory is based upon symbolic interactionism which stresses the fact that reality is a social construction. We don't project -like a movie projector- our subjective meanings on a blank screen (which would be an extreme idealistic viewpoint), nor do we simply record -like a camera- what is out there (which would be an extreme realistic viewpoint), but the relation between person and world is to be described as a dynamic process of interaction. Subject and object are no separated entities, they cannot stand alone, like poles their very being is given by their dynamic relation of interdependency (Pongratz, 1967, 12). The interactional view on reality is of great importance for the psychology of religion. Looking upon religious experience as an inner feeling or need can be unmasked as a reductionistic stance overlooking the essential interaction with religion as a cultural and historical phenomenon. While emphasizing the importance of religious tradition in the generation of religious experience it is at the same time avoided to reduce religious experience to a mere replication of a fixed bundle of revelational stories in which the roles and positions of man unto his God and vice versa are unchangeably defined forever. Both factors are taken account of: 1) the process of giving meaning to these religious stories (parables, themes, pericopes) by the individual out of his personal history and 2) the necessity of a supply of religious roles which can serve as frames of reference. The adoption of interactionism in psychology of religion helps us understand religious experience in its complexity. It makes us navigate successfully between the Scilla of uncommunicative, volatile and elusive subjectivism and the Charibdis of massive objectivism.

3. Cognitive paradigm

Sundèns theory is so attractive because of its simplicity. According to the generally accepted cognitive paradigm in psychology all human experience is the result of interpretation. Sundèn makes us realize that the same thing is true for religious experience. As in every experience models, schemes and cognitive structures are needed which function as frames of reference. To illustrate his theory in the field of perception Sundèn uses the example of ambiguous figures. We all know the picture which can be seen or interpreted by a young man either as his young and very attractive fiancee or as his old and say less attractive or even ugly mother in law. Another example is Rubins vase: an ambiguous picture either to be seen as a white vase before a black background or as two dark faces in profile say staying before a bright window. What we see depends on our perceptual set. This set is a program (a cognitive structure) stored in memory, which processes the incoming sensations into experiences: that is into meaningful figures before a background. Without these structures or frames of reference our sensations would remain meaningless: they don't develop into experiences. Experience and frame presuppose each other. By our frames of reference we can anticipate our situation and cope with it more or less adequately. Frames have the status of working hypotheses about our reality. Consequently they constantly need adjustment and readjustment. Sundèn describes a police-officer chasing a dangerous criminal on a beach. Suddenly the policeman's eye catches a rifle-barrel. He seeks cover by falling down and shortly after that, he discovers the threatening object to be nothing more than the neck of a beer-bottle laying in the sand and pointing in his direction. If I may elaborate a bit on this illustration: in spite of this obvious misperception the tendency of the policeman to perceive long, thin objects as rifle-barrels will be judged as adequate in this threatening situation. Eventually it could have saved his life. If he would go on however perceiving long thin objects as rifle-barrels in safer situations, he probably would be advised to take a holiday and if this would not help, to see a doctor. Perceiving shooting criminals everywhere and anytime is a distortion and reduction of reality due to the dominance and exclusiveness of one frame of reference which closes –if I may allude to Huxley– other "doors of perception". If we dispose only of a few frames of reference we can only experience a small number of dimensions of reality. Consequently we are doomed to live in a shrunken world.

4. Rollenübernahme and Rollenaufnahme

As I said already, our frames or cognitive structures continually need adjustment and readjustment. The interaction of the person with his situation leads to the refinement of his cognitive structures. At the same time in the process of social learning new structures are formed. In playing houses children learn the cognitive structures related with the roles and positions of father and mother, in school they learn to take the role of a pupil (Sundèn uses the concept "Rollenübernahme") and they learn to anticipate the role of the teacher (Sundèn: "Rollenaufnahme"), while studying physics they learn to take the perspective of a physician on the physical dimension of reality. Listening to fairy tales and myths, reading novels, occupying oneself with dreams, relating with friends, neighbours, colleagues, going to the cinema, expressing oneself artistically in music, dance, painting, pottery or otherwise, all these things may in the long run broaden the scope of ones reality including logical and rational, sharply defined concepts as well as poetry, novelry and other forms of symbolic language to approach personal, existential and religious dimensions of reality. Sundèn points to the fact that by reading and listening to religious stories and by taking part in religious rituals the cognitive structures, especially religious roles, are learned. If we don't learn these roles we will not have the frames or perspectives by which we can experience the religious dimension of reality. As said, theoretically religious experience is nothing special: it only needs the cognitive structures, supplied in abundance by religious tradition. But if this is so, why has it become so difficult then for modern man to perceive his situation religiously?

In terms of Sundèns theory: switching from usual, daily frames of reference to religious frames has become a rare phenomenon. Religion has lost its overarching ideological impact. Modernity implies pluralization not only with respect to division of labour, but also in the field of philosophy of life. Religion has become one option among others. Turning to religious interpretations to cope with existential questions is no more a matter of course. Besides, other frames have become dominant in modern society. These are the frames inherent to the world of labour where rational thinking, productivity and effeiciency are the dominant values.

B) The practice of bibliodrama

In the next section of my paper I will show you the relation between Sundèns theory and the practice of bibliodrama. Maybe at the end you will agree with me that bibliodrama could have been a methodological deduction from Sundèns theory.

Derksen & Andriessen (1985) look upon bibliodrama as a form of pastoral work. The aim of a bibliodrama is to stimulate the participants in their religious development. Their position in the course or training is defined as that of a believer, but not in the sense of accepting the religious dogma's. The authors view faith as a dynamic process in which belief and unbelief form a fundamental polarity together with another basic polarity of anguish and desire.

In a bibliodrama the participants are invited to take the position of a person in the Bible with whom they can identify and play his or her role. Mostly a group of 10 to 16 people under the supervision of a pastoral worker and co-worker work together to dramatize a Bible story. Because of the fact that the participants have chosen for a bibliodrama-course out of their position as believers the bibliodrama for them is not an unrealistic situation of game-playing but a serious spiritual endeavour. I will now summarize the 12 steps of the procedure in a bibliodrama as developed by Derksen & Andriessen.

1) A bibliodrama can be a situation with great impact: while playing the role in a Bible-story the participants confront themselves with the tension between the meaning of the role and their own personal situation. Such a self-confrontation which may add to ones self-knowledge, above all by sensing ones stance as a believer and getting more insight into it, is not an easy thing, especially not when it takes place in a group. It is for this reason that the first step is a short talk about the aims and procedure of the bibliodrama. This talk has the character of a contract in which the person decides if he or she really wants to engage oneself in the endeavour of a bibliodrama.

2) The information about the procedure will be shortly repeated at the

beginning of every bibliodrama-session. This is done by mentioning the 12 steps.

3) A Bible story is told, for instance "the cure of a cripple" by Luke, chapter 5, verses 17-27.

4) The story-teller invites the group-members to gather the roles they have heard in the story. These roles are written down on a blackboard or flap. In the case of "the cure of a crippled" we get for instance the following roles: the pupils of Jezus, Jezus himself, the Pharisees and lawyers from Judea, Galilea and Jerusalem, the power of the Lord, the cripple on his way to Jezus, the cripple in front of Jezus, the cripple glorifying the Lord, the bearers, the crowd, God, those who glorify the Lord, those who have witnessed unheard things.

5) The Bible-story is told a second time. This is done to enable the group-members to get involved emotionally with the story and to sense which of the roles is the best representation of ones personal situation.

6) The story is put in scene. The story-teller shows the spots in the room where everyone can take position according to the role one has chosen. In doing so the room becomes the visualized world of the Bible-story told a moment ago. It is important that one is very careful in finding out what is the right place to go to in the room. To facilitate the attention to this task things are preferably done in silence.

7) The pastor turns to everyone to ask which is the role one has chosen. In doing so everyones participation in the drama is confirmed and consolidated. Now everyone knows who is who in the drama at hand.

8) The pastor tries to get in touch with the "tension" between the people who have taken their roles in the story. This enables him to choose some of the role-players for a pastoral interview. The interview consists of four components. I will mention these components now.
- The aim of the first component is to get clearness about the situation of the role-player and the way he or she is feeling about the choice of the role. Possible questions are for instance: May I ask you what it means for you to be on this spot? How does it feel like? How certain are you? Are you becoming uncertain? Is this the right place for you? Would you prefer to go to another place? How about your being alone here? Do you enjoy people being close to you here? Your are a pupil standing right next to the bearers; can you tell me what you are expressing with this position? You are a cripple; was it you who asked to be brought to Jezus or was it the

116

bearers who pushed you to do so? Where are you, still outdoors, already on the roof, in front of Jezus? These questions make the role-players sense the atmosphere.

- The second component of the interview is meant to find out what is the role-player's problem now and with which questions he or she does or does not want to confront himself or herself. A Bible-story appeals to people. The question is to discover what is the specific appeal now for this role-player in his or hers particular life-situation. For example: the pastor says: "could you express your growing desire being a cripple by moving yourself, acknowledging your inner paralysis?"

- The third component of the pastoral interview is the response to the interview of those who are not directly interviewed. Sometimes they show their inner response by moving to another spot. The pastor will pay attention to this move and ask for the meaning of it.

-- The fourth component of the interview is the willingness of the others to take an active part in it at the moment they feel touched by it. Though the pastoral interview normally takes place with one or two role-players, the scope of the interview sometimes can be broadened by letting other role-players participate in it. It is important that the other participants don't take over the role of the pastor-interviewer but that their interventions emanate from their role-position. So far for the four components of the pastoral interview.

9) The pastoral interview creates the atmosphere from which scenes can be actually played. Bibliodrama is meant to help improve peoples' self-knowledge: who am I as a believer, how do I experience myself, how am I relating to others in this Bible-story, in this group? Bibliodrama tries to stimulate the inner developmental process of the participants. By actually moving in the room the role-player can get in touch with his or her inner dynamic process. The combination of verbal and non-verbal expression of the inner movements is an essential element in a drama and this is true for a bibliodrama as well. The expression of the inner process from the position of the role in a specific Bible-story can enable the role-player to perceive the grounding questions in his or her life-situation more clearly.

10) Together the nine steps I just mentioned will take about 90 minutes. Than there is a 15-minutes' break to recover ones breath.

11) After the break the participants are invited to communicate their experiences during the play. This communication is meant to let speak those who have actually played a role as well as those who have not taken initiative during the play. The explicit formulation of what one has

discovered can be of great help to the others.

12) The final step is an evaluation of the session.

These twelve steps give us an impression about the procedure of a bibliodrama. We can now ask ourselves why listening to a sermon or reading a Bible-story rarely leads to a religious experience whereas playing a role in a Bibliodrama does. One of the answers is that the active playing of the role deepens the identification with the world of the Bible-story. I will mention some facilitating factors with respect to this identification. 1) CONFIRMATION OF ONES ROLE AS A BELIEVER. By participating in a bibliodrama one is confirming his or her position as a believer. As said, a bibliodrama is not an "as if"-situation. The role and position of believer function as a frame of reference. Within this frame the activities will not be looked upon as games without any commitment. On the contrary, they will be perceived as serious steps in ones life-situation. I need not say this seriousness does not exclude humour! 2) DEFINING THE ROLE OF A BELIEVER AS A DYNAMIC PROCESS. From the concept of man underlying this bibliodrama the role of a believer is not defined as a static one but as a dynamic process implying the polarity of belief and unbelief as well as the polarity of anguish and desire. Being defined as a believer in this way will not impair ones personal freedom. 3) RESPECTING EXPERIENCE. The attitude of the pastor and co-pastor is such that they don't try to change the experience of the participants. They are not pushing them in one or another direction. A central value is to respect the process of experiencing. 4) INTERACTION OF PERSONAL AND TRADITIONAL HISTORY. The participants choose a Bible-role because of its relatedness to their own life situation. From this a process of interaction between personal and traditional history starts. In this process the Bible-story is not to be reduced to the personal history. It keeps its inner appeal or direction and the role-player is reminded of his or her freedom to respond to this appeal or not. 5) INTENSIVE GROUP. The role-playing takes place in a group. What is at stake is the quality of the relatedness to others. The inherent polarity of self and other intensifies the process of experiencing. The impact of the group may impair the dominance of the usual daily frame of reference. 6) NONVERBAL EXPRESSION. The nonverbal expression of inner movements enhances the clearness and the intensity of the experience. 7) SYMBOLIC FUNCTION OF THE BIBLE-STORY. A Bible-story has a symbolic meaning. A symbol has many meanings including fundamental polarities. The symbolic function inherent to a Bible-story allows for a multitude of interpretations. Thus everyone can understand a Bible-story in his or her own way, out of his or her personal history. This is not to say that a Bible-story is like a blank screen without a meaning of its own. It has, as said, an inner appeal, but the character of this appeal is an expressive one. The function of a good story is to point to the grounding questions in human life, not to solve them.

I conclude this paper with a Bible-story which points to the fundamental problem of human misery. Before I do so I will draw your attention to attributional psychology. One of the interesting questions in this field of research is how people perceive their own contribution to their life events. Do they think they are the masters of their situation or do they see themselves as the victims. Let's be a bit more precise. Some people may tend to attribute the good events to themselves and the bad ones to others. There will also be people who will do the other thing around: ascribe negative results to themselves and positive ones to others. To systematize: 1) an event can be experienced positive or negative, 2) an event can be beyond human control or not, 3) the amount of personal influence on the event can be perceived as great or small. If we combine these three dichotomies we get eight possibilities. I won't annoy you by enumerating them all. But you will agree with me that some of the possibilities will be evaluated as adequate and some as inadequate attitudes toward life. We all know the convinced victim who thinks he has never had any part in his misery. We also know the optimist overestimating his possibilities and his counterpart the pessimist underestimating them. There is a prayer in which the healthier attitude is hoped for:
"Oh Lord, give me the courage to resign myself to what can not be changed in my life.
Give me the power to change what in effect can be changed.
And give me the wisdom te differentiate between both".

To face ones limitations is not an easy thing. We tend to repress our vulnarablity. And this was already the case in the time of Job. One preferred the fantasy of a cosmic order wherein everything was in balance, in control. But, we have to acknowledge the dark side of the human condition, that is absurdity. In the final section of my paper I will review the Book of Job and I will introduce it by a little poem.

BOOBY-TRAP

Do you know what's a booby-trap?
It's not what it seems to be:
a ball-point, cigarette-lighter or another
harmless looking object.
It's a bomb meant to produce

personal loss on the side of the enemy.
Achmed, Mohammed, Kahlil
or whatever may be the name of the little boy
has gladly and eagerly picked one up.
Now one side of his face shows a hole
as big as a man's fist.
The inside of his mouth
can be seen through it
like on an anatomical picture.
Sitting on the arm of a Red Cross nurse
he looks at our world,
not understanding.
Did he not always brush his teeth properly
as his parents instructed him to do,
did he not wash his hands before meals
and did he not at the end of the day
clear away his toys
and recite his evening-prayer?
Was he not a good boy?
Why this?
Violation feel upon the flesh of
Achmed, Mohammed, Kahlil,
Ben, Samuel, Jezus
or whatever may be the little boy's name.
Those who try to look at him
shut their eyes in shame.
After all it is God
who lost face.
Achmed, Mohammed, Kahlil,
Ben, Samuel, Jezus,
Iwan, Andrej, Pjotr
or whatever may be the name
of the little boy
will be able to speak no more.
But Job has spoken for him.
He has wept, cried and sweared.
It is Job who has charged the Allmighty
and who has called him to account
and Job will continue to do so
all to eternity,
God damn it.

(Gerritsen, 1984b)

120

C) The book of Job

Why did I choose Job? Well I think that the Book of Job can function as a model of religious experience and of religious development. I am planning now to do research on bibliodrama about the Book of Job.

This summary of the Book of Job (Gerritsen 1984a, 1984b) is based on a commentary and translation of Pius Drijvers and Pé Hawinkels. (1978). The authors see the Book of Job in the context of the way of living and thinking of historical Israel which beliefs in a living and dynamic God. They relate the Book of Job to one of the cultural movements of that time: the so called "Wisdom thinking". Wisdom thinking meant to learn from the events and experiences in life, not to pass on the acquired insights to the next generation without any change, but to give the opportunity to listen to it and to shape it in its own way. In turn the next generation will learn to be wise, that is to accept and reject things out of its own responsibility. Running counter to its original aim the Wisdom thinking grew gradually into an abstract and systematized view on man and his world. The Wisdom thinking became a closed minded system estranging itself gradually from real life. In the days of Job this system dictated as a general and unshakable truth the doctrine that all suffering is caused by moral guilt. From this point of view a suffering person ought to confess and to submit to God to change things for the better. Job, though suffering from a great loss, does not bow to this doctrine, but he dares to trust his own experiences which learn him that innocent suffering indeed does exist, that man's fate does not always emanate from his deeds. He fully confronts himself with the reality of absurd suffering in this world. He dares to become wise by not sheltering under the familiar system, but by really facing the absurd. In spite of his friends who are no companions in his misery but moralisers of the settled system, Job goes his own hard but independent way: Job continues to look for the meaning and connection of things and in his hopeless situation he even looks for the meaning of the absurd. He experiences the indifference of life and from this he cannot but conclude that God does not care. Therefore Job accuses God. Not only does he completely talk himself out unto his Creator, but he also in all intensity and straight forward gives expression to his feelings of diminishing hope and shrinking trust, to his anger and rebelliousness, to his bitterness and disappointment, he deplores the day of his birth, he gives way to his sorrow until, after deeply and painfully sensing his infinite forlornness, he finally becomes silent. There is nothing more to say. Job has opened his heart completely. And we must add, he did it without the least guarantee for an answer. But Job's experience does lead to an answer. An answer in which he finds hope and new courage to face life. It is given to him in the form of a vision of God. He hears his God in a "storm of wind": "And than the Unspeakable gave an answer to Job. A storm of wind rose, and through it His voice sounded". To be sure God radically rejects Job's claims, among other things by referring to His greatness and inscrutability and by confronting Job with the fact that everything has its place and time and that nothing is without meaning, but what He does not reject is Job as a human being who fully dares to face his experience of reality: that is the unshakable fact of innocent suffering.

JOB'S RELIGIOUS DEVELOPMENT AND RELIGIOUS EXPERIENCE

Job's experience can be understood as a process of religious development leading to a religious experience: the apparition of God in the "storm of wind". As such to my opinion it can be taken as a paradigm. Let me summarize the important aspects to be differentiated in the developmental process:

1) While looking for the meaning and connection of things Job discovers that his experience (of innocent suffering) does not fit in the usual frame of thinking (suffering as a punishment).

2) Job breaks through the settled pattern of thinking: he lets prevail his personal and concrete experiential knowledge above the impersonal and abstract moral values at the dominating culture.

3) The abandonment of the familiar frame of thinking necessitates more than a process of cognitive restructuring. What is at stake is the very existence of Job. Leaving the old worldview to acquire a new understanding of things demands a cognitive, as well as an affective and emotional process of assimilation, which can be understood psychologically as a complete grief process.

4) The structure of the developmental process is characterized by communication. Job inquires into his reality by talking himself out to his friends (independently of their understanding) and in accordance with Jewish faith-tradition to his God (also without the certainty of being heard).

5) Not until Job has talked himself out completely and has become silent, God returns to him. From this it is reasonable to suppose that the religious experience (that is Jobs meeting with God in the "storm of wind") is related to an open search and feeling for reality and to facing the facts and limitations of human existence.

FROM DOMINATION TO SURRENDER

It's allowed to apply the concept of a religious developmental process because Job's experience moves between two contrasting images of God. At the beginning we find the image of God as a judge who rewards what's done right and punishes what's done wrong. Identification with this mighty deity meets the narcissistic fantasy of personal greatness and invulnerability (Uleyn, 1978). It is curious enough, but this deity may be put -unconsciously- to ones will. By abiding the law, by pious and honourable behaviour one can in a way enforce his goodwill and the acquired prosperity proofs his blessing. If one nevertheless meets with disaster, one can by submission and confession to the deity, keep the idea upright that one has a part in ones fate. Thus one feeds the fantasy of complete domination over ones lot. The haunting feelings of guilt can be beared better than the anguish with respect to a reality which can be unapproachable and which one cannot fully control. Seligman's (1975) research on depression proves that the perception of being in control over ones environment is one of the most important determinants of psychological well being. Though acknowledging the scientific as well as social relevance of this research we may question his underlying view of man: man as a succesful, always winning personality. The Book of Job departs from this limited view of man and the related limited image of God. But the poet of the Book of Job had a broader vision: he shows that man is not only a winner but also a tragic being, a looser. Like Job he may curse this aspect of life, as long as he does not ignore it, for in the rebelliousness and the grief the confirmation is enclosed. Human existence implies a double task: to learn to control the situation and to learn to let things go and eventually to leave life itself. At the end of his experience Job arrives at the point of surrender and related with this essential moment is a new understanding of God: a God who lets himself be experienced, who is close bu -Job hears His voice through the storm of wind-- and who is at the same time an awe-inspring God, a God who can not be manipulated, who is the Wholly Other, a transcending, unapproachable mystery.

Literature

Derksen, N., & Andriessen H. Bibliodrama en pastoraat, (forthcoming)

Drijvers, P., & Hawinkels P. Job/Prediker. Baarn: Ambo, 1978.

Gerritsen, A.J. Religieuze ontwikkeling. Lisse: Swets & Zeitlinger, 1984a

Gerritsen, A.J. Job: het zelf en de ander. In: J. v.d. Lans. Spiritualiteit. Baarn: Ambo, 1984.

Pongratz, L.J. Problemgeschichte der Psychologie. Bern: Francke Verlag, 1967.

Sundèn, H. Religion und die Rollen. Berlin: Töpelmann, 1966.

Uleyn, A. Religiositeit en fantasie. Baarn: Ambo, 1978.

Transzendenzerfahrung – am Himmel oder in der Unterwelt?

M. Kassel
Universität Münster

Vorbemerkungen

1. Ich arbeite als katholische Theologin in der Religionspsychologie, und zwar mit dem Schwerpunkt auf tiefenpsychologischer Sehweise nach dem Modell von C.G. Jung, in dem die physische und psychische Zusammengehörigkeit aller Menschen in verschiedenen Traditionen ihren Ausdruck findet, und in Verbindung mit feministischer Betrachtungsweise.
2. Die Thesen sind komprimierte Gedankengänge zu einer größeren Arbeit über tiefenpsychologisch - feministische Spiritualität, die 1986 erscheint.
3. Als Erkenntnisquellen dienten mir:
    Alltagserfahrungen und -beobachtungen in christlichen Umfeld und bei distanzierten Christen,
3.2 jahrelange praktische tiefenpsychologische Bibel-arbeit,
3.3 Erfahrungen von Frauen in und mit dem Christentum,
    Forschungen über vorpatriarchale weibliche Religionen im Entstehungsbereich des Christentums.

Thesen

1. Transzendenzerfahrung halte ich für eine grundlegende Kategorie von Religion, sowohl in religiösen Institutionen als auch von persönlicher Religion.

In tiefenpsychologischer Sicht gehört Transzendenz zum Menschsein. Sie ergibt sich als Folge des Bewußtwerdens und der Ich-Bildung der menschlichen Spezies. Das im Ich zentrierte Bewußtsein erweist sich zwar als die typische, aber als nur eine psychische Funktion. Unterhalb der Bewußtseinsschwelle bleibt das menschliche Ich verwurzelt in der Muttererde des Unbewußten, aus der es in der Evolution herausgewachsen ist und durch die der einzelne Mensch mit der Gattung "Mensch" und mit allem, was ist, psychisch zusammengehört, so wie er in seinen Körpermerkmalen physisch diese Zusammengehörigkeit aufweist. Hier ist die psychische Basis gegeben für das Theologumenon, daß der Mensch eins ist mit der gesamten Schöpfung.

Transzendenz bezeichnet tiefenpsychologisch die Fähigkeit des Ich, die Verbindung zum psychischen Unbewußten als seinen natürlichen Lebensvoraussetzungen bewußt herzustellen und zu intensivieren. Durch Transzendenz kann das Ich über seine psychisch engen Grenzen hinausgelangen, seine Isolierung überwinden und sich an ein größeres psychisches Ganzes anschließen. Transzendenzerfahrung ist für das Ich notwendig, um psychisch nicht zu verkümmern. Tiefenpsychologische Transzendenz hat keineswegs eine e.,.,.,gozentrische Engführung zur Folge, wie oft unterstellt; vielmehr weist sie in der Praxis religiöse Merkmale auf, die auf eine Erlösung aus der Ich-Zentrierung hindeuten.

2. In vorjüdisch – vorchristlichen Religionen ist die Transzendenz des Ich ins Unbewußte durchgängig in der mythischen Vorstellung von der Unterwelt symbolisiert. Wenn Mythologie als archaisch – antike Psychologie verstanden werden kann (Hillman, 1979a, 1983b), dann stellt das Symbol von der Unterwelt in seinen verschiedenen Varianten eine Projektion der psychischen Erneuerung und des Ganzwerdens des Ich durch sein "Hinuntergehen" ins Unbewußte dar. Projektion ist hierbei ein neutraler Begriff ohne negative Bedeutung.
Denn Projektion ist unausweichlich wegen der menschlichen Subjektivität, die ohne Spiegelung, z.B. im Mythos, ihrer Inhalte nicht ansichtig werden könnte.

Die Unterwelt hat offenbar vom Anfang der Menschheit an eine Rolle gespielt, wenn wir z.B. an die Höhlenbilder und Höhlenbegehungen aus der Eiszeit denken. Der Mythos von der Unterwelt ist seinen bisher bekannten Ursprüngen nach ein Symbol weiblicher Religion. Am Beispiel des sumerisch – altbabylonischen Mythos vom Gang der Lebensgöttin Inanna bzw. Ishtar in die Unterwelt, der im 3. Jahrtausend vor Christus schriftlich fixiert ist (Kramer, 1959; Brinton Perera, 1985), sei dies erläutert. Die Göttin geht aus eigenem Antrieb in die Unterwelt, die das Reich ihrer Schwester ist, einer Ausprägung des Todesaspekts am weiblich Göttlichen. Sie läßt sich dort ihre Hoheitszeichen, ihre Kleider und ihren Schmuck abnehmen und wird getötet. Nach drei Tagen wird sie durch die Speise und das Wasser des Lebens wieder erweckt. Sie kehrt in die obere Welt zurück, zieht durch das Land und bringt Leben und Fruchtbarkeit wieder in Gang. Später vertritt sie Dummuzi bzw. Tammuz, ihr Partner bei der Heiligen Hochzeit, in der Unterwelt; jährlich stirbt er dort und wird wieder zum Leben erweckt. Denselben Mythos gibt es noch in fortgeschritten patriarchalischen Religionen, wie im Alten Ägypten den Isis - Horus - Osiris - Mythos. Die Elemente des Unterwelt – Mythos gehören zu der uralten weiblichen Lebensfeier des "stirb und werde". In ihr werden das physische Leben und das Bewußtsein erneuert, indem sie zurückgebunden werden an die schöpferischen Kräfte der Natur und des Unbewußten. Für die Menschen, die an dieser Lebensfeier beteiligt waren, bedeutete das, teilzuhaben an der Ganzheit und Fülle des Lebens. Der Ritus der Unterweltsfahrt ermöglichte den Menschen Transzendenzerfahrung; denn in der Unterwelt des Mythos konnten sie ihre eigene seelische Unterwelt finden.

Der Tod wurde im Unterweltsmythos nicht als Ende des Lebens erfahren, sodern als zum Leben erweckende Macht. Das änderte sich in den patriarchalisch werdenden Religionen. Dort wurde die Unterwelt zum Ort ohne Wiederkehr, wie etwa in der griechischen Hadesauffassung. Der Tod begann, Angst und Entsetzen auszulösen (vgl. Gilgamesch-Epos).

3. Im Christentum ist die Unterwelt als Ort der Transzendenz verloren gegangen. Mit ihrer Wandlung zur Hölle ist die Unterwelt zum absoluten Negativum geworden, wie bereits im Alten Testament die Scheol ein Gottloser Ort geworden ist. Und der Tod ist zum Feind des Menschen schlechthin degeneriert – vor allem bei Paulus: "der letzte Feind, der entmachtet wird, ist der Tod" (1 Kor. 15:26). Was in archaischen weiblichen Religionen der Mutterschoß der Erde als Ort der Wandlung des gestorbenen Lebens durch Wiedergeburt war, ist in der christlichen Hölle zu einem Ort grauenhafter Torturen geworden. Tiefenpsychologisch bedeutet das: das seelisch Unbewußte ist im Christentum abgespalten vom bewußten Ich. Die höllische Unterwelt ist zu bewerten als Phantasie von Menschen, die sich in ihrem Bewußtsein getrennt haben von der weiblich – lebensspendenden Macht des seelisch Unbewußten.

Transzendenzerfahrungen werden in diesem Bereich nicht mehr gesucht; Träume und Visionen – Hauptmedium göttlicher Offenbarung in weiblichen Religionen – sind im Christentum verpönt, sogar als unchristlich verdächtigt. Das Christentum ist charakterisiert durch ein großes seelisches und weibliches Defizit.

Transzendenz ist im Christentum stets mit der Vorstellung vom Himmel verbunden worden – "oben" wird Gott gesucht und gefunden. Diese Projektion von Transzendenz ist zu Ende gegangen mit der Änderung des Weltbildes durch wissenschaftliche Aufklärung; das neuzeitliche Weltbild läßt keinen Raum für die Vorstellung von einem Gotteshimmel. Als eine Folge davon wird Transzendenz weithin kaum noch erfahren, und also bleiben Menschen – individuell und kollektiv – in ihrem engen Ich eingeschlossen; der entleerte Himmel führt zur Sinnleere. Da das Ich nur ein kleiner Teil des Gesamtpsychischen ist, werden Menschen ohne Transzendenz seelisch fragmentarisch. Ja, das Ich mit seinem Intellekt und seiner Macher-Mentalität okkupiert die Stelle von Transzendenz. Den Himmel oben, den früheren Ort der Gotteserfahrung, besetzt jetzt das Ich. Bewußtsein und Unbewußtes driften dabei immer weiter auseinander. Das von seiner seelischen Unterwelt abgespaltene Ich verfällt schließlich einem Allmachtswahn; dessen destruktive kollektive Auswirkungen sind weltweit zu sehen. Das patriarchale Christentum hat mit seiner Verteufelung des Weiblichen und der seelischen Unterwelt nicht wenig zu der fatalen psychischen Lage der Gegenwart beigetragen.

4. Es stellt sich daher die Frage: Soll das Christentum zurückkehren zur vorchristlichen Unterwelt, um dem Ich Transzendenzerfahrung wieder zu ermöglichen? Gewiß nicht zur antiken Unterwelts-Projektion, wohl aber durch Zurückholen der verleugneten Unterwelt an ihren seelischen Ursprungsort. Der "oben" leer gewordene Himmel müßte nach "unten" wandern. Dazu bietet die Jesus-Überlieferung der Evangelien viele Impulse. Ich möchte das an einem Traditionskomplex aus praktisch tiefenpsychologischer Erfahrung verdeutlichen, und zwar an der Überlieferung vom leeren Grab Jesu, die in allen Evangelien fest verankert ist.

An der Geschichte vom leeren Grab interessiert mich vor allem ihre Symbol- und Urbildstruktur, in der die österliche Transzendenzerfahrung von ersten Christen, insbesondere die der Frauen, die das leere Grab entdeckt haben, übermittelt wird. Da in Mythen das Grab Eingang in die Unterwelt ist, versuche ich bei tiefenpsychologischer Bibelarbeit, mit Hilfe dieses Symbols Menschen ihre heutige Transzendenzerfahrung machen zu lassen. Als intensive Methode bietet sich dafür die Imagination an, das ist ein bewußtes Hervorrufen seelischer Bilder, wie sie sich in den Träumen autonom einstellen. Zwei Beispiele mit solchen Urbilderfahrungen zum leeren Grab möchte ich anführen.

Ein junger Mann, dessen gleichalter Freund vor einigen Wochen plötzlich gestorben war, sieht diesen aufgebahrt. Ein befreundeter Pfarrer sagt zu ihm: "Dein Freund ist auferstanden." Er: "Aber sein Leichnam liegt doch hier." Der Pfarrer: "Das hat nichts zu bedeuten." Der junge Mann kommentiert seine Erfahrung: "Ich habe zum erstenmal gemerkt, wie sinnlos es ist, einen Leichnam zu salben." Als ich ihn einige Wochen später wieder treffe, sagt er, die Erfahrung habe den Schrecken und die Erstarrung über den Tod des Freundes gelöst; er habe jetzt Schmerz empfinden können.

Eine ältere Frau, deren Mann kürzlich gestorben war, erzählt ihre seelische Grabeserfahrung so:

"Ich trat in das Grab und sah eine Leiche. Ich ging hin und sah, daß es mein Mann war. Ich wollte ihn anfassen; aber in dem Moment, als ich ihn berühren wollte, war er weg, verschwunden. Ich habe ihn unter Tränen und Weinen im Grab gesucht; aber ich wußte, ich würde ihn nicht mehr finden."

Diese Geschichte erscheint wie eine Konkretisierung eines Satzes aus der Grabesgeschichte bei Lukas 24:5:6:

"Was sucht ihr den Lebenden bei den Toten? Er ist nicht hier, er ist auferstanden."

Ein drittes Beispiel entnehme ich der Theologie des Volkes, dem von Ernesto Cardenal (1978) dokumentierten "Evangelium der Bauern von Solentiname". Ein Bibelgespräch über die Grabesgeschichte nach Matthäus

28:1:10 endet so:

Cardenal: "Das Wichtige an dieser Erzählung ist, daß sie ein leeres Grab vorfanden...

Esperanza: "Ich glaube, das Wichtigste ist, daß von diesem Augeblick an jedes Grab, in das man eine Leiche legt, leer bleibt. Auch wenn dort eine Leiche begraben liegt, ist das Grab leer". (Cardenal, 1978: 410. Bd.2)

In allen drei Fällen wird von strukturell ähnlichen tiefenpsychologischen Transzendenzerfahrungen berichtet.

Für die Betroffenen wandelt sich der aus dem physischen Miteinanderleben in die psychische Unterwelt eingegangene Tote. Der Leichnam, gewissermaßen das Substrat des Toten und Vergangenen, ist bedeutungslos geworden. Sowohl bei dem jungen Mann als auch bei der älteren Frau zeigt die Imagination eine seelische Ablösung vom Toten an. Ohne durch Trauer und Schmerz sich vom Gewesenen zu lösen, wäre keine neue lebendige Nähe zum Gestorbenen möglich. Und Esperanza hat an der Geschichte von den Frauen am Grab Jesu genau denselben Aspekt erfaßt. Nicht der Leichnam hält den Toten präsent, sodern dessen seelische Verwandlung in den Trauernden.

5. Was läßt sich nun an der biblischen Grabesgeschichte selbst in Bezug auf Transzendenz erkennen?

'Exegetische Streitigkeiten über die Historizität des leeren Grabes und über die Priorität der Erscheinungen des Auferstandenen vor dem leeren Grab haben die spirituelle Tiefendimension der Überlieferung vom leeren Grab aus dem Blick geraten lassen. Dieser Verlust geht einher mit dem Verdrängen der Frauen als Erstzeuginnen der Auferstehung Jesu. Schauen wir die Geschichte ohne die traditionellen theologischen Vorurteile an, dann läßt sich an den Frauen ein ähnlicher seelischer Prozeß in ihrer Beziehung zu Jesus erkennen wie bei den referierten Imaginations-Beispielen. Die Frauen, die bei der Kreuzigung, dem Begräbnis und am Grab dabei sind, machen eine verwandelnde Trauer durch. Die Realität des leeren Grabes spiegelt auch ihr inneres Abschiednehmen von toten Jesus. Das schafft die Voraussetzung, Jesus als Auferstandenen zu erfahren, ihn zu sehen und eine neue lebendige Beziehung zu ihm einzugehen. Von der Symbolstruktur aus gesehen, gehört die Überlieferung vom leeren Grab daher zeitlich vor die Überlieferungen von den Erscheinungen des Auferstandenen. Die innere Wandlung, die im leeren Grab symbolisiert ist, kann nicht erst nach den Erscheinungen erfolgt sein. Die übliche umgekehrte Reihenfolge ist für die tiefenpsychologischen Prozesse, die den Ostererfahrungen auch zugrunde liegen, nicht haltbar.

Von den männlichen Jüngern wird ein ähnlicher tiefenpsychologischer

Prozeß nicht überliefert: sie gehen nicht zum Grab, sie glauben auch dem Osterzeugnis der Frauen nicht. Doch ohne die innere Wandlung nachzuholen, hätten sie ihre österliche Transzendenzerfahrung mit dem Auferstandenen nicht machen können. Die Geschichte von den Emmausjüngern (Lk 24:13-35) deutet - ebenfalls in symbolischer Aussage - auf solche Nachholprozesse bei den Jüngern hin.

Daß sowohl die Frauen am Grab als auch das Symbol des leeren Grabes in der Christentumsgeschichte aus ihrer primären Position verdrängt worden sind, ist ein Signal dafür, daß die Unterwelt des seelisch Unbewußten mit ihren Transzendenz-Symbolen geschlossen und das Ich in eine zunehmende transzendenzlose Einsamkeit gesperrt worden ist. Diese seelische Region im Christentum wiederzugewinnen, erscheint mir dringend notwendig, sowohl im Blick auf die Vollständigkeit der biblisch-christlichen Botschaft als auch im Blick auf das Ganz- oder Heilwerden des Menschen durch Transzendenz. Oben und Unten, Himmel und Unterwelt bedürfen dringend der Versöhnung.

Literature

Brinton Perera, S. Descent to the goddess. A way of initiation for women. Toronto: Inner City Books, 1983.

Brinton Perera, S. Der Weg zur Göttin der Tiefe. Die Erlösung der dunklen Schwester: Eine Initiation für Frauen. Interlaken: Ansata-Verlag, 1985.

Cardenal, E. (Ed.). Das Evangelium der Bauern von Solentiname. Gespräche über das Leben Jesu in Lateinamerika. (2 vols.). Wuppertal: 1978.

Hillman, J. The Dream and the underworld. New York: Harper and Row, 1979.

Hillman, J. Am Anfang war das Bild. Unsere Träume - Brücke der Seele zu den Mythen. München: Kösel-Verlag, 1983.

Jung, C.G. Die transzendente Funktion. Die Dynamik des Unbewußten. Gesammelte Werke, Olten, Freiburg: Walter-Verlag, 1979.

Kluger-Schärf, R. Einige psychologische Aspekte des Gilgamesch-Epos. Analytische Psychologie, 1975, 6, 386-427.

Kramer, S.N. From the Tablets of Sumer. Indian Hills, Colorado: The Falcon's Wing Press, 1959.

Kramer, S.N. Geschichte beginnt mit Sumer. Berichte von den Ursprüngen der Kultur. München: Paul List-Verlag, 1959.

Steinbart, H. Im Anfang war die Frau. Die Frau - Ursprung der Religionen. Ein Beitrag zur Geschichte der Religionen. Frankfurt a. Main: Fischer-Verlag, 1983.

Meditierende Niederländer.

O. Schreuder
Universität Nijmegen

1. Geistige Popularisierung

Durch die Praxis der Meditation versuchen religiöse Menschen, eine für sie typische Geisteshaltung zu den "meta physika" und den Dingen dieser Welt in sich lebendig zu halten. Diese bewußt, methodisch und regelmäßig durchgeführte "Introversion", deren Wesen und Formen u.a. von Jan van der Lans dargelegt wurden (1978), kann man als einen Bestandteil der sogenannten "Virtuosenreligiosität" betrachten. Max Weber (1964: 421 ff.) stellt sie idealtypisch der "Massenreligiosität" gegenüber, die von höheren geistigen und sittlichen Werten keine Ahnung hat und vorwiegend auf den innerweltlichen Nutzen der Religion ausgerichtet ist.

In unseren Tagen vollzieht sich aber ein Prozeß, der als "Demokratisierung der Kultur" bezeichnet wird, und in diesem Rahmen werden nicht nur Wissenschaft, Kunst und Philosophie, sodern wird auch die "hohe" Religion unters Volk gebracht. Das geht selbstverständlich mit einem Wandel der Inhalte und Funktionen einher, obwohl man oft nicht sagen kann, welche neuen Bedeutungen da geschaffen werden.

Dies trifft gleichfalls auf die Praxis der Meditation zu. Der Begriff an sich ist relativ weit verbreitet; man versteht so ungefähr, was gemeint ist, und es ist deshalb nicht verwunderlich, daß das Meditieren zum Beispiel in Zeitungsannoncen, in denen Wünsche bezüglich ehelicher oder nicht-ehelicher Partnerschaften vorgebracht werden, als besonderes Persönlichkeitsmerkmal angegeben wird. Die Frage ist nun, was es mit der Popularisierung dieser Praxis auf sich hat und welche Faktoren sie mehr oder weniger fördern.

2. Vier Hypothesen

Wer sich von klassischen (Troeltsch, 1912) und modernen (McGuire, 1975; Wuthnow, 1976; Campbell, 1978; Woodrum, 1982) religionssoziologischen Autoren inspirieren läßt, könnte im Hinblick auf das Phänomen der popularisierten Meditation die vier nachfolgenden alternativen Hypothesen aufstellen.

Erstens: Das Meditieren ist ein Bestandteil des Jugendmystizismus. Es wird vor allem von jungen Menschen praktiziert, die der tödlichen Langeweile und Oberflächlichkeit der Wohlstandsgesellschaft überdrüssig sind, tiefere Erfahrungen bezüglich des menschlichen Lebens und Zusammenlebens sowie der kosmischen Ordnung sammeln wollen, den gesellschaftlichen Institutionen kritisch oder gar ablehnend gegenüberstehen und zu allerlei Experimenten auf dem Gebiet der Geschlechterbeziehungen, in bezug auf Arbeit und Lebensunterhalt, Gruppenleben und Politik neigen. Meditieren stellt also ein Symptom des jungendlichen Protestes und ein Moment der "counterculture" dar.

Zweitens: Die Praxis des Meditierens grassiert vor allem in Kreisen der Intellektuellen. Diese Personen interessieren sich stark für die "höheren Dinge des Lebens", haben aber für die institutionalisierte Religion, für Dogmen, Riten, kirchliche Organisationen und Gesetze nicht viel übrig. Intellektuelle sind eher für Spiritualismus und Mystizismus zu begeistern, die besser zu ihren Werten von Individualität, Autonomie, Toleranz u.dgl. passen.

Drittens: Das Meditieren ist vor allem in Umfeld der kirchlichen Institutionen anzutreffen. Es wird von religiös und kirchlich stark gebundenen Personen praktiziert, die durch die heutigen religiös-kirchlichen Reformen in Unsicherheit geraten sind. Diese Menschen wenden sich von der lauen Masse ab und sind unzufrieden mit einer Kirche, die ihre Autorität nicht mehr gelten läßt, sich den Moden der Zeit anpaßt, durch Rationalisierung das Wesen der Religion unterhöhlt und die Riten durch gefühllosen Intellektualismus entwertet. Sie treten diesen Ubeln entgegen, indem sie in kleinen Gruppen an emotional ansprechenden Ubungen und Meditation teilnehmen, die ihnen ein lebendiges Bewußtsein von Gottes Anwesenheit in der Welt vermitteln.

Viertens: Die Meditation ist einfach eine Handelsware geworden, ein Produkt, das marktbewußte Gurus östlicher und westlicher Herkunft Personen aus der höheren Mittelklasse zu Bekämpfung von ihrem Streß und zur Wiederherstellung ihres seelischen Gleichgewichts zum Kauf anbieten.

Es ist uns nicht möglich, diese vier Hypothesen anhand empirischer Daten in allen Einzelheiten zu überprüfen. Da wir aber in Rahmen einer nationalen Umfrage (1979) einer Stichprobe von 1005 Niederländern von 18 bis 70 Jahre die Frage vorlegten, ob sie irgendeine Form des Meditierens praktizieren, sind wir in der Lage, wenigstens einige allgemeine Tendenzen zutage zu fördern und Elemente für eine neue Hypothese beizusteuern.

3. Soziale Merkmale

Auf die Frage "wer meditiert?" gibt Tabelle 1 -die Tabellen stehen am Schluß dieser Verhandlung- eine Antwort. In den ersten zwei Spalten werden sich Meditierende und Nicht-Meditierende gegenübergestellt. In der dritten Spalte wird angegeben, ob die statistischen Unterschiede zwischen den beiden Gruppen signifikant sind, während die vierte Spalte über die Relevanz der signifikanten Unterschiede Auskunft gibt.

Laut Tabelle 1 bilden die Meditierenden eine Minderheit von etwa 10% der Befragten. Diese Praxis ist aber in allen sozialen Milieus in ungefähr gleichem Masse bekannt. Meditieren ist also weder typisch weiblich noch ein Merkmal jüngerer Leute. Es ist auch kein ausgesprochenes Oberklassenphänomen und ebensowenig auf die Großstadt beschränkt. Es ist nur eine Ausnahme zu verzeichnen: Personen mit einem Hochschulabschluß meditieren relativ viel; Personen, die lediglich die Volks- und Berufsschule besuchten, tun das relativ wenig. Demzufolge sind die statistischen Unterschiede zwischen den Bildungsstufen nicht bloß signifikant, sondern auch relevant (.17).

4. Weltanschaulicher und religiöser Kontext

Wenn in fast allen sozialen Milieus in etwa gleichem Maße meditiert wird, so ist zu erwarten, daß die Meditation in verschiedenen geistigen Kontexten zuhause ist. Das ist tatsächlich der Fall, wie Tabelle 2 zeigt (für die Skalenkonstruktionen vgl.: Felling, Peters, Schreuder, 1981 und 1982).

Die Befragten, die eine starke christliche Überzeugung besitzen, d.h. an Gott oder ein höheres Wesen glauben und den Sinn des menschlichen Lebens, sowie den Sinn von Leiden und Tod in dieser Perspektive deuten, stellen bei den Meditierenden einen höheren Prozentsatz (47%) als bei den Nicht-Meditierenden (34%). Zum anderen aber sind die wenig Glaubenden in beiden Gruppen mit etwa einem Drittel vertreten. Der Zusammenhang ist deshalb wenig relevant (unter .15), wenn auch signifikant.

Dasselbe Bild ergibt sich, wenn man die Aufteilung der Meditierenden und Nicht-Meditierenden auf vier anderen welt- und lebensanschaulichen Skalen -die nicht in der Tabelle aufgenommen sind- betrachtet. Diese Skalen beziehen sich auf die skeptische, agnostizistische oder verneinende Haltung in bezug auf die Existenz einer transzendenten Ordnung, auf die innerweltliche Bedeutung des menschlichen Lebens, auf die wahrscheinliche oder sichere Sinnlosigkeit des Lebens und auf die wahrscheinliche oder sichere Sinnlosigkeit des Leidens. Die statistischen Verteilungen der Meditierenden und Nicht-Meditierenden auf diesen vier Skalen sehen ähnlich aus und etwaige signifikante Unterschiede erweisen sich als nicht sehr relevant (under .15).

Bei der Kirchenbindung zeigt sich ein gleiches Bild, wie in Tabelle 2

132

ersichtlich ist. Meditierende sind weniger konfessionslos, besuchen den Gottesdienst etwas fleißiger und gehören relativ mehr zu dem Kern der Kirchengemeinden; die Unterschiede zu den Nicht-Meditierenden sind jedoch nicht sehr relevant. Gleiches gilt in bezug auf das Beten und die religiöse Selbstbeurteilung. Etwas relevanter werden die Zusammenhänge, wenn man einen Vergleich mit dem Lesen der Bibel zieht (.17) oder die beiden Gruppen auf der Skala "salience of religion" oder "Wichtigkeit der Religion für des Alltagsleben" aufteilt (.16).

Kurzum: Meditierende und Nicht-Meditierende unterscheiden sich zwar im christlichen Glauben, in bezug auf die Kirchenbindung und im Hinblick auf das Gewicht, das sie ihrem Glauben oder ihrer Weltanschauung für die Alltagspraxis zuerkennen, aber sie leben ganz bestimmt nicht in zwei völlig entgegengesetzten geistigen Milieus, im Gegenteil. Die Meditation erscheint somit keineswegs als ein Monopol religiöser, christlicher oder kirchlich gebundener Menschen.

5. Wertorientierungen und soziale Attitüden

Die zwei Kategorien können anhand Merkmale noch etwas eingehender charakterisiert werden.

Da sind zunächst die Wertorientierungen (für die Skalenkonstruktionen vgl.: Felling, peters, Schreuder, 1983a und 1983b). Es gibt in den Niederlanden drei Orientierungen, die an der Spitze der Wertehierarchie stehen: die Orientierung auf die Natur, die Mitmenschlichkeit in den täglichen Kontakten und persönlichen Beziehungen, sowie die Pflege der Innerlichkeit. Laut Tabelle 3 unterscheiden sich die Meditierenden von den Nicht-Meditierenden auf der zuletzt erwähnten Skala: Sie betonen relativ stark das Genießen der Stille, das voll bewußte Leben, die innere seelische Harmonie und den Sinn für die Dinge außerhalb dieser Welt. Das ist kein umwerfendes Ergebnis. Interessanter ist die Antwort auf die Frage, ob sich die beiden Gruppen im Hinblick auf das sogenannte bürgerliche Wertemuster unterscheiden. Dieses Muster umfaßt einerseits die Hochschätzung von Ehe und Familie sowie die Betonung von Arbeit, Beruf, Wohlstand, finanzieller Sicherheit und sozialem Aufstieg, und andererseits die Abwendung von hedonistischen Freuden und ungebundener Freiheit wie auch die Geringschätzung von wirtschaftlichem und politischem Egalitarismus. Nun, laut Tabelle 3 sind die Meditierenden keine bürgerlichen Menschen. Einmal sind ihre Faktorenwerte auf der familiären und wirtschaftlichen Bürgerlichkeitsskala niedriger als die der Nicht-Meditierenden, wenn auch die Unterschiede nicht sehr relevant sind (.09 und .12); zum anderen ergeben sich in bezug auf Hedonismus und Egalitarismus keine signifikanten Unterschiede. Schluß: Die Meditierenden sind keineswegs ausgesprochene Vertreter des Bürgerlichen Wertemilieus; sie geben jedoch ebensowenig eine alternative Figur ab.

Andere Merkmale, die sich zum Vergleich anbieten, sind folgende: die Meinungen über die Nivellierung von sozialem Status und Einkommen, die Nivellierungspolitik der Regierung, die Militanz der gewerkschaften, die völlige Aufrechterhaltung oder Einschränkung der bürgerlichen Freiheitsrechte, das Bild der Frau, die Attitüden zum gesellschaftlichen Wandel, die Kritik an den Veränderungen in der niederländischen Gesellschaft der letzten Jahrzehnte u.dgl. Sämtliche Vergleiche –die nicht in Tabelle 3 aufgenommen sind– geben wenig her; die Meditierenden neigen in diesen Angelegenheiten zu denselben Attitüden wie die Nicht-Meditierenden.

Nicht viel anders sieht es auf der politischen Ebene aus. Das Verlangen nach politischer Information, die Urteile über den politischen "Betrieb", das Interesse für und der Glaube an die Macht bzw. den Nutzen der Politik sind in beiden Gruppen etwa gleich stark oder schwach bzw. etwa gleich positiv oder negativ. Meditierende zeigen hier kein spezifisches Verhalten auf. Und auf keinen Fall sind es Menschen, die sich von der Welt abwenden und sich einschliessen. Sie verhalten sich als normale Bürger, politisch interessiert und informiert oder nicht. Sie wählen noch nicht einmal signifikant anders als die Nicht-Meditierenden, wenn sie auch etwas mehr Mitglied in einer politischen Partei sind. Nur wenn es um die Teilnahme an ausserparlamentarischen Aktionen geht, werden die Unterschiede relevant (.18).

6. Zwischenbilanz

Fassen wir zusammen. Meditieren ist eine Verhaltensweise, die bei einer kleinen Minderheit der niederländischen Bevölkerung anzutreffen ist. Allerdings ist diese Praxis in jeder sozialen Kategorie nachzuweisen, keine Gruppe besitzt in dieser Sache ein Monopol. Zudem wird in jedem geistigen Milieu meditiert. Christen und Kirchenmitglieder können hier keine Exklusivitätsansprüche erheben. In dieselbe Richtung weisen die Daten bezüglich der Wertorientierungen und sozialen Attitüden. Insbesondere fällt auf, daß der Meditierende keineswegs das zurückgezogene, unpolitische Wesen ist, wie manchmal behauptet wird.

Diese Ergebnisse bedeuten, daß wir unsere schönen Theorien über die Meditation als Symptom des Jugendmystizismus, als Abwehrreaktion anomisierter Kirchenmitglieder oder als Anti-Streßmittel für "Leitende" vergessen dürfen. Lediglich die Hypothese bezüglich der höher Gebildeten kann sich ein wenig auf die ermittelten Daten stützen. Wenn man jedoch das Ganze überschaut, so neigt man zunächst einmal zu dem allgemeinen Schluß, daß das Meditieren als ein gleichmäßig verbreitetes und deshalb mehrdeutiges und multifunktionales Phänomen in Erscheinung tritt, das einer differenzierteren und gründlicheren Analyse bedarf.

Eine solche Analyse kann hier nicht durchgeführt werden. Dafür sind wir zu wenig über unsere Befragten informiert. Es wurde zum Beispiel nicht nach den Attitüden zu Dogmen, Riten u.dgl. gefragt, ebensowenig nach Meinungen über die Kirchenreformen oder nach Problemen des seelischen Gleichgewichts. Über solche und andere Einzelheiten müßte man genauestens informiert sein, um die oben erwähnten Hypothesen überprüfen zu können. Wir bleiben somit die Antwort auf die Frage nach den unterschiedlichen Inhalten der Meditation bei den verschiedenen Gruppen schuldig. Dafür sind wir aber in der Lage, über einen anderen Punkt Auskunft zu erteilen, und zwar über das genaue Gewicht einiger sozialer Merkmale –Alter, Bildungsstand und Kirchenbindung– für das Meditieren. Eine diesbezügliche Analyse führt zu interessanten Erkenntnissen.

7. Determinanten der Meditation

Um den Zusammenhang zwischen Meditation, Alter, Bildungsstand und Kirchenbindung zu überprüfen, wurden die Befragten nach all diesen Merkmalen aufgegliedert. Daraus ergibt sich eine multidimensionale Kontingenztabelle mit 16 Zellen: Tabelle 4. Sie wurde unter Anwendung eines explorativen loglinearen Verfahrens analysiert, wobei versucht wurde, mit möglichst wenig Parametern die Verteilung der Befragten auf die 16 Zellen zu reproduzieren.

Das Ergebnis dieses Verfahrens zeigt Figur 1. Hier erscheinen sechs voneinander unabhängige Zusammenhänge. Drei davon haben mit Meditieren nichts zu tun: Alter-Bildungsstand, Bildungsstand-Kirchenbindung und Alter-Kirchenbindung. Unter jüngeren Leuten befinden sich weniger Personen der niedrigeren Bildungsstufen, und umgekehrt; in den niedrigeren Bildungsstufen sind weniger Konfessionslose und nicht-aktive Kirchenmitglieder, und umgekehrt; unter jüngeren Leuten sind weniger kirchlich Aktive, und umgekehrt. Wenn man nun diese drei Zusammenhänge konstant hält, so dass sie bei den Berechnungen nicht stören können, so deckt man drei andere Zusammenhänge auf, die für das Meditieren direkt relevant sind: Je höher der Bildungsstand, bzw. je enger die Bindung an die Kirche, bzw. je höher das Alter, desto mehr wird meditiert. Diese Zusammenhänge sind voneinander unabhängig: Personen mit höherer Bildung meditieren mehr, ob sie nun kirchlich gebunden bzw. älter sind oder nicht; stärker kirchlich Gebundene meditieren öfter, ob mehr oder weniger gebildet, ob älter oder jünger; ältere Menschen meditieren mehr, ganz abgesehen von ihrem Bildungsstand und ihrer Kirchenbindung.

Man kann das loglineare Verfahren auch auf eine andere Weise anwenden, und zwar als ein Kausa-Effektmodell. In diesem Modell wird das Meditieren als eine Folge betrachtet, deren Ursachen in den drei sozialen Merkmalen und deren Kombinationen zu suchen sind, und es wird getestet, inwieweit die drei Merkmale die Chancen "Meditieren versus Nicht-Meditieren" beeinflussen. Aus diesen Berechnungen geht Figur 2 hervor. Der Faktor Bildungsstand liegt mit .53 am meisten unter 1.00, dem Punkt der Chancengleichheit. Bildung übt also den größten ursächlichen Einfluß auf den Drang zur Meditation aus. Es folgt die Kirchenbindung mit .64 und das höhere Alter mit .71.

8. Deutung

Abschließend wollen wir versuchen, das alles auf einen gemeinsamen Nenner zu bringen.

Das Alter ist nicht nur ein biologisches, sodern auch ein sozio-psychologisches Merkmal. Der älter werdende Mensch hat Erfahrungen gesammelt und gelernt, die Dinge zu relativieren. Er geht nicht mehr so ganz in der Welt auf, was sich auch in der geringeren Teilnahme an gesellschaftlichen Organisationen ausdrückt. Distanzierung von der Umgebung, Individualisierung und intensivere Beschäftigung mit dem eigenen Leben, das sind die Stichworte, an die hier erinnert werden muß.

Der höhere Bildungsstand wirkt in einer ähnlichen Richtung. Wer eine Schulbildung genossen hat, die erheblich über den Durchschnitt hinausgeht, hat gelernt, relativ rational und empirisch zu denken und zu urteilen. Demzufolge ist er besser in der Lage, sich einigermaßen kritisch und autonom der Umgebung gegenüber zu verhalten und sich nach seinem eigenen Kompaß auszurichten.

Die kritische Haltung zu der Umwelt und die Betonung der individuellen Verantwortlichkeit sind Themen, die auch von den Kirchen ständig betont werden. Wer mit ihnen Kontakte unterhält, wird dauernd angeregt, den Strom des Lebens einen Augenblick zu unterbrechen und einmal Pause zu machen.

In den vorhergehenden Absätzen war die Rede von einigen gemeinsamen Elementen wie Abstand nehmen, Autonomie gegenüber der Umgebung, sich auf sich selbst zurückziehen, Selbstprüfung u.dgl.. Was dies alles für die Struktur und Entwicklung der Persönlichkeit bedeutet, mag der Psychologe klären. Soziologen sind eher für die sozialen Mechanismen zuständig, die die Menschen für einen Moment aus dem gesellschaftlichen Treiben herausnehmen, um sie in der Meditation auf sich zelbst zurückzuwerfen. Von diesem Gesichtspunkt aus ist dreierlei zu betonen.

Erstens: Die drei aufgedeckten Mechanismen sind voneinander unabhängig. Eine höhere Bildung, eine stärkere Kirchenbindung und ein höheres Alter sind drei eigenständige Pfade, die zur Meditation führen; sie brauchen sich nicht zu kreuzen oder zu vereinigen. Das heißt ganz besonders, daß Kontakte mit der institutionalisierten Religion oder der religösen Tradition keine notwendige Vorbedingung für meditative Aktivitäten bilden. Natürlich sind die Chancen des Meditierens am größten für diejenigen, die sowohl höher gebildet als älter und dazu noch kirchlich gebunden sind, aber da handelt es sich um eine Summe sich addierender autonom wirkender Kräfte.

Zweitens: Der stärkste Anstoß geht zweifellos von der höheren Bildung aus; die Kirchenbindung kommt an zweiter, das Alter an dritter Stelle. Zwar führen alle Pfade zum zelben Ziel, aber der Weg der höheren Bildung ist der kürzere. Er bewirkt mehr Distanz und macht mehr bewußt als der Einfluß der Kirche oder die Lebenserfahrung.

Drittens: Die Sonderrolle der Bildung -neben dem des Alters- wurde schon öfter festgestellt. Sie fällt erheblich mehr ins Gewicht als die Rolle der Schichtenzugehörigkeit oder der Wohnortgröße. Zudem zeigt sich einmal mehr, daß die höhere Bildung nicht bloß instrumentelle Bedeutung für wirtschaftliche oder politische Ziele hat. Am Beispiel der Meditation ist nachzuweisen, daß die Menschen durch höhere Bildung eher die Chance bekommen, bewußter und autonomer ihr Dasein zu gestalten.

Literatur

Campbell, C. The secret religion of the educated classes. Sociological Analysis, 1978, 39, 146-156.

Felling, A., Peters, J., & Schreuder, O. Gebroken identiteit: een studie over christelijk en onchristelijk Nederland. Jaarboek van het Katholiek Documentatie Centrum, 1981, 11, 25-81.

Felling, A., Peters, J., & Schreuder, O. Identitätswandel in den Niederlanden. Kölner Zeitschrift für Soziologie und Sozialpsychologie, 1982, 34, 26-53.

Felling, A., Peters. J., & Schreuder, O. Bürgerliche und alternative Wertorientierungen in den Niederlanden. Kölner Zeitschrift für Soziologie und Sozialpsychologie, 1983, 35, 83-107.

Felling, A., Peters, J., & Schreuder, O. Burgerlijk en onburgerlijk Nederland. Deventer: Van Loghum Slaterus, 1983.

Lans, J.M. van der. Religieuze ervaring en meditatie. Nijmegen: Benschop en Thissen, 1978.

McGuire, M.B. Toward a sociological interpretation of the 'Catholic Pentecostal' movement. Review of Religious Research, 1975, 16, 94-104.

Troeltsch, E. Die Soziallehren der christlichen Kirchen und Gruppen. Tübingen: Mohr, 1912.

Weber, M. Wirtschaft und Gesellschaft. Studienausgabe herausgegeben von Johann Winckelmann. Tübingen-Köln-Berlin: Mohr, Kiepenheuer & Witsch, 1964.

Woodrum, E. Religious organizational change: an analysis based on the TM movement. Review of Religious Research, 1982, 24, 89-103.

Wuthnow, R. The consciousness reformation. Berkeley Ca.: University of California Press, 1976.

Tabelle 1. Meditierende und Nicht-Meditierende nach sozialen Merkmalen   (v.H.).

soziale Merkmale	Meditierende N= 95	Nicht Meditierende N=910	prob V	Insgesamt N= 1005
Männer	53	51		51
Frauen	47	49	n.s.	49
18-25 Jahre	10	16		15
26-30 Jahre	10	13		13
31-40 Jahre	28	26		27
41-50 Jahre	22	18		18
51-60 Jahre	19	17		17
61-70 Jahre	12	10	n.s.	10
Volks- u Berufs schule	35	50		48
mittlere Reife	10	15		15
Hochschulreife	26	23		24
Hochschule	29	12	.00 .17	13
Arbeiter	19	30		29
untere Angestellte und Beamte	31	30		30
kleine Selbständige	12	10		10
mittlere Angestelte und Beamte	16	17		17
höhere Berufe	22	14	n.s.	14
Land	7	12		12
urbanisiertes Land	12	19		19
Pendlergemeinden	15	17		16
Kleinstädte	14	12		13
mittelgroße Städte	20	15		15
Großstädte	27	25	n.s.	25

x ≤ .05 ist signifikant; n.s. ist nicht signifikant; V ≥ .15 ist relevant.

139

Tabelle 2. Meditierende und Nicht-Meditierende nach religiösen Merkmalen (v.H.).

religiöse Merkmalen	Meditie- rende N= 95	Nicht-Medi- tierende N= 910	prob	V	Insgesamt N= 1005
Christlicher Glaube:					
schwach	31	33			33
mittel	22	33			32
stark	47	34	.02	.09	35
Kirchenbindung:					
Konfessionslose 2. Generation	7	12			12
Konfessionslose 1. Generation	7	11			11
Ausgetretene	18	20			20
Randmitglieder	13	21			20
Kirchgänger	31	25			25
Kernmitglieder	24	11	.00	.14	12
Beten:					
oft	56	37			39
manchmal	14	24			23
nie	30	39	.00	.11	38
Bibel lesen:					
oft	32	15			17
manchmal	30	21			21
nie	38	64	.00	.17	62
findet sich selbst religiös:					
ja	62	46			48
einigermaßen	19	20			20
nein	16	31			30
weiß nicht	3	3.	01	.11	3
Relevanz Welt- und Lebensanschauung für Alltagsleben:					
groß	54	32			34
mittel	31	33			33
gering	15	35	.00	.16	33

x ≤ .05 ist signifikant; n.s. ist nicht signifikant; V ≥ .15 ist relevant.

Tabelle 3. Meditierende und Nicht-Meditierende nach Wertorientierungen
(Faktorenwerte) und politischem Verhalten (v.H.).

Wertorientierungen und politisches Verhalten	Meditie-rende N= 95	Nicht-Medi-tierende N= 910 prob	eta oder V	Insgesamt N= 1005
Wertorientierungen: Orientierung auf die				
Natur	504	499	n.s.	500
Mitmenschlichkeit	523	497 .	02 .07	500
Orientierung auf				
Innerlichkeit	558	494 .	00 .19	500
Bürgerlichkeit:				
--> allgemein	459	504	.00 .13	500
---> familäre Bür-				
gerlichkeit	472	503	.00 .09	500
---> wirtschaftliche				
Bürgerlichkeit	464	504	.00 .12	500
Hedonismus	492	501	n.s.	500
Egalitarismus	518	498	n.s.	500
Parteipräferenz:				
Linksradikale	7	4		5
Sozialdemokraten	18	30		28
Christdemokraten,				
Reformierte	42	31		32
Neuliberale	13	12		12
Altliberale	10	15		14
keine	10	8	n.s.	8
Parteimitgliedschaft:				
ja	32	16		17
nein	68	84	.00 .12	83
Teilnahme an Demos und Bürgerinitiativen:				
gering	60	82		80
mittel	22	12		13
stark	18	5	.00 .18	7

x ≤ .05 ist signifikant; n.s. ist nicht signifikant; eta oder V ≥ .15 ist relevant.

Tabelle 4. Meditierende und Nicht-Meditierende nach Bildungsstand,
Kirchenbindung und Alter.

| Kirchen-
bindung
und
Alter | Bildungsstand | | | | Zusammen |
| | niedrig | | hoch | | |
	Meditie- rende	Nicht- Medi- tierende	Meditie- rende	Nicht Medi- tierende	
Konfessionslose und Randmit- glieder:					
≤ 30 Jahre	3	114	9	71	197
> 30 Jahre	13	320	18	80	431
Kirchgänger und Kernmit- glieder:					
≤ 30 Jahre	4	60	2	19	85
> 30 Jahre	32	209	14	36	291
Zusammen	52	703	43	206	1004

Figur 1. Loglineare Analyse: Frequenzmodell (Tau).

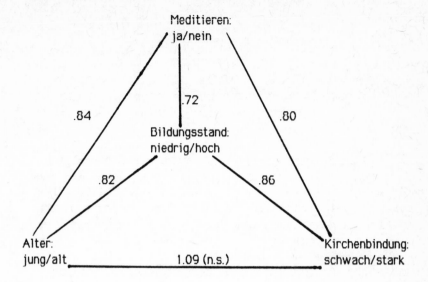

Figur 2. Loglineare Analyse: Effektmodell (Gamma).

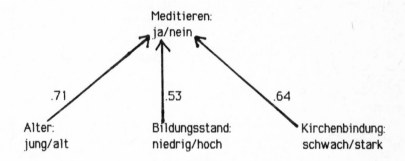

Religious attitudes and reaction time.

G.E.W. Scobie
University of Glasgow

Introduction

Any study of religious attitudes almost inevitably involves discussion of the meaning and status of the concept of attitude. Numerous definitions of the concept exist, each with its own emphasis. Most tend to look back to the comprehensive definition of Allport (1935) before producing their own distinctive contribution. Given this apparent confusion about the concept, it is not surprising that attempts to measure attitudes have met with only limited success. Questionnaires have been the most frequently used method of attitude measurement and I have discussed earlier (1982) their limitations and have argued that many of the criticisms may more properly be directed at survey methods rather than questionnaires. However so strong have been the criticisms that many attempts have been made to find an alternative for questionnaires. The rest of this paper examines reaction time as one possible alternative method of measuring attitudes.

Most current investigations tend to stress the evaluative aspects of attitude and refer to a disposition for or against subject or group (Fishbein & Ajzen, 1975). This is certainly a useful model but it is not the only one. Another possibility is the application of a cognitive model or more precisely an information processing model.

In many respects an organism's ability to survive is related to how it processes incoming information. For example the more rapidly it recognises a predator the more likely it is to escape. It is therefore in the interest of every species to be able to process information as efficiently and effectively as possible. This is particularly true of man. In general terms one could view functions like categorization and stereotyping as methods of speeding up the processing of information. However, as with most systems increase in speed leads to increase in error liability. It is also important to emphasise that the information processing system is response related. The organism has to decide how to respond to the information. A number of possibilities exist: (1) The information can be rejected as irrelevant, trivial or emotionally uncomfortable etc. and processing ceases; (2) information can be stored; (3) processing the information can continue and (4) a behavioural response can be made e.g. run, jump etc. Current developments in cognitive psychology indicate different levels of processing through which information can pass (Cermak & Craik, 1979) and any of the three options, rejection, storage or

144

behavioural response can occur at any level of processing. Processing levels can vary from simple stimulus and object recognition to more complex searches for meaning significance and relationship. In addition the behavioural response may be directed towards gaining further information in order to complete the desired level of processing. It is also worth emphasizing that it may not be necessary for information to pass through every lower level of processing before passing on to a higher (or deeper) level. It would clearly be undesirable and inefficient if every stimulus had to be processed through each and every level. The concept of "behavioural response" needs to be quite broad, it should include emotional responses such as anger or affection etc.

Without getting ourselves involved in the controversy of parallel versus sequential processing one can simply say that functions like categorization, stereotyping, belief, attitudes, values etc. are ways which enable individuals to skip certain levels of processing and thus speed up the analysis and response to incoming information. In other words there are different types of schema for processing certain types or categories of information. If a schema exists within the individual for a particular type of information then that information will be processed more rapidly than without such a schema. It is also important to note that not only should a schema exists but it should be readily available for use. Therefore included in this description of an information processing system is the concept of salience, another but often neglected aspect of attitude.

To get back to religious attitudes the hypothesis proposed is that religious people have a schema for processing religious information and that schema is highly salient. As a consequence religious information will be processed more rapidly. One method of measuring speed of processing is by using reaction time techniques.

This then is the rationale behind the investigations that we have been making over the last year or so. The experiments are exploratory, simple pilot studies conducted by students in my department. Like all good pilot studies they have highlighted more problems than they have resolved. I will discuss each study briefly and discuss the implications.

<u>The Pilot Studies</u>.
I) McCormick & McGinley (1984). The experiment can be summarised as follows:
(a) The sample: a group of university students were selected and ranked on the basis of their scores on (i) Ferguson's Religionism Scale and (ii) the Radicalism Scale of Eysenck's Social Attitude Inventory.
(b) The stimuli: the subjects' reaction times were measured to words on a balanced list of (i) religious and non-religious words (ii) political and non-political words. Words were presented sequentially on an Apple computer.
(c) The response:- the students had a choice of two keys labelled either (i) religious and non-religious or (ii) political and non-political. They were required to press the appropriate key as soon as they had decided on the category of the stimulus word presented on the computer screen.

From the responses it was possible to calculate for each subject their mean reaction time for (i) religious words and (ii) political words and produce two corresponding rank orders. Spearman rank order correlation coefficients were obtained between (i) Ferguson's Religionism Scale and religious word reaction time and (ii) the radicalism scale and political word reaction time. Neither correlation coefficient proved to be significant although the one dealing with religious words almost reached .05 level of significance suggesting that a larger student sample might reveal a relationship.

The fundamental problem was trying to select religious and political words and balancing them against non-religious or non-political words. Some words are so obviously religious e.g. 'God' that categorizing them would not vary for religious/non-religious people; other words may be so technical as to be more a test of intelligence rather than attitude. An attendant difficulty concerned the level of processing required by the task. It is questionable whether this simple word recognition task would require the application of processing associated with attitude systems. All that may be indicated is that religious individuals have a larger religious vocabulary and are therefore more likely to respond more quickly when exposed to a random list of religious words.

II) Glen and Paterson (1985). There were a number of changes in the second experiment.

(a) The sample: Glasgow University students still formed the sample in this experiment but they were selected using a different criterion. Instead of being based on questionnaire scores, a simple measure of commitment or involvement was used. Fourteen religious subjects who were members of the student Christian Union professing a strong religious conviction, eleven political subjects who expressed active involvement and interest in student and national political groups and fifteen control subjects without religious or political convictions (no subject in the experimental groups was involved in both religion and politics).

(b) The stimuli: There were sixty items in four categories, fifteen religious words (from Bible or general Church words), fifteen political words (from political terms dictionary), ten general words (from Collins dictionary) and twenty non-words (made by changing specific letters in general words to make them non-sensical e.g. INSTRUMESS).

(c) The response: The subjects again had two keys to choose from but this time they were labelled WORD and NON-WORD. They were required to press the appropriate key as soon as they had decided whether the stimulus was a word or a non-word.

The rationale behind the experimental design was to avoid cuing the subjects into their schema by the selection of either religious/non-religious or political/non-political choice but to force them to look carefully at the stimuli so that the words would be effectively processed.

Tests of significance (Mann-Whitney U Test) indicated that the religious group processed religious words more quickly than the control group processed these words but there was no significance for the religious group in processing religious as opposed to control words. There was also no significance in the two equivalent political tests.

In this experiment we had still failed to resolve the problem of selecting the stimulus words. It is difficult to balance religious words against political or control words. Should it be done in terms of letter length or frequency of occurrence in the language? The consideration of "word frequency" led to an examination of a related research area; that of value. Postman, Bruner and McGinnies (1948) had looked at work recognition and value. Words selected from the six value areas of the Allport-Vernon Study of Values Scale (1931) were presented at short duration and their exposure interval increased until they were identified by the subject. They found that subjects recognised words more quickly form their "highest value" area. But in this experiment word frequency was not controlled. Howes and Solomon (1950) repeated the experiment but used a group of frequent and infrequent words and a more extensive examination of the problem was also undertaken by Postman and Schnider (1951). In general both investigations found that high frequency words were more rapidly recognised than low frequency words and that value did not seem to influence the recognition time for high frequency words, but did for low frequency words. So these experiments indicate that word frequency is an important variable. Word frequency was assessed using the Thorndike-Lorge word count (1944). But sub-groups of the population (religious, political etc.) will have different word frequency patterns. For example in the selection of Christian/Fore names for children; Bible names seem much more popular amongst certain extreme Christian/religious groups. In this sense word frequency itself may be an attitude or value indicator and attempts to control its effect would be counter productive in terms of the purpose of the investigation.

The problem of word frequency is related to the other difficulty in this experiment. In terms of the first experiment by requesting the subjects to discriminate between religious/non-religious or political/non-political they were being asked to switch in the appropriate schema if they had it. The request however undermines the effects of salience i.e. how readily were the subjects likely to use the schema. one would assume that religious people are more likely to use a religious schema than non-religious people and by requesting both groups to be ready to use such a schema we were reducing the potential difference between them. The use of word/non-word instructions avoids this problem. Unfortunately it highlights the other difficulty mentioned in reference to the first experiment i.e. level of processing. The requirement in the first experiment required processing of information at a word recognition level i.e. is the word in the religious category or not (or political or not)? In the second experiment the processing required is simply "Is the stimulus a word or not?" This second requirement would seem to be at a more superficial level of processing than the first experiment, not even requiring necessarily an analysis by word meaning. In both experiments the focus is on word recognition and as a consequence word frequency is important. But the requirement of this investigation is a deeper level of processing involving the emotional tie associated with attitudes. If it is possible to demand by instructions to the subjects this deeper level of processing then word frequency would be a much less or even insignificant factor.

III) Betts & Glen (1985). The problems arising from experiment II led to further modifications in the design for experiment III.

(a) The sample:- Glasgow University students were not pre-selected on this occasion but the subsequent analysis would be based on their response to the Wilson-Patterson Attitude Inventory (1975) (W.P.A.I.).

(b) The stimuli:- the fifty words/catch phrases used for the WPAI were presented as in the other experiments using the Apple computer.

(c) The response:- On this occasion the subjects had three keys (or buttons) labelled "Yes", "Don't Know" and "No". Subjects were again required to respond as quickly as possible to the stimulus

item by pressing the appropriate key. The instructions given were those normally provided for subjects completing the WPAI

questionnaire but instead of indicating the appropriate response on a form they pressed a corresponding key; they thus indicated their agreement or support for the particular stimulus item. In this way subjects not only completed the questionnaire but also provided reaction time information for each item.

One of the interesting aspects to emerge from the non-selection of the sample was the recognition that reaction time is non-directional. It is possible for an individual to have a religious schema either because they are positively orientated to religion or because they are strongly opposed to it. Those not interested, the non-religious are not likely to have a schema. As a consequence one would expect faster reaction times for religious and anti-religious individuals and slower times for the non-religious. A similar pattern of reaction times would be found for the corresponding political groupings. However there are complications which will be discussed later.

The WPAI is a general conservatism scale but does include a number of sub-scales. The twelve items of the religion-puritanism sub-scale and sixteen selected items from the main Conservatism scale, (those which seem most appropriate to political conservatism) were used. Bearing in mind the observation made earlier about possible anti-religious and anti-political schemata some attempt was made to deal with this in terms of the individuals scores derived from the WPAI.

Correlation coefficients between WPAI score and reaction time for the religion sub-scale and the devised political conservatism scale were not significant. Bearing in mind the observation that it is the non-religious who have no schema for religion and such people are likely to respond "Don't know" to the religious items giving a scale score of twelve. It was

149

decided to consider those with a score above twelve as a pro-religious group, and those with twelve and below as an anti-religious group. Corresponding correlation coefficients were calculated. The pro-religious group gave a significant correlation (.05 level of confidence) but the anti-religious group was not significant. In other words for "religious people" the more religious they are the quicker they process religious material.

An attempt to treat the political scores in a similar way proved impossible. Only two individuals scored above the mid-point in the test. In addition this scale seems to discriminate between political conservatives and political radicals rather than between the political and the non-political individual. I have observed elsewhere (Scobie, 1978) that there is a tendency in the religious demension to more readily think in terms of religious and non-religious groups whereas in the political dimension it seems to be political conservatives versus political radicals.

While there were obvious advantages in the experimental design, a number of problems did arise. The unselected nature of the sample meant that the number of religious individuals and especially political conservatives was restricted. The use of the WPAI catchphrases as stimulus words also posed problems. Many of them were not obviously religious or political but were in related areas e.g. fluoridation, easy divorce, etc., in the religion scale and working mothers, women judges etc., in the political scale. While it can be argued that these concepts do indicate general conservatism and may even be valid indicators of religioius or political attitudes it is debateable whether the words would be processed through a religious or political schema. It may be that ideas or concepts correlated with a particular attitude may not be appropraite material for reaction time tests of this kind.

It could be argued that religious people would have thought about religious issues such as miracles or Bible truth and would therefore be more likely to respond rapidly to such stimuli. This argument is rather similar to the one about word frequency. The purpose of the present investigation is to detect the existence of an attitude; and word frequency patterns and rapid response to certain complex issues may turn out to be more reliable indicators than standard questionnaire methods.

Conclusions
The most obvious conclusion is that the relationship between attitude and reaction time is much more complex than one might have hoped.

Despite the numerous variables influencing the situation, the religious variable did produce significant or near significant results in all three experiments. This result in itself merits further investigation. What is equally interesting is the failure to get any corresponding results in the political area. It has always been my contention that religion and politics, at least at a psychological level, have much in common (Scobie, 1978; 1983). I would have expected to have found similar results in each area. It is possible that political issues and highly motivated political people are more difficult to investigate than their religious counterparts and the variation in terms of radicalism/conservatism and pro/anti measures contribute to this defference. Perhaps a more likely explanation would be a difference in salience. Perhaps religious people have an attitude which is more likely to be regularly used in everyday life whereas political attitudes are more specialized. However this suggestion flies in the face of the usual understanding of religion and politics i.e. the former is other-worldly while the latter is concerned with down-to-earth everyday issues. If politics focusses so much on everyday issues perhaps the vast majority of people have and use a 'political schema' and so unless a sample of non-political individuals was deliberately selected reaction time differences would be difficult to detect. There are a large number of religious people whose beliefs are all embracing but there are also many people for whom religion means nothing. In contrast there may be relatively few people for whom politics is the 'be all and end all' of their existence but for most individuals political issues of one kind or another impinge on their life.

Further research is obviously needed. In many respects pre-selected samples of religious and political individuals would seem the best sort of sample to investigate. The type of stimuli used also poses more of a problem. The use of WPAI catchphrases was less than helpful and alternative sources need to be found. The response techniques of experiment III seems the best way of entering the processing system at the most appropriate level.

Should my optimism about further progress be well founded then future developments would involve a move away from words to pictorial representation and use of the tachistoscope as well as reaction time measures.

Literature

Allport, G.W. In: A handbook of social psychology. Worcester, Massachusetts: Clark University Press, 1935.

Allport, G.W., & Vernon, P.E. A study of values. Boston: Houghton Mifflin, 1931.

Betts, S., & Glen, E. Unpublished undergraduate research project. Department of Psychology, University of Glasgow, 1985.

Germak, L.S., & Craik, F.I.M. (Eds.). Levels of processing in human memory. Hillsdale, N.J.: Erlbaum, 1979.

Fishbein, M., & Ajzen, I. Belief, attitude, intension and behaviour. Reading Mass.: Addison-Wesley, 1975.

Glen, E., & Paterson, C. Unpublished undergraduate research project. Dept. of Psychology, University of Glasgow, 1985.

Howes, D.H., & Solomon, R.L. A note on McGinnies "Emotionality and perceptual defense." Psychological Review, 1950, 57, 229-234.

McCormick, A., & McGinley, R. Unpublished undergraduate research project. Department of Psychology, University of Glasgow, 1984.

Postman, L., Bruner, J.S., & McGinnies, E. Personal values as selective factors in perception. Journal of Abnormal and Social Psychology, 1984, 43, 142-155.

Postman, L., & Schneider, B.H. Personal values, visual recognition and recall. Psychological Review, 1951, 58, 271-284.

Scobie, G.E.W. The religion of politics. Conference paper. First Correlation on Implicit Religion, 1978.

Scobie, G.E.W. Methods of investigating religious attitudes. In: Proceedings of the Second European Symposium on the Psychology of Religion. Nijmegen: University of Nijmegen, 1982.

Scobie, G.E.W. The origin and development of political and religious attitudes. Paper presented at the 6th Annual Scientific Meeting of the International Society of Political Psychology, 1983.

Thorndike, E.L., & Lorge, I. The teachers' word book of 30,000 words. New York: Teachers College, Columbia University, 1944.

Wilson, G.D., & Patterson, J.R. Manual for the Wilson-Patterson Attitude Inventory. Windsor, England: NFER Publishing Company, 1975.

Mental imagery and religion. Theory and experiment.

O. Wikström
University of Uppsala

Let me introduce this topic with three quotations from three different fields; neuropsychology, literature and psychology of religion.

Roger W. Sperry wrote after he had recieved his Nobelprize:
"Cognitive introspective psychology can no longer be ignored or written off as a science of epi-pheonomena, nor either as something that must in principle reduce everything to neurophysiology. Mental phenomena are explanatory causal constructs on their own right, interacting on their own level, with their own laws and dynamics." (Le prix nobel, 1982, 82)

Hermann Hesse says in one of his papers on literature:
"Eine neue Dichtung beginnt für mich in dem Augenblick zu entstehen, wo eine Figur für mich sichtbar wird, welche für eine Weile Symbol und Träger meines Erlebens, meiner Gedanken, meiner Probleme werden kann. Die erscheinung dieser mythischen Person ist der schöpferische Augenblick as dem alles entsteht." (Hesse, 1982, 80)

and Spilka, Gorsuch and Hood claim in their newly released textbook:
"Imagery is a central fact of the content of religious experiencing and one ought to anticipate studies of the elicitation of this imagery by psychologists interested in Psychology of religion. ... The issue of the presumably spontaneously occuring experiences has become of immense importance". (Spilka et al, 1985, 161-162).

These quotations stress the importance of Mental Imagery constructs. What is the psychological function of inner pictures and images, and the "fantasy persons" who in inner fictive landscapes, (consciously or unconsciously created) seem to live their own lives and develop according to specific psychological laws? These kinds of experiences have during the last few years become the topics of psychological research and seem to be important to observe especially for the psychologist of religion.

Of course it is with great hesitation that one takes new theories and applies them to the Psychology of Religion. Our science already seems too broad and too eclectically oriented. However according to my opinion, theories dealing with Altered States of Consiousness, and their implications for a new and deepening understanding of, for example **visionary** and **mystical** experiences, are important to take in consideration.

In my paper I will first discuss some basic theories of Mental Imagery.

Then I will describe an explorative experiment and its results. Lastly I will point to the possibilities and limits of Mental Imagery Research in Psychology of Religion.

Mental Imagery

When one hears the rumour of the newborn scientific interest in Mental Imagery and scrutinizes papers and journals on Mental Imagery, one is at first very suspicious. We all recall the old Dorpat School with their introspective and speculative psychology. We have learned that science must be impirical, a science of behaviour or attitudes or motivations, not of "inner subjective idealistic thoughts" or speculative fantasies.

In this situation, it seems odd that it was not primarily from psychologists that the new interest in imagery arose, but rather from the hardcore "brainsciences" like neurophysiology and neurology. Especially experimental studies on dreams, sleep, sensory deprivation (Hilgard, 1981, 5-66) and brain researchers (Sperry,1970, 123-138), studied the spontaneously occuring picture- producing-- capacity of the brain. Or as Holt says "All revield Imagery and held it up to the psychologists views as an honorable subject coming from hard sciences rather than from metaphysics. Radar operators, truckdrivers, jet-pilots, all told about perceptlikening imaginations". (Holt,1981, 39) One found that ordinary people, free from mental illness, seemed to have the potential to create out of themselves inner images, and to experience these inner fantasy landscapes with such realism that it sometimes changed their lives. The inner images were not products of psychotoxic effects, neither were they produced in the sleeping state of mind but are rather Mental Imagery Constructs.

Of course, these new theoretical concepts are of interest for the science of religion. Both transculturally and transhistorically the world religions are full of visionary and ecstatic experiences. Spontaneous mystical or other perceptlike states are common, in which the "inner eye" (or whatever the individuals theological legimationsystem labels it), has given the religious person an opportunity to be taken to the "seventh heaven" or to see "the glory of God".

In the antique sleep temples of Greece, the priests induced a state of relaxation and gave small suggestions to create an altered state of consciousness in which dreamlike visions, with their symbols, figures and persons were legitimated and reinforced by the theological or mythological systems.

In the tantristic buddhism, it is important for the initiate to be taught how to observe dreams and mental imagerys. It depends on the tantristic world view or legitimation system which underlines the realm **mano** which is the realm of human consciousness where man is coexistent with the divine forces. In psychological concepts there is a theological qualification and legitimation of this kind of ASC. The religious context seems to stimulate, reinforce and interpret these dreamlike visions.

Let me give a "microhistory" of the science of mental imagery.

At the end of the 1900 century A. Meyer claimed that the unconsious Mind or the subliminal Self has an inherent capacity or tendency to solve psychic conflicts through mental pictures in dreamlike states. In symbolic representations the psyche seemed to express emotionally loaded conflicts. T. Flournoy, pupil to W. Wundt, went a step further and postulated that the function of the picture- producing- capacity of the mind was not only to express problems but also to permit man to stimulate other than verbal-cognitive functions, it was more creative. P. Janet called this the "mytho-poetic function", H. Bergson labeled it "la function fabulatrice". In Germany the Würzburggruppe studied provoked introspection and there C. Happich used the concept Geistiges Auge, Spiritual Eye. (Jordan, 1979)

However it is especially in therapeutic and clinical work that the use of inner pictures has been reintroduced. It has become a tool by which one seems able to diagnose disturbances and to treat emotional disturbing material on the primary process level through *non* interpreted fantasy images. It is especially because of C. Schulz with his medical relaxation system close (Autogenic training) and the tradition from R. Desoilles therapeutic system (Réve Eveillé) and Hans Carl Leuner (Symboldrama or Guided Affected Imagery) that the interest has grown in Europe. Leuner and Desoille used light relaxation and induced suggestion of inner pictures in order to enable patients with mainly neurotic disturbances to project their feelings into these inner landscapes and then to walk in fantasy, so to speak, into this landscape. Then he observed the development of the fantasy material. (Desoille, 1945; Leuner, 1977)

C.G. Jung, in the depth psychological tradition, was interested in the tantristic yoga tradition and used their concept of the picture-stimulating strata of the mind. He often worked with active imagination as a therapeutic technique. Patients were asked to relax in the therapeutic setting and observe their inner fantasies. He observed that persons in relaxed states were more and more involved and absorbed by their inner mental constructions.

Active imagination was discovered and used as a very potent tool in uncovering unconscious material. The brain seemed to be able to express emotional conflicts more easyly in primary processes than on a verbal cognitive level. Leuner, professor in psychiatry in Göttingen and research director (he wrote, by the way, the very interesting Die experimentelle Psychose long before Stanislaf Grofs books on LSD-therapy) has developed a whole psychotherapeutic theory and technique around a few symbols which he let patients imagine during light relaxation.

Of interest for our purpose is his theoretical approach; he says that Mental Imagery is a sort of projection. But it is not like TAT or Torschah an external object; a multidimensional picture, but rather the inner emotional loaded impulses etc. are projected onto an inner scene. The symbols of the inner landscape are the condensation and symbolic representation of emotional material. The more one concentrates on ones inner world the more it seems living, vivid and the more you will remember it. It developes after exercises of inner concentration to be more vivid, more plastic, has more colors, one can experience it in three-dimensions (Ramonth, 1985).

For the Religionswissenschaft it reminds one of the meditation schools of St. Ignatius, St. Juan de la Cruz or St. Theresia from Avila; all the meditation practices of the cataphatic theologies in and outside the christian tradition. The spiritual exercises in these theological contexts seem from this psychological angle, to be a kind of supported legitimation system to provoke theologically initiated symbols and persons.

From our point of view it is of interest that one observes a sort of reciprocal dynamics. Leuner and his co-workers found that the client not only seemed to project himself onto the inner pictures, the opposite was also the case. The fantasies were very impressive and "spoke" to the patient. It seemed, however, not as important as in psychoanalytical or insight-oriented psychotherapeutic strategies to interpret or understand the material on a secondary level. Instead the active conscious effort to interpret could even destroy the therapeutic benefits of the imagined world. (Reyher, 1977)

In the medical and clinical uses of inner fantasies the main focus seems to be that symbols have a capacity to impress the subjects and change the subjects affects and lives even when these fantasies are not as worked-through.

And then we come closer to psychology of religion. In these therapeutic sessions it has been extensively observed over a long period of time that patients spontaneously have religious feelings experiences, mystical feelings and often create and view religious symbols. (Fabre, 1981) It has been reported that persons who on the conscious level were not interested in religion at all for themselves unexpectedly experiencing the greatest change and having the most spiritual/transpersonal experiences they had ever had. (Gödan, 1963; Shaeffer, 1979)

In this tradition dr. Klaus Thomas (now President in the European Society for Clinical and Experimental hypnosis) 1967 reported about spontaneously occurring religious symbols.

Klaus Thomas have described that the most religio-provoking inner picture is climbing a mountain. "Fast sämtliche Teilnehmer berichteten von religiöse Erfahrungen in weitesten Sinne des Wortes". He reports that in his group patients have "met angels, God, Grace, Temple, Jerusalem etc" even those with no former religious interest. (Thomas, 1967)

The state of mind in itself seems to start experiences of a "religious character". Thomas like other clinical psychologists or psychiatrists has just observed these things by the way. As far as I know no one has made a more formal and controlled experiment on the border Guided affected daydreaming – religious experiences.

Experiment

In order to study the problem a little bit further, I have undertaken a tentative, explorative investigation on the claims of spontaneous religous experiences during guided affected daydreaming.

Questions

1. Do individuals during an imaginative ascent of an "inner mountain" have "religious experiences"? If that is the case; of what kind are they; religious, mystical or existential? Number, differences between groups? (I operationalized later in content analyses of experiment protocol statements where the subjects in the test used an explicit religious language as *religious experience* (Temple, God, Spiritual, Jesus, Church, Altar, Kneel, etc) and *existential* those where they expressed searching for meaning, goal of life, dealing with responsibility or guilt-feelings, choice, fate, and *mystical* experiences of oneness, ineffability, noetic dimensions, wholeness).

2. When is the experience labeled religious; during the drama, afterwards in the interview and what kind of religious "aftereffect" does it have?

3. What is the relationship between the religious experiences during the relaxed states of mind and the subjects conscious religious attitude and activity?

Material and method

In order not to create any associations with my person I used two different groups. 12 psychologists from the department for applied psychology participated in one session each with their ordinary associate professor in psychology as research leader. The other group consisted of 12 theological students who all were active in different churches but had no experiences of hypnosis or Symboldrama.

One session lasted about 40 minutes for each subject. The session started with an introduction in Symboldrama. The main symbol was fantasies about climbing a mountain. During the session the research leader noted all utterances. After the session the person related in his own words what he remembered, and after that followed a semistructured interview. In this way I had material from psychologists, all nonreligious with no religious socialisation or actual religious activity. This material encompasses 83 pages.

For the group of theologians I added two other symbols a) a chapel b) a "wise man or woman". One of the theologians dropped out. The written material from the theologians were 117 pages. Since one of the theologians left the experiment the material was 23 persons, 200 pages.

Results

It was very easy to note every single world. In that relaxed state of mind one speaks very slowly. The main result is that all, both the psychologists and the theologians had in this broad sense clear religious experiences. The most impressing results were not expecxted nor anticipated in my preliminary questions. Spontaneously *all* the theologians (and I don't think it was to be polite) and more than half of the group of psychologists after three of four weeks told me, either directly or by letter, that these inner pictures, where they walked quite spontaneously and where the only thing the research leader asked was "What do you see?, What do you want to do?, Can you look closer?, Can you describe your feelings?" and were utterly restricted from giving any suggestions in any direction, had been an *immense spiritual experience* It has made an impression on their life of prayer or on their feelings towards religion. They remembered the inner voyage very exactly.

The content was analysed in an hermeneutic mode. I tried to find common themes and common levels (primary, secondary or tertiary processes) by which they expressed their experiences. Because of the tentative character of the experiment I did not quantify the results but only observed the main trends in the material. I quote from this very impressive and interesting material.

"It is calm, it is blowing, I feel endless, there is no boundary but I can't express it. I see a gloria just around the mountain. I feel like I am finding something like a mirror in myself, it is great, you can call it holy, frightening, and wonderful. No, I can't explain it" (Psych)

"I see an old temple in the valley, a small bell is ringing. It's warm stones on that temple I would like to enter. It is light, very light in the temple. I would like to cry now, it's beautiful. This is not like in our time, it feels like in the antique times, the beginning of the world" (Theol)

"It's a very rare state, I can't explain it, it is clear in a way, I have no limits, I feel like I am the tree and the sea and the temple, it's very mysterious but wonderful. It is unchangeable. It is something very new

and very old I can't explain it but these mountain, the wind and the clouds is a heavenlike feeling for me" (Psych)
"I am flying, I am a bit over the ground, I feel like water poured out in the sea, may be I am both the sea and the mountain, mysterious!
"I feel that I am flying, I am over the ground" (Psych)

To put the mountain experience on a more proper level, in the analyses of the protocol, the spontaneous story and the semistructured interview, I differed between perceptlike experience in the drama, associations around these imagerys during the drama (what does this remind you of? etc.) and associations and commentary to the experiences after drama. It was a way of controlling whether the pictures were on primary or secondary or tertiary level.

To summarize: For the psychologists 6 of 12 had religious imageries and "saw" very clear symbols with strict religious connotations in the session, but only 4 of them described in the interview afterwords their session in religious terms. 5 psychologists described existential feelings of choice as I operationalized them above during the drama but 10 described in the interview after the whole drama in existential terms. 8 of the psychologists described mystical experiences during the drama but only 2 of 12 described their experiences afterwords in terms of mystical character. I will later discuss the results.

To conclude, the psychologists experiences were on the primary process level mystical, or religious as I earlier stipulated these experiences but as soon as they tried to label it in intellectuell concepts they seemed to avoid both classical and mystical concepts but chose words with existential connotations.

If we then turn to the theologians only 2 had religious perceptlike or visionary excperiences during the session but 7 of 11 described mystical experiences and only 2 of 11 existential excperiences during the drama.

But provoking and surprising for me was that out of the theologians 10 of 11 labeled their experiences as an existential experience of great importance in the interviews. 8 of 11 in the interview talked about the session as a religious experiences but only 1 of 11 labeled the experience as in terms of mystical experiences **in spite of the fact** that they had very vivid and living mystical feelings and statements during the session. (*Observe* we did not ask for any specific kind of experience in the interviews in order not to provoke any specific understanding of the session. We found these results afterwards when the independent co-researchers coded the material).

This was rather contradictory that the theologians in spite of their mystical experiences during the drama afterwards seemed to label their experience as not mystical. Why?

159

It seems that persons who are used to labeling feelings etc. in explicit religious symbol systems are "prepared" or "set" to perceive and label this multidimensional freefloating percept- and dreamlike state in explicit religious terms and to suppress concepts of more mystical or non-traditional religous character. Maybe the ordinary theological legitimated symbolic universe "filters" so to speak the inexact paradoxical mystical language. One hypotheses could be that the theological concepts in classical Christian tradition does not permit subjects to label experiences with paradoxical and diffuse mystical symbols.

As to the specific suggestions of a church and an old man/woman for the theologians I did not find any result that could support Jungs proposals about the archetypical Animaprojections in the unconscious of the man and Animus of the women.

Of course, the material also contained a lot of other observations. Here I restrict myself to these basic preliminary findings: relaxation in combination with light suggestions to climb a fantasy mountain creates a state of mind in which both secular and especially consciously religious people seem to spontaneously label their experiences in religious, mystical but above all in existential terms.

Discussion
Hood and Morris, (1981), found that intrinsically oriented persons (whether given a religious set before participation in an experiment in isolation tank or not) tended to experience more religious imageries than extrinsicaly oriented persons. This means that suggestions, or in other terms, the set that is given to an individual before or during an Altered State of consciousness of course has importance for the outcome of the experience. But it is not the only explanation of religious imagerys. The state in itself seems to actualize dimensions of perceptlike states at least for some personalities.

Of course, the meaningful status of mental imagery varies depending on the context where it is interpreted and depending on the ontological status that is given to them. In that sense, is it important to distinguish between cataphatic and apophatic theological traditions.

In order to shed light on the psychological processes behind mystical experiences especially in the apophatic traditions (either on the exploration of the unintended or the desired or on the intended experiences), theories from mental Imagery Research could be helpful. The old Good Friday experiment (Pahnke 1963) needs to be completed with studies on altered states of consciousness which concentrate on ordinary, not chemotoxically created altered states of mind.

As far as I can see, we can never separate an experience from the interpretation of that experience. It seems that our results point in the direction that secular subjects, with no religious socialisation tend to label Mental imagerys as unusual, overwhelming but even utilize vocabulary from the classical theological or mystical traditions.

This does not mean that Mental Imagery is or even resembles the classic religious mysticism. We know nothing about the consistency or the vulnerability of these momentous experiences. In order to further the scientific approach in the study of this realm it is presumable necessary to make in-depth interview in order to understand how the individual's particular symbolic universe is working in imagination and to try to grasp its relation to the subjects affective and existential conflicts.

Literature

Desoilles, R. Le rêve éveillé en psychotherapie. Paris: 1945.

Fabre, N. Vécus corporales et vécus dits mystiques Rêve-Éveille. Etudes psychotherapeutiques, 1981, 45, 215-221.

Gödan, H. Religiöse Interferenzphänomene beim Autogenen Training. Ihre beurteilung und Vermeidung. Zeitschrift für Psychotherapie und Medizinische Psychologie, 1963, 13, 6-97.

Hesse, H. Schriften zur Literatur. Ges. Werke 11. Suhrkamp, 1982.

Hilgard, E. Imagery and imagination in american psychology. Journal of Mental Imagery, 1981, 5, 5-66.

Holt, A. A note on the philosophy and the history psychologies concern with imagery. Journal of Mental Imagery, 1981, 538-40.

Hood, R.W., Jr., & Morris, R. Sensory isolation and the differential elicitation of religious imagery in intrinsic and extrinsic persons. Journal for the Scientific Study of Religion, 1981, 20, 261-73.

Jordan, L. The potential of fantasy and mental imagination. New York: Harper & Row, 1979.

Jordan, L. Le prix Nobel, The nobel Prizes. Stockholm: Almkvist-Wiksell, 1982.

Leuner, H.C. A guided affective imagery. An account of its development. Journal of Mental Imagery, 1977, 73-92.

Reyher, J. Spontaneous visual imagery: Implications for psychoanalysis, psychopathology and psychotherapy. Journal for Mental Imagery 1977, 2, 253-274.

Ramonth, S. Multilevel consciousness in meditation, hypnosis and directed daydreaming. Doct Diss. Dep of Psychology University of Umea, 1985.

Sperry Roger, W. Perception in the absence of the neocortical communications issures. Perception and its disorder, 1970, 48, 123-138.

Spilka, B., Hood, R. Jr., & Gorsuch, R. The psychology of religion. An empirical approach. New Jersey: Prentice Hall, 1985.

Schaeffer, J.T. The experience of the wholistic mind. New York: 1979.

Thomas, K. Die Bedeutung der hypnotischen und autogenen Bilderschau für die Religionspychologie. Archiv für Religionspychologie, 1967, 9, 282-297.

Research on the celibacy of priests and grounded theory approach. Some preliminary results.*

A.M. Hoenkamp-Bisschops
Catholic Theological Faculty, Heerlen

My lecture consists of 4 parts:
In part one I will present a short review of earlier research on the celibacy of priests; in part two I will explain the design of my own research.
Part three contains a description of the grounded theory approach of Glaser and Strauss, with illustrations taken from my own research. In the last part I will present some preliminary results of this research project.

Many people consider the priestly obligation to remain celibate in the Roman Catholic Church to be an anachronism. Very little however is known about what this obligation means to priests, monks or nuns. My discussion here will be limited to priests, but of course many of the questions raised will also be applicable to the situation of monks and nuns.
In the sixties and seventies a great deal was published about priests who have left the church and in the last few years more has become known about priests who choose to have intimate relationships. The media however do not cover how the silent majority of priests experience their celibate life.
How do they feel about their state in life? How does this influence their lifes? What effect does it have on their contacts? How do they deal with the inevitable sexual tensions? What limitations do they impose upon themselves in their contacts with others? What role does their own religiosity play in experiencing and shaping their celibate life? These are only a few of the subjects we still know very little about.

As a psychologist of religion, working at a divinity school for priests and pastoral workers, I became more and more interested in priest's experiences of being celibate. It puzzled me that we know so little about such a central domain of life, a domain moreover which undoubtedly influences their work greatly.

Earlier research
Earlier social-scientific research on the experience of being celibate consisted mainly of large-scale opinion polls and sociological survey research. However such research provided little insight into the experience of being celibate.
From the few qualitative psychological studies of celibacy seven factors

have appeared to be important: extreme mother-fixation, strong ideal self, undeveloped affectivity, religious meaning of celibacy, influence of the seminary training, lack of correction by a partner, and finally the age at which the choice for celibacy is made. Below I will give a short overview of these results.(1)

In a number of research projects the common characteristics of priests have been investigated (Christensen, 1969; Hurter, 1969; Rey, 1969). In short the conclusion is that priests often come from families with a dominating mother and a father who was absent in their (sexual) upbringing. However the discriminating value of this factor in and of itself is unclear: men may have grown up in a similar situation and may not become a priest.
Rulla (1971) found that priests are strongly influenced by their ideal selves.
Traditionally, overcoming genital sexuality by repression, sublimation or integration has been looked upon as the main problem of celibacy. Not until the sixties did researchers become aware of undeveloped affectivity as a problem of at least the same size. Trimbos (1955) was one of the first to point to the more general problem of affective development in celibacy, that is the capacity to entertain satisfying relationships. Likewise Plé (1969) speaks of an immature affectivity, which can be expressed in different forms, varying from an unhealthy mother-fixation to narcissism and homosexuality (sic!)
Although Trimbos considers celibacy, when looked upon from a mere psycho-biological point of view, as a foolish and dangerous venture, he thinks that giving a religious meaning to it can save celibacy.
The cause of the fact that celibacy is such a problem to many priests may lie outside, as well as inside celibate life itself. Independent of the celibate experience itself, the training at the seminary may deform affective development. Further it is inherent to celibate life that one does not have the opportunity to be corrected by a partner; something that constantly takes place in a dual existence.
The general consensus of opinion is however that celibacy is in itself not necessarily harmful, provided that certain conditions are met. These conditions concern nature of training and the moment at which the decision is made to become a priest, i.e. celibate. Calon (1956) for example considers the protected education and training of priests to lead to their clumsiness in social contacts. Vergote (1967) sees the avoidance of conflicts in the seminary training as a main cause. He also points out that the usual repression of sexuality at seminaries damages the complete personality and above all affective development.
Mitchell (1970), who takes as a starting-point the developmental stages of

Erikson, thinks that most of the problems with celibate life are caused by the fact that the choice is made at too early an age. The choice to become a priest is an identity choice and traditionally takes place at the end of training, usually before the age of 25. Mitchell claims that a well thought through choice for celibacy can not be made until Erikson's intimacy phase is reached, this means approximately at the age of 30.

So far for this short overview of earlier research into celibacy. We can see that its results are quite poor. Even in a relatively well studied area as the consequences of celibacy, the output is dissappointing. Moreover this research is on the whole quite old. We don't know how the situation of celibate priests in the eighties looks like. How about for example the new class of priests who nowadays do not undergo seminary training? But above all, questions like what celibacy means to priests and what kind of place it occupies in their lifes remain unanswered.

My own research project

I will now briefly describe my own research project on the celibacy of parish priests.
One of our first problems was: how to collect the relevant data. We decided to use depth-interviews, although in the beginning it was not clear at all to what extent priests could be expected to talk in an open-minded way about the intimate things concerning their celibate. Also there was the possibly complicating fact that the interviewer was a woman. It was therefore decided to do the interviews together with an elder priest who had a long practice in counseling priests and nuns.
Now we also had doubts as to whether it was sensible to do the interviews with two persons. This combination however turned out to lead to a great openness on the part of the interviewed persons. This is partly due to the co-interviewer who enjoys great confidence among his colleague priests in Holland. It may also have to do with the fact that the two interviewers combine different characteristics, such as old and young, male and female, colleague priest and outsider. For some people for example it is easier to open up to a woman than to a man, or vice versa. It also resulted in more in-depth probing on the part of the interviewers, since both interviewed from different points of view and from different attitudes towards life.

We did not only want to know what kind of place celibacy occupies in the life of priests, but also wanted to gain some understanding in subjects like their growth toward celibacy, their sexual and affective development, the relation with their religiosity, etc. For this purpose a detailed semi-structured questionnaire was constructed. This questionnaire contained subjects like: family of origin, reasons for becoming a priest, years of training, history of work (including satisfaction in work), religiosity, sexuality, self-image, significant others, attitude towards the churchly legitimation of celibacy, and personal meaning of celibacy.

Through this elaborate list of questions we got a quite complete overall picture of the person under study. This was necessary because nowadays celibacy is quite a delicate subject for many people, especially for priests themselves. So they might easily tend to defend their choice. Since in the interview method our only source of information is the celibatarian himself, we have no direct means of double-checking his information. Not until we have a more complete overall picture of the interviewed person, we are able to fully evaluate and understand his allegations in some subjects. Besides we did need to know whether the respondent is capable of seeing himself realistically, that is whether he can recognize the good as well as the bad sides of himself. In combination with the impression the respondent makes on the interviewers along with his answer to the question about his self-image, it indicates his capability of reality perception and thus indicates the reliability of his information.

When it became clear that the interviews yielded an unsuspected wealth of material, we looked for 25 priests of different ages, who were willing to talk to us about their experiences of celibacy. The respondents were approached by the before mentioned elder priest.

So far for the collecting of the data.

The interviews which took about five to six hours time were taped and then typed integrally. This resulted in an average of hundred pages of text per interview, so altogether about 2500 pages. It is clear that one can not handle such a quantity of material. Therefore we decided to condensate each interview to an average of 20 pages. This resulted in so called 'analyzing summaries'. I will not go into the procedure by which these summaries came about.(2) Suffice to say that the list of subjects that had to be included in these summaries was quite broad and long. For example one of these subjects reads: "All significant experiences and persons in past and present of the respondent", which is of course a rather rough description applicable to many subjects. It is however chosen to avoid the material not being done justice due to a preconceived schema. The points for attention in such schemes easily tend to act as spot-lights which put the rest of the empirical field in the dark.

The grounded theory approach

Since we did not want our study to be a mere descriptive one, but also wanted to develop some theoretical insights, we considered the use of the grounded theory method of Glaser & Strauss (1967). However since their research procedures as described in 'The discovery of Grounded Theory' is quite vague, we could not estimate very well the usefulness of their method in our material. We therefore first tried it on some of our interviews.

The results of this first, tentative application of grounded theory were so promising, that we decided to settle for this method.

In this third part of this lecture I will try to give you an idea of the grounded theory approach and illustrate it with some preliminary findings from our own research. I will start by giving a short summary of the most important elements of this method (see also Wester, 1984 and Glaser, 1978).

Glaser & Strauss object the general trend within social sciences to restrict oneselves to testing hypotheses by means of purely quantitative research methods. These quantitative statistical methods are not always suitable. The need for discovering and explorative research is often far more urgent than that for research on a strictly scientific argumentation. On the other hand Glaser & Strauss do acknowledge that not much qualitative research is done systematically. Therefore they suggest a research strategy in which theory is built upon qualitative research data by means of a systematic procedure. By theory they mean: ideas on a higher level of abstraction than the level of the qualitative material.

In brief their method comes to this: In the process of researching, a continuously developing of ideas takes place by continuously comparing the incoming data -in our case interviewdata on respondents- with each other. This constant comparison of cases quickly draws the researchers attention to many similarities and differences among cases, thus contributing to the generation of theoretical categories. By continuously stating similarities and differences, elements of the theory, such as categories, concepts, variables, their dimensions, the conditions under which they exist and their major consequences, are being developed. After thus tracing the apparently important elements of the developing theory one continues to look for more data that can verify or correct earlier findings.

In this way one tests and builds up the theory to be. The comparisons continue until no further insights are discovered. The concepts will then be defined and formed into a consistent structure.

It is clear that in this approach one stays very close to empirical reality, since the theory is built in direct contact with the empirical field.

An important difference with the more common analytical procedures is that here the data are not first all coded and then analyzed. In stead while studying the material the theoretical notions – concepts or codes – are constantly being revised and reformulated.

Glaser & Strauss distinguish between 3 types of concepts.
SENSITIZING CONCEPTS are those concepts with which the researcher starts to explore the empirical field. They are necessary to guide datacollection and analysis, but at the same time should be as open as possible.
EMERGENT CONCEPTS are those possibly important concepts that emerge in the proces of comparing cases. They gradually become well defined.
CORE CONCEPTS finally are more abstract concepts. They reduce the complex picture of the research field to one or a few themes or processes, that appear to be central in the field under study.

These three types of concepts correspond to three of the four phases that can be distinguished in a grounded research project:
1. In the EXPLORATIVE PHASE concepts are being discovered, starting from the sensitizing concepts.
2. In the SPECIFICATION PHASE the concepts are being developed and defined, so as to contain in their definition a list of characteristics that fit every instance of that concept.
3. In the REDUCTION PHASE the core concepts are defined.
4. Finally in the INTEGRATION PHASE the theory is formed by relating the important concepts to the core concepts.

Now, in order to prevent my account of grounded theory being too abstract I will illustrate it with examples taken from our own research.
At the moment we are in the second – specification – phase. When we started the project, some of our sensitizing concepts were: significant others, personal meaning of celibacy and self concept.
As you will remember we began by comparing our first two cases, in order to check the usefulness of grounded theory on our material. These cases consisted of an interview with a 44 year old priest with a girl friend and a 34 year old convinced celibatarian. This comparison of extreme cases turned out to be quite conducive to the development of research ideas. Here I will present two of them.(3)
A striking difference between the priest with the close relationship – let me call him John – and the convinced celibatarian – let us call him Paul – is their experience of detachment. Both feel that as a priest one has to keep a certain distance between oneself and other people. Whereas Paul experiences this aloofness very positive – as giving a greater freedom in relationships – John gradually became more and more unhappy about his detachment from others. He wanted to be part of ordinary life and of ordinary people. That is why he eventually decided to live together with his partner.
So in this comparison between these two cases the concept of 'experience

of detachment' emerged. Looking for an explanation for their different experiences, it suddenly occurred to me that both, when asked about their childhood years, recollected childhood memories, which bear a striking resemblance with their later experience of detachment. John, talking about his mother, was always very pleased to be with his mother when they had to collect money. He says: 'Just the two of us, together (...), that you were together then (...); it was real physical with your mother's arm hooked into your's as a child'. So nearness and physical contact already appealed to John when he was a child. Paul on the contrary speaks about the fact that his father often sent him upstairs as a punishment and how he enjoyed staying upstairs longer than the required hour. So in a way Paul enjoyed being set apart from others already when he was a child.

This would mean that an early childhood relation with a (significant other like the) parent might play an important role in the experience of being celibate. So we discovered not only the tentative concept of 'experience of detachment' but also the concept of 'early childhood relationship with a (significant other like the) parent'. Of course these concepts, discovered in this first exploration phase, have to be better defined in the second specification phase.

In later comparisons we came across many other emergent concepts. For example in one case we tried to answer the question as to why respondent X became so terribly stuck in his doubts about starting a relationship. We had the impression that among other things the lack of a warm mother figure and a resulting basic distrust had something to do with it. But on comparison with Y, another respondent with a more or less similar mother figure but with a different experience of celibacy, we discovered that although both became priests out of love for this work, X in his time did not have the opportunity to choose between becoming a priest or becoming a pastoral worker. Moreover, X underwent a long psychotherapy, which – in his own perception at least – was aimed at helping him to live a good celibatarain life.

Thus the possibly important concepts of 'having had a choice between priest or pastoral worker' and 'influence of psychotherapy' are discovered. They may become key categories in our developing theory.

As I said right now we are in the specification phase of our research project. This means that all passages in the interviews pertaining to a specific concept are compared with each other. In doing so these concepts become more specified and better defined. Usually this is done by the method of analytical induction: starting from a global description, one systematizes those characteristics that always occur when the phenomenon appears. By doing so a description that fits all the cases is being developed. Also different aspects, dimensions, characteristics and

even different variants of the category can be discovered.
For example the concept 'choice between priest or pastoral worker' seems to have only two dimensions: present or absent. 'Influence of psychotherapy' probably has several variants, one of them being 'therapy lasting as long as five years and having the purpose of adapting client to celibacy'. Further comparisons with other respondents who also underwent psychotherapy will have to lead to a more precise description of this subcategory.
So far for this illustration of the grounded theory approach.

<u>Some preliminary results</u>
As a conclusion I will now present some preliminary but notable results of our research. Having interviewed only 25 respondents, we can of course make no claims of generalizability to a larger population. Nevertheless it may interest you to hear some facts about these 25 Dutch priests.
The first conspicious result of our research concerns the sexual discipline of the respondents. Their sexual moral shows a remarkable change from some decades ago. With two exceptions, all our respondents consider sexuality as a normal human need, just like eating, drinking and sleeping. Thus it comes as not suprise that we found hardly any feelings of guilt about masturbation among them.
A second surprising fact about our interviewes is the relatively great amount of homosexuals among them: 8 out of 25, that is alomst 32%. These are between 30 and 44 years of age, so most of them have never been to a seminary. This would indicate that seminary training is not as crucial in causing homosexuality among priests, as is often assumed.(4)
A third interesting result I would like to present here concerns the role the duty to remain celibate has played in the lifes of these 25 priests.
We can distinguish between roughly four types: Those who have more or less accepted this duty. Those who have been struling with it for already quite some time. Then there is a third group of priests who all have an intimate relationship with someone. And finally we have the group of convinced celibatarians.
I will give a short description of each group, ending with a more elaborate discussion of the group of convinced celibatarians.

The group of those who have accepted the demand to remain celibate consists of 8 persons. Half of them are homosexuals.
The second group of 5 persons who struggle with their celibate is quite heterogenous. One respondent for example became involved with women several times already – more or less against his own will. These were usually women who were about to disappear from his life – through removal or through impending death. Another one had great problems with

loneliness. He did have a girl friend for some time – even lived with her, but put an end to this relationship, because he could not reconcile it with his being a priest. Again another one had several nervous breakdowns and many short relationships with women. He finally found some peace of mind with the help of a psychotherapist. Yet he remains unhappy with his situation.

The third group consists of respondents who are all having a steady intimate relationship. All the six persons in this group feel they learned a great deal from this relation, especially in their work. It is interesting to note that all except one would not want to marry of live together with their partner, not even should the official celibacy demand be abolished. This is because for them their work is so important, that it comes first of all.

The last group consists of six persons who are celibatarians from conviction. This group is remarkably homogeneous in a number of aspects. I will shortly discuss their similarities:

First of all: these CONVINCED CELIBATARIANS are all quite young. Four out of six are younger than 35 years; the other two are 40 and 44 years old.

Then: All except one decided for celibacy at a relatively late time. You may remember from the first part of this lecture that a responsible choice for celibacy should not be made at too early an age.

This is connected with the next point: all except one have been doing pastoral work for some time prior to their ordination.

Although all are very positive about their own celibacy, 5 out of 6 are definitely against the official demand for celibacy, just as by the way all the rest of our respondents.

All emphasize the fact that not everybody is fit for the celibate life. As for themselves they feel that they just happen to have a character that goes well with celibacy. For example most of them are quite capable of being alone and even like it.

Friendships are most important to them. They definitely need people with whom they can be wholly themselves.

Another remarkable similarity between the priests in this group is that all once seriously considered becoming a monk. They all still pay regular visits to abbeys.

Finally a last point I want to mention here is their sober lifestyle. Without forgetting about their own happiness in life, they want to look as much as possible for the needs and wants of other people. This soberness, which is indissolubly connected with their celibacy, also shows in their renunciation of having a partner.

(1) A literature study by Kerssemakers (1984) was very helpful in this.

171

(2) This procedure is discussed in Hoenkamp-Bisschops, 1987.
(3) See Hoenkamp-Bisschops (1984) for a more detailed description.
(4) See for a possible explanation for this high amount of homo-sexuals in our research group Hoenkamp-Bisschops (1985).

Literature
Calon, P.J.A. Priesterschap en celibaat. Brochure van katholiek leven. Nijmegen, 1956.

Christensen, C.W. The occurrence of mental illness in the ministry. In: E.M. Pattison (Ed.). Clinical psychiatry and religion. Boston, 1969.

Glaser, B.G. & Strauss, A.L. The discovery of grounded theory. Chicago: Aldine, 1967.

Glaser, B.G. Theoretical sensitivity. Advances in the methodology of grounded theory. California: The sociology Press, 1978.

Hoenkamp-Bisschops, A.M. Priesters en het celibaat: drie case-studies. Praktische Theologie, 1984, 5, 522-544.

Hoenkamp-Bisschops, A.M. Die gegenwärtigen Zölibatserfahrungen katholischer Priester in den Niederlanden. Archiv fur Religionspsychologie, 1985. (forthcoming)

Hoenkamp-Bisschops, A.M. Priests and celibacy: a qualitative research project. In: F. van Zuuren (Ed.). A qualitative approach to empirical psychology. Lisse: Swets & Zeitlinger: 1987. (forthcoming)

Hurter, O. Das Zolibat des Weltpriesters im Aspekt der Sozialpsychologie. In: F. Henrich (ed.), Existenzprobleme des Priesters. Munchen: 1969.

Kerssemakers, J. Het ambtscelibaat; een overzicht van de sociaal-wetenschappelijke literatuur. Praktische Theologie, 1984, 5, 502-521.

Mitchell, K.R. Priestly celibacy from a psychological perspective. Journal of Pastoral Care, 1970, 24, 216-226.

Plé, A. La vie affective du celibataire consacre. Supplement de la Vie Spirituelle, 1969, 22, 217-234.

Rey, K.G. Das Mutterbild des Priesters. Einsideln und Koln: Benziger, 1969.

Rulla, L.M. Depth psychology and vocation. Chicago: Loyola University Press, 1971.

Trimbos, C.J.B.J. Het priesterlijk celibaat. Enige psycho-hygienische beschouwingen. Nederlandse Katholieke Stemmen, 1955, 51, 320-337.

Vergote, A. Das Werden des Priesters als Mensch und Christ in psychologischer sicht. Der Priester in einer saekularisierten Welt. Akten des 3. internationalen Kongresses zu Luzern, 1967, 54-75.

Wester, F. De gefundeerde theorie-benadering. Een strategie voor kwalitatief onderzoek. Nijmegen: Sociologisch Instituut, 1984.

*The research was supported by the dutch Catholic Centre for Studies in Mental Health (KSGV).

Pilgrimage: motivation and effects.

Oosterwijk, J.W., Uden, M.H.F. van, & Hensgens, L.
Theological Faculty, Heerlen

Introduction

One of the characteristic changes in our society nowadays is the decreasing influence of traditional religion on the lives of most people in Western society (van Uden, 1985). Less and less people express their religiosity by going to churches.

But there is one form of religious expression that is an exception to this tendency. We are referring to the phenomenon of going to churches and chapels during a pilgrimage. It seems that this kind of religiosity is still alive and even becoming more popular in many places (Bart 1984).

This in one of the reasons why some time ago the department of social sciences of the H.T.P. at Heerlen decided to investigate this phenomenon (H.T.P. stands for Hogeschool voor Theologie en Pastoraat, A Catholic Theological Faculty, specialized in pastoral work). Pilgrimage is an interesting subject for the H.T.P. because this faculty has chosen "popular religion" as a main topic in their research program, and the phenomenon of pilgrimage is a prospering branch of popular religion, where many of its features can be studied.

For a psychologist of religion it is an interesting subject because of the mental health aspect involved. Is pilgrimage detrimental no mental health because pilgrims push off causalities and responsibilities to forces outside themselves? (Proudfoot and Shaver, 1975). Or is it beneficial because it gives hope, relieves depressive feelings, and reduces existentiel anxieties?

These are among the questions yet to be answered.

One of the starting points of our project was reading an article by Morris with the title: The effect of pilgrimage on anxiety, depression, and religious attitude (Morris, 1982). Morris finds it surprising that, though there have been many hundreds of papers written about the physical condition of patients before and after visits to shrines, there is, for example, no record in the Medical Bureau of Lourdes on any investigation into the emotional state.

Morris argues that the majority of people visiting shrines go for the spiritual upliftment to be expected from the pilgrimage. His survey was an attempt to quantify the benefits, on an emotional level, of such pilgrimages for people who were sick in the body. Morris' investigation aimed to ascertain the levels of anxiety, depression and religious attitude, by means of rating scales, in a group of physically sick men and women planning to go on a pilgrimage to Lourdes. These levels were reassessed one month and ten months after the pilgrims had returned. Morris found a significant decrease in anxiety and depression which was sustained.

After studying this article, we wondered if this effect was due to the fame of Lourdes, or that it was possible to find the same positive effects in other, less-known places of pilgrimage.

We decided to do an exploratory study in Wittem, a little place of pilgrimage in the south of Holland, only about 20 kilometers from Heerlen.

First we will tell you something about Wittem. Then we will give some information about our way of data collection, followed by an impression of the first results.

Wittem as a place of pilgrimage

Wittem is a very small village, mainly consisting of a monastery, some souvenir shops, a restaurant and a few houses. It is beautifully situated in the rolling hill landscape of the south of Holland. The monastery is a grand old building. It's church is abundantly decorated, especially if you compare it to the sober furnishing we are used to in most modern churches. Apart from the church it has several chapels which are internally connected. There are two chapels devoted to Mary and a big chapel devoted to Saint Gerard Majella. Outside the building is another tiny chapel with a sculpture from Gerard and a big garden which is used for processions. Because all chapels and the church are internally connected, people visiting the monastery can have a kind of "internal pilgrimage". As you have understood already, the devotion to St. Gerard plays a prominent role in this pilgrimage.

In the nineteenth century Wittem was a place of devotion to Mary. When in 1836 the congregation of Redemptorists took their residence in Wittem, they brought with them the devotion to Gerard.

Gerard lived in Italy at the end of the eighteenth century. He was a poor and lanky boy, and even had some trouble when he wanted to enter the Congregation of Redemptorists in 1749. But in the few years of his live (he died in 1755 at the age of 29), he proved to be a real saint. He was beatified in 1893, and canonized in 1904. After starting the monthly magazin "Het St.-Gerardus klokje" in 1920, more and more people started to come to Wittem. How and why this pilgrimage became so big that nowadays it attracts about 200.000 pilgrims a year, remains unclear.

Although people are visiting Wittem at any time, there are a few months (from june till october) when most people go to Wittem. At a typical pilgrimage sunday, you will find at least a dozen busses at the parking place, plus a lot of cars, from all over Holland and even some from Belgium and Germany. At ten or eleven o'clock the pilgrims follow a simple mass in the Gerard chapel. Then they have to wait a few hours till the procession and the benediction in the afternoon. This time is used for an internal pilgrimage, the lighting of candles, praying, or just relaxing. After the benediction there is a final gathering with blessings of people and objects, after which the busses and cars leave.

Purposes and methods

In this study:

-we wanted to know more about the people who go to Wittem on a pilgrimage

-we wanted to know more about the motivations of the pilgrims

-we wanted to see if we could also find in Wittem the positive effects that Morris found in Lourdes.

In order to replicate Morris' research, we had to collect the names of potential pilgrims before they went to Wittem. We asked the fathers in Wittem for the adresses of the people everywhere in the country who organise the busses for the pilgrims. June 2-nd 1985 was chosen as the day to investigate. We managed to get a selection of busses from all parts of Holland. We phoned the local bus organizers and asked for the names of people who had booked for the trip.

These people we first sent a questionnaire one week before June 2nd, and a second one 3 weeks after their pilgrimage. A follow-up 9 months later, as Morris did in his research, would be useless because our pilgrims might -and as the first results showed, probably would have- visited Wittem again in the meantime.

The first questionnaire dealt with topics concerning:

the population, their motivation (38 preformulated items plus an open-end question), and their religious commitments. This first questionnaire also contained, as a pretest, two psychological inventories: the Z.B.V. (a Dutch version of Spielbergers Trait Anxiety Inventory), and the Zung-d (a depression inventory).

The second questionnaire, 3 weeks after pilgrimage, asked for an evaluation of all kinds of aspects of the pilgrimage. It also contained a religious attitude scale: Frans Derks' adaptation of Batson and Ventis (Batson and Ventis, 1982) and again as the post-test the two psychological inventories.

Response

For this kind of questionnaire research the response was quite satisfying. We had sent 175 questionnaires and both times we got back nearly 90 questionnaires (about 50%).

This response was so high, we almost believed Gerard' blessings were upon us. It was a pity however that not all questionnaires were filled up adequately, especially the two inventaries. One reason was that many of our respondents couldn't handle multiple choice alternatives, despite our clear and simple instructions. When we asked explicitly to choose only one response possibility, an x was put in front of several alternatives.

In filling up our motivation inventory it was hard for several of our respondents to discriminate between "very applicable", "applicable", "don't know", "not applicable" and "completely unapplicable". Many respondents only put some marks in the first row ("very applicable") leaving the other response alternatives blank. These respondents obviously couldn't or wouldn't make a finer distinction then "yes" and "no."

In general, we were rather often puzzled by the way some respondents performed their task. But still more than enough of the data were adequate and helped us to reach the following first results.

First results

Let us start with the population data.

We only partly analysed the population data so far.

What we did analyse reveals that the mean age of our respondents is 63 years. Regarding the male-female ratio: as expected, three quarters of the population consisted of women.

About the educational level of these pilgrims: with the one exeeption of an elderly priest, none of the pilgrims did go much beyond primary school. The occupational level of our respondents and their partners was that of unskilled workers.

Regarding their religious commitment: in general our population consists of people who on the average go to church more than once a week. They are usually actively involved in their parish. The opinion of the pope is important for them.

Our pilgrims go more than once a year on a pilgrimage, usually not only to Wittem, but also to other places of pilgrimage.

Now about the motivation of the pilgrims for going to Wittem.

To investigate this, we formulated 38 motivation items, trying to be as exhaustive as possible.

From the literature, we supposed that the following 5 motivational complexes would play a role. To make things more clear, we will give an example of each category.

1. First what we called religious pilgrimage-related motivation. F.e.: because of Gerard.

2. religious not pilgrimage-related motivation. F.e.: because Jezus of Nazareth appeals to me.

3. traditional motivation. F.e.: because I have grown up with it.

176

4. social motivation. F.e.: because my husband/wife (or other member of the family) likes it.
5. recreational motivation. F.e.: because Wittem is situated in such a nice environment.

Taking into account that several of our respondents only gave yes/no responses, all responses in our first analysis were treated as if only yes-no response categories were given.
In a later stage of our research, we will factoranalyse the responses of the pilgrims who discriminated properly.

What were the main motivations?
The item which got the highest score was: "Because of St. Gerard" (of Majella). This is not so surprising, considering the fact that Gerard is the key figure of this pilgrimage.

If we draft a "motivational top-ten", we see the following list:
1-because of Gerard
2-to give thanks
3-to beseech God's blessing
4-to beseech help/assistance
5-to pray for the curing of others
6-because of Mary
7-to pray for a better world
8-to gain new strength
9-to pray for the need and misery in the world.
10-giving thanks for acquired favours

All of these items fall in the religious motivation categories. Most of these are pilgrimage-related motivations, some are general, not specifically pilgrimage-related items.
Two observations attract our attention.
In the first place: if we look at these items we see two devotional figures, Gerard and Mary, and the other items deal with asking for support and giving thanks for support.
Speaking in terms of types of religiosity, this looks like Allports "extrinsic religiosity" or Batson and Ventis' "means orientation" or Frans Derks' "support orientation".
In the second place we see that not even one single item of the other three motivational complexes are found here. We can see what happened to these items if we look at the bottom-ten of our motivational items:
-here we find all the social motivation items
-we also find, with one exception, all the recreational motivation items

here
-and here we find, with one exception, all of the traditional motivation items.

This is contradictory to the view that people would go on a pilgrimage because their other family members go, or for the touristic aspects of the trip. This confirms the findings concerning pilgrims to Lourdes, who also scored lowest on the recreation motivation (Pelgrims Onderweg, 1983). Secondly the pilgrims do not go for traditionalistic reasons: a definite and intrinsic choice seems to be at stake.

Finally, the item with the lowest score was : "because I feel less and less at home in my own parish". Actually, we expected that more of these elderly people wouldn't agree with the changes in their churches after Vaticanum 2 and would find the more traditionalistic aspects of Wittem appealing. Obviously, the discrepance between their own parish and Wittem is not as big as we thought: Wittem does not function as a place of refuge for these pilgrims.

In general, when we look at the differences between males and females, we see that there is a clear difference with regard to the items that acknowledge a social or recreational motivation. On everyone of these items the females score relatively higher. Examples of these items are statements like "because I find the collective journey so pleasant" or "because Wittem is situated in such a beautiful environment." Possibly women, more than men, see a pilgrimage also as an opportunity to be able to leave their household. This corresponds to a finding of Iso Baumer in his analysis of several pilgrimages (Baumer 1977). However, because the recreational aspect in general appears not to be that important, this in only a minor reason for going.

Apart from the 38 preformulated motivations we also gave room for individual motivations. About one fourth of our respondents made use of this possibility, but all of these where variations of our items, with a single exception like: "for the Saving of many souls who are lost otherwise, because nobody prayes for them".

We hope the factoranalysis will shed more light on the preceding issues concerning the motivation.

Our third important topic deals with the hypothesis that going on a pilgrimage enhances the pilgrims' sense of wellbeing.

As said before, we used two inventories for this purpose, in a pretest-posttest design. Our analysis was based on 26 respondents who adequately filled in the pre- and posttest of both inventories.

The first inventory was the Z.B.V., a Dutch version of Spielbergers Trait Anxiety Inventory (van der Ploeg, Defares and Spielberger, 1980).
This scale consists of 20 items, like "I am happy" or "i feel at ease". The respondents have to choose between 4 alternatives: hardly ever, sometimes, often and nearly always. They can get 1 to 4 points for each item, so they score somewhere between 20 and 80 points.
Now if we look at the data from the first questionnaire, the one the pilgrims filled in during the week before they went to Wittem, we find an average score of 36,5. This is quite a low score to begin with. At the post-test, 3 weeks after going to Wittem, the mean value was 34,5, which means a decrease of 2 points. This decrease in general anxiety level appeared to be significant on a .05 level.

The second inventory we used to measure their sense of well-being was the Zung-d, a self-rating depression scale (Zung, 1965). The Dutch version we used had 21 items, like "I have trouble sleeping at night" and "I am restless and can't keep still". It has the same 4 response categories as Spielbergers Anxiety Inventory. The scoring is between 0 and 3, so the range will be between 0 and 63.
The mean score of the pretest on the Zung-d was 17.7. Again this is a very low score. One would have to be quite euphoric to score that low.
Still their average score drops with nearly 5 points, from 17.7 to 12.8. In statistical terms this is highly significant. ($p < .01$)
So on both inventories there was a significant change, both in the direction of a higher sense of well-being.

A fourth topic in our analysis is the kind of religiosity of the pilgrims. For this purpose we used items from the inventory that is recently being developed by Frans Derks. As explained in his paper yesterday this inventory consists of 4 scales labeled: the support orientation, the witness orientation, the quest orientation and the non-religion orientation. This last one, the non-religion orientation, we didn't use for time reasons and because of the assumption that in this particular population this scale would not be relevant. Since these scales are not mutually exclusive, a person can score on all 3 of the scales, which in fact they did. Every respondent can have as a maximum score on each scale 1.0
The principal orientation turned out to be the support orientation, with a mean of .94. Second was the witness orientation with .83 and third, at a great distance, the quest orientation with .57.
These results correspond to our findings in the analysis of the motivational top-ten, where the support items also played a dominant role.

<u>Discussion and conclusions</u>

With this exploratory study we had four main objects in mind.

First: we wanted to know more about the kind of people that go to Wittem.

Second: we wanted to have an impression of their motivational structure.

Third: we wanted to replicate the study of Morris and see if we could find the same positive and measurable effects in this pilgrimage.

Fourth: we wanted to know more about the type of religiosity of these pilgrims.

With regard to the <u>first</u> topic: we have only partly analysed our data so far.

It is important to point out though, that we took our sample from the pilgrims who went to Wittem by bus. We don't know yet how different this sample of organised pilgrims is from a sample of pilgrims who go there by private car. We didn't contact these people because in this stage of research, we needed to have their adresses <u>before</u> they actually went to Wittem (because of our pretest-posttest design). Getting access to this group before their pilgrimage was not possible however.

Concerning the <u>second</u> topic: we shed some light on the motivational structure of our sample of pilgims.

-first: the pilgrims go to Wittem because they want something. They ask for strength, they come with special intentions, they pray for a better world in general and they render thanks for received favours.

-they are asking this in the first place from Gerard, in the second place from Mary and God. Jezus does not appear in our motivational top-ten. This underlines the minor Christocentricity of this population, in contrast with the popularity of Mary or a saint like Gerard. This phenomenon has often been observed (see f.e. "Pelgrims Onderweg", a publication on the pilgrimage to Lourdes) and seems to be a common characteristic of popular religion (Blijlevens et al, 1982).

This fact was recognized by the fathers in Wittem. They point to the fact that the main sculpture of Gerard is placed opposite to the crucifix. Also the candles and devotional lights are arranged in such a way, that the rows of lights in front of Gerard are widening in the direction of the crucifix, in that way symbolically pointing to Jesus. Obviously they use this arrangement to make the pilgrims more aware of Gerard's place in relation to Jesus.

Concerning the <u>third</u> topic: we wanted to see whether the effects found by Morris could also be discovered in this pilgrimage. For the measurement of a reduction in depression level, we used the Zung-d scale. Here we found highly significant improvement, applying the so-called t-test, (p<.01).

Regarding the measurement of a reduction in anxiety level, we used the same anxiety inventory that Morris used, and although Morris found stronger effects, our effects were still significant at .05 level.

One problem in this context is: to what extend is a conscious or unconscious pilgrimage-promoting tendency involved. The pilgrims might have tended to overemphasize the positive effects of the pilgrimage, which then might have influenced their scoring on the second questionaire. Nevertheless such an effect could't totally explain our results. We feel that the way in which the Z. B. V. and Zung-d were presented made it very difficult for the pilgrims to manipulate the results (considering the nature of the items and the 4-weeks interval between the pre- and posttest).

Our fourth topic, concerning the type of religiosity: we found the support orientation scoring very high and the quest orientation quite low.

This is in accordance with our findings regarding the motivational structure of the pilgrims. Our pilgrims are not searching for answers: they know what they want and where to find it.

There is one last issue we want to discuss.

In our first questionnaire our sample of pilgrims reported to be very healthy, both physically and psychologically. Their initial anxiety level was very low: it can be compared to the anxiety level of an average Dutch student (van der Ploeg et. al. 1980). Their initial depression level was also very low. As said before, one would have to be quite euphoric to reach their level.

How can this be explained?

The first questionnaire was sent the week before they went to Wittem. Possibly the pilgrims were already looking forward to the uplifting effect they expected to experience. These expectations might have been so strong, that the pilgrims improved at the mere anticipation of what was laying ahead of them. This being true, it would imply that in this kind of research it is necessary to take the first test a longer time before the "treatment" -in this case the pilgrimage- takes place.

It would also mean that one could expect an even greater improvement than the one we found.

All in all, we feel we have been able to discover in this less wellknown place of pilgrimage the positive effects Morris found in Lourdes: pilgrimage seems to have a beneficial effect on the anxiety and depression levels of the pilgrims.

Literature

Bax, M. "Officieel geloof" en "Volksgeloof" in Noord-Brabant. Sociologisch Tijdschrift, 1984, 10, 621-647.

Batson, C.D., & Ventis, W.L. The Religious Experience. New York: Oxford University Press, 1982.

Blijlevens, A., Brants, A., & Henau, E. Volksreligiositeit: uitnodiging en uitdaging. H.T.P. studies, Averbode: 1982.

Pelgrims Onderweg. Boxtel, Uitgave Y.N.B.: 1983.

Baumer, I. Wallfahrt als Handlungsspiel. Frankfurt/M: 1977.

Herwaarden, J. van. Pelgrimstochten, Bussum: 1974.

Morris, P.A. The effect of pilgrimage on anxiety, depression and religious attitude. Psychological Medicine, 1982, 12, 291-294.

Ploeg, H.M., Defares, P.B., & Spielberger, C.D. Handleiding bij de Zelf-Beoordelings Vragenlijst. Lisse, Swets & Zeitlinger, 1980.

Proudfoot, W., & Shaver, P. Attribution theory and the psychology of religion. Journal for the Scientific Study of Religion, 1975, 14, 317-330.

Uden, M.H.F. van. Religie in de crisis van de Rouw, Nijmegen: Dekker & van de Vegt, 1985.

Zung, W.K. A Self-Rating Depression Scale. Archives of general Psychiatry, 1965, 12, 63-70.

Marrying in church: a rite of passage?

J.Z.T. Pieper
Catholic Theological Faculty, Heerlen

1. Introduction

Sociological and psychological studies of religious life of modern, western man very often arrive at the conclusion that religion, faith and especially church have become less and less important. The recent study of the values and norms of the European -besides publications for each country there is an overview of the whole project by Stoetzel (1983): Les valeurs du temps présent: une enquête européenne- also points in this direction. The church-attendance figures for Sundays in the Netherlands as measured by KASKI (the office of research of the Roman Catholic Church in the Netherlands) are another illustration of this. Still in 1973 an average of 37.5% of Roman Catholics older than seven attended church on Sundays. Ten years later, in 1983, this percentage had decreased just below 20 (KASKI, 1984): a decrease of almost 50%.

Nevertheless in case of important occasions in their lives, such as birth, marriage and death, many people still ask for the religious rituals associated with these occasions as offered by the church. Statistics about baptisms, marriages in church and burials clearly indicate this phenomenon. As for marrying in the Roman Catholic Church in the Netherlands, in 1983 60% of all the Roman-Catholics solemnized their civil marriages in church (1). If we disregard the mixed marriages this figure increases to almost 75% (KASKI, 1984). In the countries surrounding the Netherlands a solemnization in church is even more popular. Elsewhere too the special position of these religious ceremonies has been pointed out. Zulehner (1983) found that in 1980 Catholics in Austria expected the church above all to baptize, solemnize marriages and bury people. Felling, Peters and Schreuder (1981) noted that the religious "rites of passage", at least as far as the Netherlands are concerned, are the line of demarcation between people who have and people who don't have any tie with the church. If people do not marry in church or do not want their children to be baptized, they loose to a high degree the possibility of staying Christian and, as for the children, of becoming Christians.

With this knowledge in mind a rather extensive research-project has started at the Catholic Theological Faculty te Heerlen in 1981 (2) concerning one of these religious rites of passage: church marriage and, more specifically church marriage in the Roman Catholic Church in the Netherlands. One of the purposes of this project was to explore the motives for a church marriage. Why do people marry in church; what does this mean to them? In this paper we shall concentrate on one of the few elaborate theories about the meaning of church marriage: church marriage as a rite of passage. In this theory marrying in church is an answer to a need for meaning and religious (possibly in the form of specifically Christian) interpretation in relation to a life-event with strong existential consequences. We will examine two forms of this theory. The first form points especially to social transition, in which the actor takes a new role in society. The second form points especially to the cognitive and emotional changes that take place within the individual. At the same time we shall see that each of these forms has its own implicit notions of what marriage looks like. The next step is a confrontation of this theory with empirical evidence, gathered within the framework of the above-mentioned research-project. At the end we will try to answer the question whether marriage today is still a rite of passage.

2. Church

2.1. Social change

Studies that emphasize the change of social status follow the propositions of anthropologists about how rites of passage function. Pickering (1974) summarizes these propositions. The most important ones are:
a) Rites of passage are essentially rites of change in which actors assume new roles in society.
b) The rites display a basic structure of separation, transition and incorporation.
c) The social changes are accompanied by emotional changes. These in turn may give rise to personal tensions, feelings of inadequacy, feelings of guilt or fear for the unknown. The personal crises are often at the heart of the rites of passage.
d) The ritual techniques define social reality. They emphasize what is happening to the actor and to the participants. They may give the actor courage to deal with fear or personal crisis and invest him with the authority to play the intended role.

Renner (1979) follows the French anthropologist Arnold van Gennep (3) in grouping the rituals under three main headings: pre-liminal (a state of relative equilibrium), liminal (the state of crisis) and post liminal (the re-emergence of relative equilibrium). The ritual keeps the desintegrating human being together and also sustains communities.

Besides attention to the function of the ritual there is in these studies also attention to those who are involved. Pickering (1974) notes that rituals are social occasions, occasions where kin and friends, even a local community, are part of what takes place. Tomka (1982) argues that rituals today are especially connected with family life and the local community, while the connection with society in general has become less important. Steck (1974) too believes that the family is the point of reference. Marrying means leaving one's parents and founding a family on one's own. In former days this was a very marked transition: the bridegroom changed from son into the head of a new family and the bride was introduced into the "enlarged family" of the bridegroom.

With regard to marrying in church this explanation means: There is a critical change of social status in the life of the individual, accompanied by fear and concern. The fear frequently arises from the uncertainty whether the individual will be able to function adequately in the prescribed role. The religious ritual offers help in dealing with this fear and uncertainty, offers consolation and self-confidence and brings God's blessing on what is going on. The church functions in this process as an institution endowed with enough power and confidence to make its rituals in situations of crisis acceptable.

It is a remarkable fact -while the studies themselves do not talk about it- that behind this explanation seems to hide a notion of marriage that resembles what in the studies of marriage and the family is called "ideal-typical" the traditional marriage. Characteristic of this type of marriage is that its functions are of vital interest for society. Marriage has to provide for economic security and continuity between generations. It also has a socializing function: bringing up and educating the children. It plays a significant role in stabilizing the social structure. Gy (1976) presents a number of characteristics of the traditional marriage, of which we select the following: Marriage is an institution, which prescribes the different roles of man and woman; procreation is one of the main functions of marriage; marriage is a place of production as well as of consumption; there is a continuity between generations; marriage is indissoluble.

2.2. Cognitive change

The previous explanation emphasized social change, here we find an emphasis on the cognitive and emotional changes within the individual. In general, as far as marriage is concerned, this explanation says: Rites of passage offer meaning and religious interpretation when a husband and wife begin to construct a shared world-view. Let's develop this a bit further. Our startingpoints are philosophical-anthropological notions that are introduced into the social sciences by the sociology of knowledge (Wissenssoziologie). Berger (1969) argues that man is born, while still developing biologically. Man's instinctual organization may be described as underdeveloped. Man's relationship to his environment is characterized by world-openness. Man has to construct his own world. A human being must continually externalize itself in activity. This externalization or reality-construction happens through interaction with significant others, especially in face-to-face communication.

Berger and Kellner (1965) apply this view to marriage. They treat marriage as an important domain in which this reality-construction takes place. The marriage companion is the most significant "significant other". The face-to-face communication with this significant other creates "nomos". The fact that two strangers with different reality definitions meet each other constitutes the transitional character of marriage. First there is a breakdown of "nomos"; later on the reconstruction of "nomos" starts. These two strangers are building up a new reality definition, a "we"-world. This creation of a "we"-world is all the more important since marriage in our western, industrial civilisation is the most important domain of self-affirmation and self-realisation. It also offers identity. It is the relation upon which someone's identity is based. While it is uncertain whether this construction of a "we"-world will succeed, in some aspects the beginning of a marriage resembles a crisis.

Zulehner (1976) argues that two different backgrounds have to become one. This is a kind of crisis. It is for both partners a rupture with the old background. On the one hand there are hopeful expectations of a successful life in love, on the other hand one is anxious about not being able to manage the tasks of marriage. Zulehner especially emphasizes the integretation of a close bond of love which gains stability by connecting it with the stable cosmos of religion and faith.

In these studies there is also a shift with regard to those who are involved in the ritual. The two marrying people are at the centre. Relatives and friends form the surrounding choir.

With regard to the religious rites of passage, in this case the marriage-ceremony, this explanation means: Human beings need meaning, especially in marginal situations. These marginal situations show how fragile the existing "nomos" is. History shows that in this kind of situation religion is the most widespread and effective system of meaning (symbolic universe). The church is the mediator par excellence of this symbolic universe. This is why people want to solemnize their marriages in church.

Here too there seems to be an implicit notion of marriage, that can be called "ideal-typical": the romantic marriage. In this type of marriage the relation between husband and wife has become the focus of marriage. Marriage offers emotional comfort and security and possibilities of self-actualisation. Gy (1976) notes, among other things, the following characteristics of the romantic marriage.

Marriage is a bond of love _and_ an institution, by which the emotional bond is especially served. The institution consolidates the bond; marriage stands apart from the outside world; marriage is no longer a place of production, but still a place of consumption; the husband provides the income and the wife stays at home; marriage is rather stable.

Weeda (1984) distinguishes between the traditional, closed marriage and the modern, open marriage. The characteristics she gives of the traditional marriage fit in our description of the romantic marriage. The most significant characteristics are: The marriage-bond is based on love and affection; marriage is meant for life; there is a strong feeling of "we together"; children are an essential part of marriage; the man earns the money, the woman raises the children; there is a special stress on privacy.

3. Empirical evidence

3.1. Collecting of the data

First our data were collected by means of a national survey among Catholics in the Netherlands. In 1982 we sent 1,768 questionnaires to newly married couples. About 700 questionnaires were filled out and returned. This is a response of 40%. An important question, of course, is whether there are substantial differences between people who did and people who did not send the questionnaire back. We have a number of indications that show that the response is fairly representative.

Secondly, in 1983 and 1984 16 persons (8 couples) were interviewed. These persons were selected out of a group of 84, who, by putting their names at the end of the questionnaire, indicated that they were willing to be interviewed.

3.2. Results

The questionnaire contained 28 motives for a marriage in church, selected on the basis of the literature. The newly married couples were asked to indicate to what degree each motive was relevant to their own marriage in church: very relevant, relevant, I don't know, not relevant, not relevant at all. By the way, this questionnaire was not explicitly meant as a test of the "rite of passage" theory. It was an exploration, as thorough as possible, of all the motives that could play a role in marrying in church. A factor-analysis showed the structure in the answers of the respondents. 4 factors or basic-motivations were found: Christian-religious embedding of the nuptial-tie; social-traditional motivation; explicit choice to belong to the church and the additional atmosphere of a marriage in church. The last three basic-motivations are hardly interpretable in the light of the "rite of passage" theory. Basic-motivation 1 (table 1) on the other hand, the Christian-religious "embedding" of the nuptial-tie, that is on an average relevant for 56% of the respondents, seems to point in the direction of what Zulehner called the need to stabilize the bond of love by putting it below the shield of the stable cosmos of religion and faith. In the words of

Berger (1969) religion and faith function as a sacred canopy. Especially motives 2,4,5,6, and 8 are good examples of this. At the same time we wonder whether this religious "embedding" has something to do with fear of an uncertain and unknown future. To what degree did the couples actually experience their marriage in church as a help for a difficult transition? When we explicitly ask whether this was the case: "By marrying in church the transition to married life is facilitated", then only 12% of the respondents agree. Together with the fact that this item is not part of factor 1, this means that the religious "embedding" is probably not to be understood in the context of help for an transition.

Let's look whether the in-depth interviews can shed some more light on the subject we are dealing with. Recently we started analyzing the interviews. One of the questions was whether the above-mentioned theories were reflected in the experiences of the newly married couples. It showed that only the marriage of two persons posessed some characteristics that could be interpreted in the framework of a social change within a traditional marriage. One person experienced the marriage-ceremony as a kind of ritually leaving parental home and announcing in public his new status. Another person married at the very moment that he could take over the farm of this father and could found a new family with his wife.

The marriage of eight other interviewees showed characteristics that could be interpreted as belonging to the romantic type of marriage. These persons emphasized the construction of a solid, indissoluble nuptial-tie that has to last for life. There is a rather strong feeling of belonging together: "we together". They relatively frequently talk with respect to their marriage in church about the help and blessing of God for their marriage. Most of these persons did not cohabit before their marriage. So, we notice that they talk about marriage as a beginning, the start of a long life together. They experience a certain kind of transition. At the same time we didn't notice any signs of an emotional crisis. Nobody speaks of fear of not being successful in marriage, or, as some one said: "To talk already at the start of your marriage about problems in the relation... No, I can't imagine that. In that case you had better not marry at all."

The remaining six persons have many characteristics of a type of marriage not yet mentioned: the companionship marriage. Gy (1976) mentions, among other things, the following characteristics of this type of marriage: Marriage is an emotional bond, with little institutional protection; the roles of man and woman are at least in principle alike; both partners are economically independent; marriage is more open for the outside world. According to Weeda (1984) a few important characteristics of what she calls the modern, open marriage, and that fit in our description of the companionship marriage, are: marriage is based upon companionship; it should last as long as possible, but not necessarily for a life-time; besides joint activities the partners also engage in activities without the partner; children are no longer the crown of marriage; role differences between man and woman lessen; besides a certain amount of privacy, there should also be openness to the outer world.

Our grouping of the interviewees is especially based upon the degree of identification with the relation. If the identification with the relation (a feeling of "we together") prevails, then the person is assigned to the romactic type of marriage. If the self-identification (a feeling of "you" and "I") prevails, then the person is assigned to the companionship type of marriage.

Indeed, we found the remaining six persons to be less dependent on the relationship with regard to their identity, than the eight persons in the romantic type. But with regard to emotional security they are still very much committed to the relationship. Another striking fact is that they all cohabited before marrying. In fact, to them marriage means more a consolidation of or a final settlement of an already existing state of affairs rather than a start. These people too refer to the help of God in behalf of strengthening their nuptial-tie, but are less clear about this than the people of the romantic type.

4. Conclusions

Let us return to the question we started with: to what degree does marriage in church today function as a rite of passage?

First, we noticed that it is hard to speak of a transition in which economic security and social status are involved. It is also hard to speak -a few cases excepted- of marriage as leaving the parental home in the sense of becoming independent and adult. Today leaving parental home even often does not coincides with marriage at all. The development behind these facts is the ever increasing de-institutionalization and individualization of marriage, by which the social dimension (community and family) becomes less and less important.

Secondly, we did notice a few facts that fit in the picture of a romantic type of marriage accompanied by a transition, that has to do with the construction of a new common identity and emotional security. With regard to the questionnaire we saw that the Christian-religious embedding of the nuptial-tie seemed to point in this direction. We may add that, on the average, this factor was more relevant to the respondents than the other three factors. With regard to the in-depth interviews we saw that half of the interviewees had many characteristics of the romantic type of marriage. But we didn't find any signs of a transition with "crisis" proportions, neither in the data of the questionnaire nor in the interviews.

Marriage is indeed a time of personal importance, but does not have the appearence of a crisis.

Thirdly, the companionship marriage has less a meaning of transition because here it is less necessary to construct a new "we"-world. The individual identity remains intact. Marriage is no longer a "nomic" break. Here the above-mentioned individualization is also noticeable inside the relationship. The individual becomes the point of reference. Where we can speak of a construction of a common world of living and in this type of marriage this has to be situated on the plane of emotional security, this must be seen as a gradual process. Because the interviewees of this type cohabited first, they had a long time to thoroughly get acquainted with each other. Still, the church marriage for these people too has, besides other meanings, the meaning of a religious "embedding". What could be the nature of this religious "embedding"? According to the interviews an answer could be: At a certain moment people that already cohabit feel some need to confirm their relationship. They fall back on the wedding-ceremony of the church, a traditional form that is deeply rooted in our culture. In this case the wedding-ceremony means that the ongoing or already finished process of building up a stable bond of love is emphasized once again. Marriage is no longer a rite of passage, but, in the words of Lewin (1982) a rite of confirmation, a reassurance of the already at least partially constructed "we"-world.

Notes:

1. On the other side there is also a gradual decline in the wedding ceremonies in church. Since 1965 (at that moment 83,3%) the figures have dropped about 1% a year.
2. Since 1 March 1984 this project is supported by the Foundation for Research in the field of Theology and the science of Religions in the Netherlands, which is subsidized by the Netherlands Organization for the Advancement of pure Research (Z.W.O.).
3. V. Gennep first used the phrase: "rite de passage" in 1909 in his study "Les Rites de Passage" (Pickering, 1974).
4. A further explanation of these 4 basic-motivations is to be found in Pieper, v. Uden, Hoenkamp-Bisschops (1985).

Literature

Berger, P.L. Het hemels baldakijn. Bijdrage tot een theoretische godsdienstsociologie. Utrecht: Ambo, 1969.

Berger, P.L., & Kellner, H. Die Ehe und die Konstruktion der Wirklichkeit. Eine Abhandlung zur Mikrosoziologie des Wissens. Soziale Welt, 1965, 16, 220-235.

Felling, A., Peters, J. & Schreuder, O. Gebroken identiteit. Een studie over christelijk en onchristelijk Nederland. Jaarboek van het Katholiek Documentatiecentrum, 1981, 25-81.

Gy, P.M. Le mariage en France aujourd'hui. A propos d'un livre de L. Roussel. La Maison-Dieu, 1976, 127, 161-173.

Kaski. In: Biltstraat 121, Speciale uitgave december. 1984.

Lewin, B. Unmarried cohabitation: A marriage form in a changing society. Journal of Marriage and the Family, 1982, 44, 763-773.

Pickering, W.S.F. The Persistence of Rites of Passages: Towards an Explanation. The Britisch Journal of Sociology, 1974, 25, 63-78.

Pieper, J.Z.T., Uden, M. van, & Hoenkamp-Bisschops, A. Trouwen in de kerk. Resultaten van een landelijk onderzoek in Nederland naar de huwelijksmotivatie. Blijlevens, A. & Henau, E. Huwelijkssluiting: gelegenheidsverkondiging, Averbode/Apeldoorn: Altiora, 1985.

Renner, H.P.V. The use of ritual in pastoral care. The Journal of Pastoral Care, 1979, 33, 164-174.

Steck, W. Die soziale Funktion der kirchlichen Trauung. Wissenschaft und Praxis in Kirche und Gesellschaft, 1974, 63, 27-46.

Stoetzel, J. Les valeurs du temps présent: une enquête européenne. Parijs: Presses Universitaires de France, 1983.

Tomka, A. Les rites de passage dans les pays socialistes de l' Europe de l'Est. Social Compass, 1982, 29, 135-152.

Weeda, I. Huwelijksleven. Ideaal en praktijk. Persoonlijke ervaringen en enquêteresultaten. Utrecht: Spectrum, 1984.

Zulehner, P.M. Heirat. Geburt. Tod. Eine Pastoral zu den Lebenswenden. Wenen: Herder, 1976.

Zulehner, P.M. Ritual und Symbol in volkskirchlicher Situation. Pastoral-theologische Informationen, 1983, 3, 257-273.

TABLE 1

FACTOR 1: CHRISTIAN-RELIGIOUS EMBEDDING OF THE NUPTIAL-TIE

	factor-loading	% relevance
-- I have married in church because one experiences the neighbourhood of God when two people love each other.	0.72	(49%)
-- I have married in church because one's marriage has a better chance to succeed by the help of God.	0.69	(39%)
-- I have married in church because I have experienced that our feelings for each other also have to do with something devine.	0.61	(50%)
-- It is by marrying in church that you really belong to each other.	0.59	(49%)
-- I have married in church to get God's blessing upon my marriage.	0.58	(81%)
-- I have married in church because by doing so you feel much more united.	0.55	(59%)
-- I have married in church because marriage is a symbol of the covenant of God with man.	0.55	(55%)
-- I have married in church because there is a new future in view with all kinds of questions, and faith can help to find an answer.	0.53	(48%)
-- By marrying in church you show that the life of Jesus is important to your marriage.	0.49	(58%)
-- I have married in church to make God witness of my promise of marriage.	0.49	(70%)
		(56%)

Religious attitudes: a practical approach. (1)

F. Derks
Catholic University Nijmegen

In the opening paper of this session I raised the question of the psychological status of the means-, end-, and quest-orientation. Such theoretical problems however do not necessarily have to keep investigators from doing their job. Indeed, most of the time such theoretical – and related conceptual – problems are discovered only while doing research. The main purpose of this paper is to communicate some problems I had to deal with when I tried to make use of the Religious Life Inventory, the instrument Batson constructed for differentiating the three religious attitudes of religion as a means, as an end, and as a quest.

In search of central characteristics

I started my research with the intention of just translating the Religious Life Inventory into Dutch, allthough I immediately felt uneasy because, in my view, the instrument had two shortcomings. First of all, because of the Doctrinal Orthodoxy Scale which is included in the instrument, it's applicability in research with populations other than Batson's American Protestants was not clear, while I had planned to include Roman Catholics and even Hinduistic Hare Krishna devotees as samples in my investigations. Secondly, in my view the instrument was unable to deal with the problem of what Vernon (1969) called "the religious nones". I had the feeling that for individuals without any religious interests most of the items in the instrument were utterly irrelevant – as is the case in almost any religious attitudes scale. One might argue that such individuals score low on every subscale (which is the solution Allport and Ross ,1967, seem to prefer when they state that those scoring low on both the extrinsic and intrinsic scale should be regarded as "indiscriminately anti-religious"), but this argument is not necessarily correct. So from the beginning I favored the elimination of the Doctirnal Orthodoxy scale and the inclusion of what might be called a 'non-religiosity' scale.

But soon I started to have even more serious doubts about the instrument. I wondered why Batson developed such an extremely artificial way of measuring the religious attitudes he had conceptualized. Batson specifies a large number of differentiating characteristics, but then constructs an instrument `in which these characteristics are not operationalized. Instead he operationalizes additional characteristics – which he never theoretically reasoned to be relevant. And he does not operationalize them in scales measuring the three attitudes directly, but in scales that have to be weighted and combined when computing an individual's score for each attitude. I came to the conclusion that I should try to measure the three attitudes directly by constructing a scale for each of them in which their central characteristic are operationalized. But then, what are these central characteristics? In order to get an answer to this question I started to read Batson's publications on this subject.

As already mentioned in my introductory paper, Batson started as a theologian and developed a theological theory (Batson, Beker & Clark, 1973) that may be considered as - at least - a first step towards his psychological theory. His next step might perhaps be conceived as a "psycho-theological" theory. This next step is his well-known study of the relationship between religiosity and helping behavior, co-authored with Darley (Darley & Batson, 1973). The authors argue amongst others that the religious quest orientation is strongly influenced by a "Samaritanlike" component. Their interpretation is that Jesus by means of this Biblical parable wanted to show the people that the Levite's and priests piety was only extrinsically motivated: they are "virtuous for what it will get them, both in terms of the admiration of their fellowmen and in the eyes of God" (Darley & Batson, 1973; 101). Only the Samaritan is - in terms of Allport's typology - intrinsically motivated: he "responds without other motivation". This intrinsic motivation may be equated with Batson's quest orientation, as becomes apparent in Darley & Batson's formulation of one of their hypotheses both in terms of extrinsic-intrinsic as well as in terms of means, end and quest. It becomes even more apparent in the name they give to the scale measuring the quest orientation: the Religious Life Inventory Intrinsic Scale, and in the names they give to the scales measuring the means and end orientation: the Religious Life Inventory Extrinsic External and Extrinsic Internal scales.

We may conclude that at this point in the development of his theory, Batson favored an interpretation of both the means and the end attitude as being essentially extrinsic and an interpretation of the quest attitude as being identical to the traditional concept of intrinsic religiosity, the only difference maybe being a stronger emphasis in the quest orientation on "Samaritanlikeness". But when we remember Batson & Ventis (1982) arguments, we cannot help but wonder why Batson later derived both the end and the quest orientation theoretically from Allport's original concept of intrinsic religion (By the way: in the meantime also the names of the scales changed: the term extrinsic was dropped from the names of the external and internal scales, while the RLI-intrinsic scale was renamed into "interactional scale").

Another conceptual-methodological problem with the scales is the question why Batson included the Allport-Ross scales as well as the Religious Life Inventory Intrinsic Scale as separate scales in his instrument, instead of just adding some "Samaritanlike" items to the Allport-Ross intrinsic scale. This question becomes even more pregnant when we take a look at Batson's formulation of what the RLI Intrinsic (later: Interactional) Scale is supposed to measure and at the items of which it is composed. The scale is "designed to measure the degree to which one's religiosity involves a questioning of the meaning of life arising out of one's interaction with his social environment" (Darley & Batson, 1973; 102). This not necessarily implies any "Samaritanlikeness", and, consequently, there is nothing "Samaritanlike" in the items. The majority of the items seems to tap some kind of "questioning" attitude (items concerning religious doubts and uncertainties, and items concerning questioning the meaning of life) rather than a "Samaritanlike" attitude.

So after reading Batson's earlier publications there still was considerable uncertainty about the exact nature of especially the quest attitude, but also the end attitude. This uncertainty   not to say confusion - became even worse after reading some other articles Batson wrote between 1973 (the Darley & Batson article) and 1982 (the Batson & Ventis book). I won't elaborate on them, but it's surely no understatement to say that I often regretted not to have chosen the probably much easier way of just translating the scales - allthough, as we have just heard, such an endeavor has it's own typical difficulties.

Tentative definitions
However, after a certain period of reading and thinking about the concepts I came to tentative definitions, formulated a list of differentiating characteristics and started the search for items, using these characteristics as a guide-line.

I defined the **means orientation** as a functional way of being religious, aimed essentially at social well being. It's central characteristics are that although the person's religious belief has a positive influence on his psychological and social functioning, these beliefs are relatively unimportant in his life.

I defined the religious **end orientation** as a way of being religious that is based on the experience of a transcendental God, an experience that directs and permeates the person's way of living and thinking. It's central characteristic is a religious experience, which is the ground for certainty of belief (rejection of doubts), religious particularism (the claim of having found eternal truth while disclaiming the possibility of any truth in opposing beliefs), readiness to 'live' one's religion (and relative ease with which this is done because the belief supplies the person with a spirituality that makes life easier to live), and the feeling of 'meaning' in life stemming from faith.

I defined the **quest orientation** as a questioning and social-minded ("Samaritanlike") way of being religious, that supplies the person with the possibility of answers to 'ultimate', 'existential' questions, but in itself is full of questions (in other words: the answers are not taken for granted uncritically). Here again a religious experience is central, but any religious particularism is absent while doubts and uncertainties are valued as possibilities to grow spiritually. Moreover there is an emphasis on the ethical aspects of faith and a mistrust of religious institutions.

The **non-religious attitude** I defined as religious indifference, characterized by a negative evaluation of the influence religion has in various domains (e.g. the social, political or scientific domain).

The construction of scales

On the basis of these definitions and characteristics I selected, translated and invented more than 200 items, most of which came from various religious attitude scales. After a reduction to approximately 100 items, the list was sent to 13 experts, all of them Dutch psychologists of religion. The instruction read that they should indicate for every item whether in their opinion an ideal-typical extrinsic, intrinsic, quest or nonreligious person would answer yes or no to the statement.

All the lists were returned and analysed for discriminating ability of the items. This resulted in the selection of 45 statements as possible items for the four subscales:

9 items for an **extrinsic-means scale**, mainly items concerning the support and comfort that the person's belief supplies, such as e.g. the originally Allport-Ross extrinsic item "what religion offers me most is comfort when sorrow and misfortune strike";

11 items for an **intrinsic-end scale**, mainly items concerning the behavioral consequences of the person's faith, such as witnessing (e.g. the self-invented item "I want to witness even though I might lose some good friends by doing so") or 'living' one's religion (e.g. the item "I am not as strict in my religious practices as I feel I should be", which is an item adapted from Funk's Religious Conflict Scale);

14 items for a **religious quest scale**, mainly items concerning ethics (e.g. the self-invented item "My religiosity shows more from the fact that I help my fellowman when he is in need, than from the fact that I fulfill my religious duties"), doubts (e.g. the originally Batson Interactional Scale item "It might be said that I value my religious doubts and uncertainties"), and openness for truth in other beliefs (e.g. the Putney & Middleton

Fanaticism Scale item "I believe the world would really be a better place if more people held the views about religion which I hold" on which a denial indicated a quest orientation);

11 items for a **nonreligiosity scale**, mainly items emphasizing the irrelevance of religion for the individual (such as "I am not interested in religion", "In my life I have little use for religion", and "In my opinion religion is outdated", all developed from items originally included in the Funk Hostility to Church Scale).

These scales, constructed on the basis of the expert-ratings, had sufficient face-validity to warrant the hope that I might succeed in my attempts at constructing a new instrument. At the same time as I sent the itemlists to the experts, I had them filled out by 57 psychology students and - somewhat later and in sometimes slightly different formulations - by 55 Roman Catholics selected by two pastors as representing the three pro-religious attitudes. The data were analysed factor-analytically which, after some additional analyses and regroupings, resulted in four scales, interpreted as means, end, quest, and nonreligiosity.

The **means scale**, for which I would prefer the name **religious support scale**, consists of six items, all of them indicating beneficial effects of the person's belief on various domains. The most important items in this scale are the statements "My belief gives me a feeling of certainty, safety and security" , "My belief gives me peace of mind" and "My belief supports me when I feel down".

The **end scale**, for which I would prefer a name like **witnessing scale**, consists of four items, all indicating readiness to inform people of one's beliefs, notwithstanding possible detrimental effects in social or societal functioning. The most important items in this scale are "I should dare to witness at any time" and "I want to witness, even though I might lose some good friends by doing so".

The **quest scale** consists of six items, most of them referring to some kind of **cognitive approach** to religion (items concerning reading and thinking about religion), the others expressing a positive attitude towards doubt (the item "For me spiritual growth is only possible when I doubt regularly") and an awareness of behavioral restrictions imposed by the belief (the item "Religion often seems like a drag to me").

The **nonreligiosity scale** consists of eight items, expressing first of all a general negative attitude towards religion (the most important items being " In my life I have little use for religion" and "I can no longer have any trust in religion because it has been used so often for the justification of prejudice and discrimination"), and expressing secondly the absence of religious experience (a negative answer to "Quite often I have been aware

197

of the presence of something I could refer to with the term 'God' or 'something divine'").

In tabel 1 the correlations between these scales are represented, as well as their homogeneity-coefficients (Cronbach alpha).

tabel 1

	support	witness	quest	nonrelig.
support	.88	.05	.14	-.47*
witness		.73	.06	-.10
quest			.69	-.44*
nonrelig.				.85

Note: * = sign. at .00; all other correlations non-significant. Cronbach alpha's represented at the diagonal; N=112 for correlations and for alpha for nonrelig. scale; N=79 for all other alpha's because before computing these alpha's the extreme high scorers on the nonrelig. scale were eliminated from the sample.

Discussion

Coming to the end of my paper, it's time to draw some conclusions from the theoretical part (my introductory paper as well as the opening paragraphs of this paper) and from the practical part (the foregoing paragraph, including the correlational data and the reliabilities)

Concerning the theoretical part we may conclude that there is still considerable uncertainty about the exact nature of the various "ways of being religious". Should they be regarded as theological or psychological concepts? And if they are psychological, are they then motivational or attitudinal? And if they are attitudinal, should they then be regarded as separate attitudes or as one attitude with any of the three traditional components of attitudes being central for different individuals at different times. In other words: why shouldn't we conceptualize the **means** orientation as the predominance of the emotional component in the attitude towards religion, the **end** orientation as the predominance of the behavioral component, and the **quest** orientation as the predominance of the cognitive component, instead of conceptualizing them as separate attitudes?

These are all theoretical problems. There are also considerable problems concerning conceptual content. I have spent a large part of this paper on a paragraph titled 'in search of characteristics'. It's still not exactly clear what the differentiating characteristics of the religious orientations are. Allport wasn't very clear and consistent in his formulations, nor was Batson, as I hope to have shown. I chose to reconceptualize the concepts and tried to develop new scales for measuring them, but allthough I'm reasonably satisfied with the results, serious criticism is possible. One important critique will probably be that I narrowed the conceptual content of the orientations too much. Isn't there really more to the end orientation than just witnessing? And isn't my interpretation of cognitive religiosity as being the central aspect of the quest orientation somewhat overdone because it implies a neglect of content characteristics of this orientation?

Another critique might concern the correlational data and the reliability coefficients. A Cronbach alpha of .69 for the quest scale and .73 for the end scale isn't very high, allthough they are not unacceptably low. But what to think of some of the correlations I presented. For example: how can we explain a negative correlation of -.10 between the end scale and the nonreligiosity scale when at the same time we find highly significant negative correlations between nonreligiosity and the means orientation (-.47) as well as between nonreligiosity and the quest orientation (-.44). And shouldn't we expect a much higher positive correlation between means and end (.05) than between end and quest (.06) or between means and quest (.14)?

These are serious criticisms that deserve further attention, but I'm confident that, with your help during the discussion, I will be able to present a definite instrument for the measurement of religious attitudes in three years - at the fourth Symposion of European Psychologists of Religion, in Nijmegen or anywhere else.

Literature

Allport, G.W. & J.M. Ross (1967): Personal Religious Orientation and Prejudice. Journal of Personality and Social Psychology, 16, 431-443.

Batson, C.D.; J.C. Beker & W.M. Clark (1973): Commitment without Ideology. Philadelphia: Pilgrim Press.

Batson, C.D. & W.L. Ventis (1982): The Religious Experience: A Social-Psychological Perspective. New York: Oxford University Press.

Darley, J.M. & C.D. Batson (1973): "From Jerusalem to Jericho": A Study of Situational and Dispositional Variables in Helping Behavior. Journal of Personality and Social Psychology, 27, 100-108.

Vernon, G.M. (1969): The Religious "Nones": A Neglected Category. Journal for the Scientific Study of Religion, 7, 219-230.

1) The investigations were supported by the Foundation for Research in the Field of Theology and the Sciences of Religions in the Netherlands, which is subsidized by the Netherlands Organisation for the Advancement of Pure Research (Z.W.O.)

Religious attitudes: a theoretical approach. (1)

F. Derks and J. M. van der Lans
Catholic University Nijmegen

Since the publication of Gordon Willard Allports (1950) seminal work on 'mature' and 'immature' religious sentiments in the early fifties, there have been numerous efforts to differentiate various religious attitudes theoretically. Although several typologies of ways of being religious already existed long before Allport formulated his famous distinction between intrinsic and extrinsic religion, these differentiations were not based in any well formulated psychological theory but were only the product of more or less intuitive interpretation of religious practices. At best some theological evaluation served as an 'objective' standard.

In the early fifties Adorno and his co-operators (1950) were the first to theoretically differentiate religious types on a psychological basis. As a side-product of their study of 'The Authoritarian Personality' they concluded that it would be more important to know in which way a person is religious (or non-religious) than it would be to know if a person is religious anyhow. Sanfords famous formulation of the problem ("it may be that the mere acceptance or rejection of religion is not so important as how the individual accepts or rejects it"; Adorno et al., 1950; 52) still serves as some kind of a dogma for those working in one of the most important branches of the modern psychology of religion. When Adorno – using his Authoritarian Personality-data – further elaborated Sanfords observation that it is important to know "what the acceptance or the rejection of religion means to the individual"; Adorno et al., 1950; 220), he differentiated between 'neutralized' (aka 'conventional') and 'interiorized' religion. Essentially this is the difference between functional and experiential religion.

At the same time Allport published his 'The Individual and his Religion', in which he formulated his opinions about the mature and immature religious sentiment. Probably because his starting-point was the same as Adorno's (viz. the curvi-linear relationship between religiosity and prejudice) – or maybe even because of some acquaintancy with Adorno's typology – his concepts of immature-extrinsic and mature-intrinsic religiosity strikingly resemble the neutralized-interiorized dichotomy, the most important difference being Allports linkage of the concepts to his developmental theory of personality. According to Allport all religiosity is basically extrinsic in nature; only when the religious motivation becomes functionally-autonomous it may grow out to be of the mature-intrinsic type.

The main difficulty with Allports typology is that he never ever formulated any clear definitions of the extrinsic and intrinsic religious motivation. Spitting through his many publications one can find several circumscriptions of the concepts, and there even is a whole chapter in The Individual and his Religion in which he differentiates intrinsic from extrinsic religion by summing up several characteristics of mature religion, but a shorthand definition of the concepts is lacking. Even their theoretical status is not clear. One might e.g. wonder why Allport sometimes referred to extrinsic and intrinsic religion as separate religious *motivations*, while at other times he referred to them in terms of religious *sentiments*. He almost never - in The Individual and his Religion only once (at page 26 in the 1954 edition) , somewhat like a slip of the pen - referred to them as religious *attitudes*.

Nonetheless, from his many circumscriptions one may get an impression of what Allport tried to differentiate. It is fairly easy to conclude that he interpreted extrinsic religion as being some kind of functional, utilitarian way of being religious. For people whose religious sentiment is of the extrinsic type, religion serves to satisfy non-religious needs, especially non-religious social needs. Diametrically opposed to this way of being religious as an end-to-a-means, we find the intrinsic religious sentiment in which religion is an end-in-itself. This difference sounds clear enough, but aren't we delusioned by nicely formulated rhetoric? For when one askes 'what *in concreto* is a religion as an end in itself?', Allport doesn't give an answer. Possibly because any answer would only multiply the confusion, as e.g. is shown by the answer Weima (1984) gave: "intrinsic religion is the final product of a developmental process that never ends".

This confusion gave rise to many different interpretations of intrinsic religion and to many efforts to reformulate the concept. I won't elaborate on them, but will jump instead immediately to C. Daniel Batson's reinterpretation of Allports typology, as formulated in his The Religious Experience: A Social-Psychological Perspective, co-authored with Larry Ventis, published in 1982.

Batson & Ventis' starting-point is Allports list of differences between extrinsic and intrinsic religion. According to Allport (1950; chapter III) the mature religious sentiment is:
1) **Differentiated and Complex**; the mature religious person accepts religion in general, yet is able to criticize it, while the immature religious person identifies with a religious reference group as a matter of course, without thinking much about it (adapted from Sanford in Adorno et al., 1950; 53 and 219).

201

2) **Derivative yet Dynamic**; the mature religious sentiment has become functionally autonomous. The dynamic that characterizes mature religiosity is, according to Allport, it's most important differentiating aspect.

3) **Consistently Directive**; a mature religious sentiment furthers high and consistent standards of moral and ethical action.

4) **Comprehensive**; mature religion includes the whole of an individual's horizon. It permeates his life with meaning.

5) **Integrative**; a mature religious sentiment is characterized by an harmonic and balanced design of the affective, cognitive and behavioral aspects of life.

6) **Heuristic**; in a mature religious sentiment any notion of 'absolute certainty' or 'having found eternal Truth' is absent: "a heuristic belief is one that is held tentatively until it can be confirmed or until it helps discover a more valid belief" (Allport, 1950; 72 in the 1954 edition).

According to Batson (see Batson & Raynor-Prince, 1983) these characteristics can be summarized into five aspects of intrinsic religion: 1) **single-mindedness**, 2) **centrality**, 3) **integrativity**, 4) **readiness to doubt**, and 5) **incompleteness/tentativeness**. However, when he and Ventis classify Allport & Ross' (1967) Religious Orientation Scale-items according to these characteristics, they find that the Allport-Ross extrinsic scale is a valid measure of Allports original concept (they only propose a new name: **Religion as a Means**), but that the Religious Orientation Scale intrinsic items are invalid because only the first and second aspect of Allports theoretical concept (viz. single-mindedness and centrality) are operationalized in them. This leads them to the conclusion that this scale only measures "intens, rigid devotion to orthodox beliefs and practices" (Batson & Ventis, 1982; 147). According to them, the ROS-intrinsic scale is nothing more than a measure of the "true believer's" (Hoffer, 1951) rigid way of being religious, a way of being religious that is characterized by unquestioned subordination to the Truth found. And because this Truth is uncritically accepted as eternal Truth, it is central (aspect 2) for the true believer, whose life is single-mindedly directed (aspect 1) towards fulfilling the prescriptions of his religion. Batson and Ventis refer to this way of being religious as **Religion as an End.**

Had they stopped their analysis at this point, their contribution to the psychology of religion would already have been of value since any substantial operational critique can only enhance the applicability of theoretical concepts, but they went even further. They still have left three characteristics of mature religion (viz. integrativity, readiness to doubt, and tentativeness) and they propose a new, third way of being religious: **Religion as a Quest**, which is an open state of mind for "honestly facing

202

existential questions in all their complexity, while resisting clear-cut pat answers" (Batson & Ventis, 1982; 149-150). It is the religion of the person who is religiously inspired, but who knows that any definite answer to existential questions is impossible; it is the religion of a person who can better live with the dynamic of a question without an answer than with the rigidity of an answer with no question. The outstanding example of such a way of being religious is – ofcourse – Siddharta who, according to Batson & Ventis (1982; 150), "searched for seven years before attaining the enlightenment that made him the Buddha. And even then he had not found the ultimate answer; he had found a path, a direction to go".

From Batson & Ventis' way of presenting their typology of religious attitudes one might get the impression that the primary inspiration for their theorizing was some kind of discontent with Allport's original dichotomy. But their formulation of the means-, end-, and quest-way of being religious was not the first time this typology appeared in the scientific literature. From 1973 on, Batson wrote several books and articles in which these religious orientations were mentioned. One of the first was Batson, Beker & Clark (1973) in which he formulated "an outline of an experiential theology based on existential phenomenology". I will try to summarize this outline as briefly as possible.

Batson poses the question of 'what it means to be a Christian', his answer being that for being a Christian it is not sufficient, nor neccessary, to espouse Christian dogma's. The nucleus of the Christian religious life is the experience of Jesus' influence in one's life, an experience that leads to a radical change in the way of living, not only a change of conduct, but also – and even more so – a cognitive change. Man is challenged by Christ "to see his world in a new way, centrifugally rather than centripettaly" (Batson, Beker & Clark, 1973; 45). Being a Christian means being centered on 'thy neigbour's needs' instead of striving for one's own happiness.

This Batsonian theology strikingly resembles another theological interpretation of 'true' Christianity, a resemblance that should be mentioned because it sheds new light on Batson's psychological theorizing. When we compare Batson's formulation of 'truly being a Christian' and his formulation of the quest-orientation with Goen's (1970) description of the Social Gospel Theology, one might easily substitute one for the other. To quote Goen (1970; 87): "(the social gospel theology) was a determined effort to come to realistic terms with the contemporary world through freedom of inquiry, openness to new truth, and tolerance of variant beliefs, while continuing to retain the authority of Christian experience and the centrality of Jesus Christ in nominal loyalty to historic

203

Christianity". Does this characterization of the late nineteenth century forerunner of modern liberal American protestantism differ substantially from integrativity, readiness to doubt, and tentativeness – the three characteristics of the quest–orientation? And does it differ in any way from Batson's definition of 'true' Christianity as being "commitment to a growth process in the direction of responsible action expressed in increased concern for others and openness to future change" (Batson, Beker & Clark, 1973; back–cover)?

In other words, isn't Batson's **psychological** theory of religious attitudes essentially a **theological** theory of true Christianity? And if so, what then is the psychological status of the means-, end–, and quest way of being religious? I think these are questions that we might try to get an answer to this morning.

Literature

Adorno, Th.; E. Frenkel-Brunswick; D. Levinson & R. Sanford, The Authoritarian Personality. New York: Harper & Row, 1950.

Allport, G.W., The Individual and his Religion. New York: MacMillan, 1950.

Allport, G.W. & J.M. Ross, Personal Religious Orientation and Prejudice. Journal of Personality and Social Psychology, 1967, 16; 431-443.

Batson, C.D.; J.C. Beker & W.M. Clark, Commitment without Ideology. Philadelphia: Pilgrim Press, 1973.

Batson, C.D. & L. Raynor–Prince, Religious Orientation and Complexity of Thought about Existential Concerns. Journal for the Scientific Study of Religion, 1983, 22; 38-50.

Batson, C.D. & W.L. Ventis, The Religious Experience; A Social Psychological Perspective. New York: Oxford University Press, 1982.

Goen, C.G., Fundamentalism in America. In P. Hammond & H. Johnson (eds.) American Mosaic. New York: Random House, 1970, p.85-94.

Hoffer, E., The True Believer. New York: Harper, 1951.

Weima, J. Researchproblemen rond het begrip 'intinsieke religiositeit'. In J. van der Lans (ed.) Spiritualiteit; sociaal wetenschappelijke en theologische beschouwingen. Baarn: Ambo, 1984.

1) The investigations were supported by the Foundation for Research in the field of Theology and the Sciences of Religions in the Netherlands, which is subsidized by the Netherlands Organisation for the Advancement of Pure Research (Z.W.O.).

Batson's religious life inventory: a pilot study.

C. Donders
Catholic Theological Faculty, Amsterdam

1. Different ways of being religious.

This paper on Batson's new theory about the different ways of being religious deals with the instrument with which Batson supports his theory. Following the presentation of the instrument, Batson's Religious Life Inventory (RLI) (2), the translation of the instrument will be considered (3). Next, the sample is described to which a translation of the scales is administered (4) and the psychometric findings made in this context are reported (5). The paper concludes with a discussion of some RLI-profiles (6).

2. Batson's Religious Life Inventory.

This paper on Batson's theory confines itself to an introduction to the instrument developed by Batson. He called it the Religious Life Inventory (RLI). The instrument maps out three religious orientations: the external, the internal and the interactional religious orientation. The first or External scale, comprising six items, measures the degree to which the external environment has influenced the individual's subjective religion. This orientation reflects an extrinsic motivation, since it is based on a wish to gain social approval. The second or Internal scale, comprising nine items, measures the degree to which internal needs for certainty and direction have resulted in the individual's personal religion. These needs reflect an intrinsic motivation, since they are based on a need to find clear answers to existential problems. And the third or Interactional scale, comprising six items, measures the degree to which an individual's religion involves an open-ended dialogue with existential questions raised by the contradictions in his or her own life (Batson, 1982, 152).
Lastly, the RLI contains six buffer items, so that in total it comprises 27 items, which are provided with nine-point rating scales.
In his investigation Batson made continual use of the scales of Wilson and Allport (measures of Extrinsic and Intrinsic religion) and a scale following Lenski (1960, 382) for Doctrinal Orthodoxy. Thus the factor analyses related to both the subscales of the RLI and these other scales. Batson every time resolved the analyses into three factors, each defining a religious orientation: religion as means, as end and as quest.
These orientations form three new variables, for they consist of factor scores and no longer of scores on the RLI. Nevertheless, for various reasons it seemed justified to confine this paper to a short discussion of the RLI, firstly because the other scales are not Batson's, secondly because the

other scales are sufficiently known, and thirdly because a narrowing down to the RLI does not conflict with the results of the factor analyses. Thus, for example, Batson gives this comment on the relationship between the RLI and the three factors: "this pattern of results was considered supportive of the RLI as a plausible map of the dimensions the subjects were using in responding to the 27 items". (Batson, 1976, 33)

The attractiveness of the results on the RLI resides in the fact that they consist of three scores, so that each time they form a profile of orientations toward religion. The results thus lend themselves to a profile analysis. In principle it is possible to distinguish different groups, which are known in advance, in terms of their scores on the three scales. And the RLI provides also the basis for a classification of individuals in terms of their profiles on the subscales.

3. The translation of the instrument.

For the translation of the 27 statements the procedure which Brislin (1980, 427) called "a pragmatic translation", a literal translation was chosen.

An investigation of Allport's scale for religious orientation has adequately shown that the formulation of the items in this field demands the greatest care (Donders, 1980). The clearest example of a pragmatic translation is in the treatment of technical documents in which information, e.g. about repairing a machine, is translated into another language. To achieve this aim as best as possible, the method of back translation was used for the translation. First, the 27 items were translated by two persons independently of each other into Dutch. Then the two translations were compared to see which was the most exact.

Thereupon, a bilingual American was asked to translate the Dutch text into American. Lastly, he was asked to compare the new American text, the back translation, with the original statements of Batson and to indicate on what points the Dutch translation might be improved. In short, care was taken that the statements were translated with as little change as possible. To be sure, for practical reasons the nine-point rating scales were changed into five-point rating scales.

The disadvantage of a too literal translation is that it does not take into account the emotional world of the target group.

American Protestants probably respond differently to the items than Dutch Roman Catholics. Here a word must be said about the denominational roots of the RLI. With his RLI Batson aimed at approaching Allport's concept of "mature religion", "religion as quest" (Allport, 1969, 1). He believed that Allport himself had only partly succeeded in this. Other authors also have pointed out that Allport with his scale for intrinsic religion had remained stuck in a measurement of the puritanical conscience of small-town Middle

America (Dittes, 1971, 383). Batson failed to see that Allport's concept "religion as quest" was just as much denominationally determined. According to Beit-Hallahmi (1985, 25) Allport's concept of "mature religion" made the self-image of liberal Protestant America the norm of authentic religiosity. Batson's social-psychological approach to religion correctly assumes that the religious actor's ideas are part of the data. Incorrectly it holds that those ideas are also a useful analyses of the religion being studied. His own ideas, Batson's religious opinion, resulted in his thesis on external religion as an extrinsic, instrumental or means orientation, thereby overlooking other beliefs and opinions on the significance of external religion. Three statements of Batson's external scale concern the church and the pastor or priest. But for a Roman Catholic for example church and priest manifest the sacred and are efficacious channels of grace. One is dealing here with a vastly different emotional world. That Batson, and thus also the literal translation of his statements, does not take Catholicism into account is clear. And that nor the Protestant, nor the Roman Catholic ideas about external religion are scientific tools is clear as well.

4. The sample.

The composition of the sample is closely connected with the problem on hand. The question does not only determine the requirements which the research instrument must fulfill, insight into the question is also indispensable for judging the representativeness of a sample. As regards the demand on the instruments, there is, for example, a clear difference between basic and applied research. In basic research the concern is with the size of the correlations and with the differences in means for different experimental treatments, for which purpose reliability of .60 for a measurement is adequate. But in applied problems, a great deal hinges on the exact score made by a person. In most applied setting a reliability of .90 is not nearly enough. And as regards the representativity of the sample, essential is that the sample represents the target group of the investigation. The question, then, concerns the selection procedure of students for pastoral schools. Pastoral schools provide courses for parish-assistents working as volunteers. The schools attempt to deepen the religiosity of the students and to increase their ability to exchange their thoughts about religion and religious feeling with others.

As schools for volunteers, they do not require previous schooling for admission. The selection occurs on the basis of a detailed conversation. For various reasons, the staff of the schools decided to have the candidates tested in future as well. The most important reason was, that time and again about thirty per cent of the candidates who were passed could not follow the courses, making it hard for the rest of the students. According to the staff, these incapable volunteers had difficulties in overcoming sets of too strict beliefs. These sets had made them highly resistant to change from inputs, appropriate for a good parish--assistent. "Victims to _rigidity_", the staff called them. In this context rigidity is seen as a relation among regions of the life space, as a rigidity of the boundaries between the religious and the other regions of this space, resulting in a resistance to a mutual and fertile contact. Searching in the literature for an approach of this quality, the third scale fo the RLI offered itself as a possible solution. But first it had to be seen whether the RLI came up to the requirements of reliability and validity.

When the RLI meets these requirements, then it is administered to adults working as church volunteers. The psychometric qualities of the RLI would have to be tested on a sample which was as much as possible representative of the target group.

In any case it had to consist of adults who fully enter into the life of the church. For this reason a sample is composed of adult church-goers. The sample thus consists of _committed regulars_, of persons who on an ordinary Sunday attended the services in their parish church. Following the services, those persons who were willing to do so filled in the RLI-form. It had been arranged that within the sample different groups could be distinguished. Each of these groups invariably consists of 35 persons. To group A belong those who attended a traditional, conservative Latin High Mass. Group B are visitors at an attractive modern celebration. Group C are the choir. And those who work as volunteers in the parish are in group D. In total the sample consists of 269 adult church--goers.

5. Psychometric qualities of the Religious Life Inventory.

The comments on the psychometric qualities of the translated RLI will be easy to follow in English, since the translation is a strict literal one. First, the reliability of the translated scales is entered into, then their content of domain, and lastly their validity. Table one (see appendix) shows, that the three score--distributions are skewed toward the lower end. This considerable skewness can be improved by adding a number of difficult or less popular items.

Also it is possible to construct new rating scales that center around the category "I agree", and not around the question mark with its meaning of "Would agree and disagree equally". This assymetrical category scheme can lead to a somewhat symmetrical distribution of responses. The table further shows that the _reliability_ of the translated scales is much lower than that of the American scales.

The primary way to make scales more reliable is to make them longer. The Spearman-Brown coefficient for test-lenght (Guilford, 1969, 465) shows, that translated scale two, the internal scale, reaches an alpha of .90 upon doubling its number of items, and translated scale three, the interactional scale, an alpha of .87. These are acceptable reliabilities, while the size of the scales remains relatively small upon doubling the number of statements. The reliability of scale one, that for external religion, will be considered shortly. Table two (see appendix) shows that the correlations among the translated scales reveals another pattern than the American scales. But on the basis of one investigation with the translated scales these differences cannot be fully assessed. In assessing the validity or the extend to which the three scales measure what they purport to do, Batson used amongst other instruments Allport's scale for intrinsic religiosity. In the context of this pilot study a translated scale for intrinsic religiosity was used. Contrary to Batson's intent, in this sample the scale for intrinsic religiosity correlates positively (.31) with the interactional scale. In parenthesis: the translated scale for intrinsic religiosity has a nice coefficient alpha of .67.

To determine the nucleus of the translated scales, the item-total correlations as well as the relationships between the items are taken as points of departure. Compared to items with relatively low correlations with total scores, those that have higher correlations have more variance relating to the common factor of the items (Nunnally, 1967, 261).

The structure of the relationships between the items as an indicator of the nature of the scale (Carmines, Zeller, 1979) is investigated with a linkage-analysis and a factor analysis. Within a strict linkage-analytic framework, the best indicator of the nature of the scale is the item that is identified as the cluster nucleus (Bennett, Bowers, 1976, 70). The three linkage-analyses moreover guided the choice of the factor analytic models for a more definite analysis of the scale-structures. In the first case it had to be a multiple group solution. For the internal and interactional scales a general factor solution was chosen on the basis of their linkage analysis. Since translated scale one, the external scale, also gave complications on this point, the two other scales will be entered into first. According to table three (see appendix), which contains the item-total correlations, the translated internal scale is carried by item 7 (20). It is as follows:

7 (20) I have found it essential to have faith.

And according to the linkage-analysis, item 7 (20) is the nucleus of a cluster that includes all the items of this scale. These results clearly support Batson's presumption that the items of this scale refer to a unitary personal predisposition. Moreover, it appears that the general factor of the items, factor G, conforms to Batson's conceptualization of internal religion. The same is true of scale three, the interactional scale. This scale also supports both Batson's conceptualization of interactional religion as an open-ended dialogue, and his presumption that the items of

209

this scale refer to a unitary personal predisposition.

In this case, according to table three, item 1 is the statement with the highest item-total correlation, while in the linkage-analysis this item also forms the nucleus of a cluster that includes all items of the scale. Item 1 (4) is as follows:

1 (4) It might be said that I value my religious doubts and
uncertainties.

In this case too, the general factor of the items, factor G, supports the thesis of a unitary disposition and the conceptualization of an interactional religious orientation.

And lastly, scale one, the <u>external scale</u>; from table three it appears that item 2 (5), albeit with a minimal difference, heads the list of item-totalcorrelations. Linkage-analysis pointed to item 1 (1) as cluster nucleus of the first cluster. This cluster includes four items: 1 (1), 3 (11), 2 (5) and 4 (15). An agreement with these statements implies a recognition of the role played by parents, clergy and the church in the individual's personal religious development. Around the cluster nucleus the individual's own parish - "the church" of 1 (1) -- group the parental home -- "the parents" of 3 (11) - and the rectory or parochial house of the individual's own parish -- "a pastor" of 2 (5).

Moreover, within this cluster there emerges the outline of a reciprocal relationship between this group of variables around the nucleus and item 4 (15). Item 4 (15) is as follows:

4 (15) My religion serves to satisfy needs for fellowship and
security.

In this context it probably acquires the meaning of feeling at home in and being on good terms with the parish. The second cluster consists of items 5 (9) and 6 (26), statements that refer to having been normalized and modelled. All in all it is not very clear whether this scale is a measurement of Batson's conceptualization of external religion, nor does the splitting up of the items into two clusters form a support for his theory of a unitary dispostion. The results of the multiple group factor analysis, with its solution in two groups, points to the same negative conclusions (see table 3). To improve the scale following the theory of Batson, one would have to base oneself on the second cluster, or on factor B, consisting of the items 5 (9) and 6 (26). An elaboration of the first cluster or of factor A, will probably result in a new scale for intrinsic "church-mindedness".

6. Some profiles on the Religious Life Inventory.

The RLI is translated, in a pilot study administered to a sample of 269 committed adult regulars, and analyzed, all for the purpose of developing a better selection procedure for admittance of new candidates to the pastoral schools. But before the test can be applied, the teachers and students of these schools must give their operation: the teachers to indicate which students are doing well and which are not; the students to fill in the RLI. If the scores on the RLI of the good students do indeed appear to differ from those of the poorer sttudents, these differences can be maximized via a multiple discriminant function. Only then will the RLI-scores of the new candidates indicate in which group these candidates belong, with the good or with the problematic students. Moreover, the RLI-scores do not yield more than a contribution to the judgement about possible suitability, for besides the RLI, tests for intelligence, emotional stability and empathy are also administered.

Apart from profile distances or profile similarities (Overall, Klett, 1972, 385), the RLI-profile gives two major types of information: the level of the profile (its mean) and the shape (its ranking of the scores). Elevation and pattern. A person or group with a higher level, with more high scores on the RLI-scales, tends to be more involved with religion than persons or groups with lower scores (if, and only if it is demonstrated that scores do provide this information). And the shape or rank order of the RLI-scores indicated the particular religious orientation of that person or group (s.s.). To get an idea of the relevance of these data, four groups of 35 persons each were lifted out of the large sample, and for each group the RLI-profile was once more calculated in z-scores.

The groups involved were:
A. visitors of the Latin mass;
B. visitors of the modern celebration;
C. choir members, and
D. volunteers.

What were the levels of the four profiles, what their shapes? What their elevations and what their patterns? The four levels were the same. There were no significant differences between the profile-means of the visitors of the Latin mass, those of the modern celebration, the members of the choir, or the volunteers. The strengths of their involvement did not vary. The shapes of the four RLI-profiles were different, and that not by chance. Each group has a mean on three scales. 21 Differences among the means are significant (t-tests) and the CR (Critical Ratio = -3.00) indicates that this is not by chance at a total of 66 differences. For the shapes see fig 1 (appendix): the underlined positions have minimally eight significant differences with other profile-points. For the visitors of the Latin Mass and the modern celebration, groups A and B, the shapes were indentical: 1 (external), 2 (internal) and 3 (interactional). It is their external orientation which distinguishes them from the other groups. Are these results supportive of Batson's conceptualization of external religion? Certainly, the shared symbolisms of being committed regulars in the Latin

Mass and of spontaneity in the modern celebration diffuse mutual affection. Is it enforced from without? Or is this form of religion for them not <u>intrinsically</u> communal and organic? The other two shapes do seem to support the validity of Batson's theory on internal and interactional religion. Choir members sing with their whole heart and soul, they stand apart and above all try to keep it festive: 2 (internal), 1 (external) and please not 3 (interactional). It seems that the staff of the pastoral schools are right when they claim that volunteers have an antenna for grasping and solving problems in a religious perspective; the shape of the volunteers is: 3 (interactional), 2 (internal) and 1 (external). The profiles form a double support for Batson's conceptualization of internal and interactional religion, both by the choir and the volunteers.

<u>Literature</u>

Allport G. <u>The individual and his religion</u>. New York: MacMillan, 1969.

Batson C. Religion as Prosocial : Agent or Double Agent? <u>Journal for the Scientific Study of Religion</u>, 17, 31-41.

Batson C., & Ventis, W. <u>The Religious Experience</u>. New York: Oxford University Press, 1982.

Beit-Hallahmi B. Religiously based differences in approach to the psychology of religion. In: L. Brown (Ed.). <u>Advances in the Psychology of Religion</u>. New York: Pergamon, 1985.

Bennett S., & Bowers, D. <u>Multivariate Techniques</u>. London: MacMillan, 1976.

Brislin R. Translation and content analysis of oral and written material. In: H. Triandis & J. Berry. <u>Methodology. Handbook of Cross-Cultural Psychology</u>. Boston: Allyn, 1980.

Carmines E., & Zeller, R. <u>Reliability and Validity Assessment</u>. London: Sage University, 1979.

Dittes J. Typing the typologies. <u>Journal for the Scientific Study of Religion, 4</u>, 375-383.

Donders C. Gesoekulariseerdheid en intrinsieke godsdienstigheid, een nadere analyse. <u>Gedrag, 4,</u> 229-239.

Guilford J. <u>Fundamental Statistics</u>. New York: MacGraw-Hill, 1965.

Lenski G. <u>The Religious Factor</u>. New York: Anchor Books, 1963.

Nunnally, J. <u>Psychometric Methods</u>. New York: MacGraw-Hill, 1965.

Overall J., & Klett, C. <u>Applied Multivariate Analysis</u>. New York: MacGraw-Hill, 1972.

Table 1   Sample values of the RLI-scales (N= 269).

scales	number of items	means	var.	skewness	alpha	Batson's alphas
1 external	6	3.61	.33	-.25	.40	.60
2 internal	9	3.41	.29	-.59	.66	.80
3 interactional	6	3.26	.42	-.09	.64	.63

Table 2a   Correlations among the scales, z-scores (N = 269)

	1 extern	2 intern.	3 interact.
1		.31	.19
2			.22

Table 2b   Batson's correlations among the scales (N = 258)

	1 extern	2 intern	3 interact.
1		.55	.09
2			.09

Table 3   Item-total correlations; factor solutions (N = 269)

1 external item r_{it}	Factors A	B	2 internal item r_{it}	Factor G	3 interactional item r_{it}	Factor G
1 .46	.76	-.12	1 .42	.56	1 .62	.70
2 .52	.61	.09	2 .54	.59	2 .39	.15
3 .49	.63	.07	3 .66	.91	3 .62	.63
4 .49	.65	.05	4 .35	.14	4 .54	.43
5 .47	.12	.76	5 .42	.34	5 .61	.57
6 .46	.04	.76	6 .55	.67	6 .59	.58
			7 .68	.97		
			8 .54	.64		
			9 .09	.12		

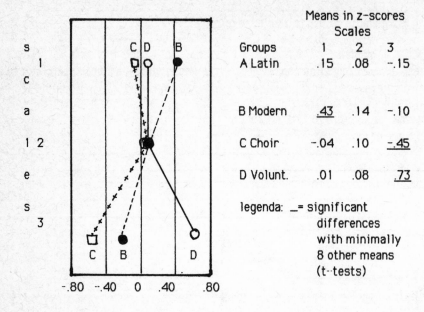

Figure 1   Score profiles for three groups on the RLI (N= 105)

Means in z-scores
Scales

Groups	1	2	3
A Latin	.15	.08	-.15
B Modern	.43	.14	-.10
C Choir	-.04	.10	-.45
D Volunt.	.01	.08	.73

legenda: __= significant
          differences
          with minimally
          8 other means
          (t-tests)

Batson's three-dimensional model of religious orientations.
Some critical notes and a partial replication.

J. Weima
Catholic Theological Faculty, Tilburg

The concept of "intrinsic religiosity" that for years in the psychology of religion possessed an almost undebatable status, seems to have lost some of its prestige in the last few years. In particular the researches of Batson et al (1976, 1978, 1982, 1983) raise questions about the interpretation of the data and on the way the intrinsic orientation correlates with other personal and social variables. Taking their point of depart in Allport's theories on mature religion, Batson et al hypothesize that the concept of intrinsic religiosity as operationalized in the Intrinsic Religious Orientation Scale (I.R.S.) lacks three characteristics that played an important role in the original theories of Allport: First, Allport suggested that the mature religious sentiment was integrative in the sense of encouraging the individual to face complex issues like ethical responsibility and evil without reducing their complexity. Second, mature religion involved a readiness to doubt and to be self-critical. (The mature religious sentiment is ordinarily fashioned in the workshop of doubt (Allport, 1950: 73)). Third, there was an emphasis on incompleteness and tentativeness; the mature religious orientation was seen as involving a continual search for more light on religious questions. (Batson and Raynor Prince, 1983) According to Batson these characteristics are present in the quest dimension of his three-dimensional model of religious orientations. This model, amply elaborated in Batson's publication of 1982, comprises:
a. Religion as a means (related to the original concept of "extrinsic religiosity"),
b. Religion as an end (related to the original concept of "intrinsic religiosity" as operationalized in the I.R.S., but with the emphasis on "the degree to which an individual's religion is a result of internal needs for certainty, strength, and direction" and
c. Religion as a quest (the degree to which an individual's religion involves an open-ended, responsive dialogue with existential questions raised by the contradictions and tragedies of life. (Cf. Batson et al, 1982: 152f)

Batson's criticism of the I.R.S. is not without any foundation. Indeed, the scale does not include items which clearly indicate what Batson calls a quest-orientation; as far as this quest-orientation is implicated by Allport's theory on mature religion, this orientation seems insufficiently represented in the scale. However, this does not mean that Batson is right when suggesting (1982: 146) that "as measured by the Religious

Orientation Scale" (the I.R.S.) "intrinsic religion has more in common with Eric Hoffer's (1951) concept of the "true believer" than Allport's concept of mature religion".

The true believer is really a fanatic: "He embraces a cause not primazily because of its justness and holiness but because of his desperate need for something to hold on to". (Hoffer, 1951: x, 80, cited by Batson)

But religious orthodoxy or a high measure of religious participation cannot simply be put on a par with fanaticism in the sense of Hoffer and most researchers agree that intrinsic religiosity is rarely related to fanaticism, authoritarianism, and prejudice. In addition, somewhat paradoxically, Batson is inclined to attribute extrinsic motives to the intrinsic believer when he hypothesizes that: "this orientation seems to be based on a need to find firm, clear answers to existential questions". In reality however, the I.R.S. does not include items which unequivocally indicate a similar motivation. But, strangely enough, this motivation seems to be indicated by some items of the Interactional Scale (e.g. item 5: God wasn't very important to me until I began to ask questions about the meaning of my own life).

A fundamental question however concerns the problem if that what is measured by the I.R.S. may directly be translated in terms of a motivation theory. In fact this is suggested by the adjective "intrinsic", but this suggestion may lead us on a wrong track. The unsatisfying attempts to generalize the intrinsic motivation to other fields of behavior (e.g. the field of work motivation) might be significant. (c.f. Morris and Hood, 1981; Claudia Peloschek, 1983)

An alternative possibility would be that intrinsic reliosity (the kind of religiosity measured by the I.R.S.) has mainly, or in a large measure, to do with the experiential aspects of religion. Particularly the researches of Hood et al (1970, 1975) point in this direction. Hood constructed two scales with which he tried to measure the presence of more or less intense religious experiences. One scale, the Religious Experiences Episodes Measure (Hood, 1970), was based on 15 descriptions of specific religious experiences, borrowed from James (W. James, 1902). High scores on the I.R.S. recognized the description of James more often than low scores as descriptions of experiences comparable to their own (r=0.51).

The same correlation between intrinsic religiosity and the presence of religious experiences was found when using the Mysticism Scale, likewise constructed by Hood (Hood, 1975).

In this case the correlation even reached the level of 0.81, which not only confirmed the hypothesis of Hood, but was also in agreement with the contention of Allport (Allport and Ross, 1967), that intrinsic religiosity has something to do with the experiential espects of religion and that "the inner experience of religion is an important causal factor in developing a

216

tolerant or prejudiced outlook on life" (o.c.: 435).

Indeed, also Batson himself (1982: 162) hypothesized "that higher scores on the end and quest orientations should correlate positively with the presence of dramatic religious experience in a person's life". But this hypothesis was not tested in his research. He postulates however that: "since the end orientation involves devout, true belief, the new vision would probably be one that provides clear, final answers and is adhered to in a rigid, absolutistic fashion. The person would be likely to believe that religiously he or she has found it, that there is no need to consider new information or points of view."

As consequently the Interactional Scale would correlate with the presence of religious experiences as well as with flexibility, the I.R.S. would correlate with the experiential aspect of religion but also with rigidity. This conclusion is of course only then inevitable when religious participation and orthodoxy are seen as valid indications for a rigid fanaticism.

On the other hand there seems to be little empirical evidence for the supposition that the presence of religious experience in respondents who participate in religion of who have orthodox religious beliefs, would correlate with rigidity.

Besides, one should take into account that according to most authors in this field, e.g. William James, these experiences have a noetic quality, they are states of real knowledge, "states of insight into depths of truth unplumbed by the discursive intellect, and as a rule they carry with them a curious sense of authority for aftertime" (James, o.c.: 371). Religious experiences, probably themselves the product of diffuse emotional states and of religious interpretive schemes (cf. Proudfoot and Shaver, 1975), give answers to religious questions and the person who has them is more or less sure that these answers are true. As such, this has nothing to do with fanaticism or rigidity, though in some cases these experiences might lead to it. Neither is this to say that in the life of the person concerned, doubt and uncertainty did not play an important role, especially before the time when the experience took place. Indeed, as Allport says: "The mature religious sentiment is ordinarily fashioned in the workshop of doubt." But one may suppose that religious questions play a different role in different age–periods and that they should not always be evaluated in the same way. Moreover, doubts and questions need not always be dominant and their presence need not always run counter to the simultaneous presence of religious convictions.

Finally, all depends on the way in which religious answers and religious convictions are held. They may be held in a more rigid or in a more flexible way. But a rigid, defensive way of dealing with one's own religious convictions is an indication of the absence, i.c. the defective integration

217

of religious experiences rather than of their active presence.

In order to obtain more information relevant to the above mentioned questions, we decided, within the framework of a research-project on intrinsic motivations in a work-situation (C. Peloschek, 1983), to include a number of scales used by Batson in the test-battery to be submitted to our respondents.

These scales were:

a. The Interactional Scale and the Internal Scale of Batson.

b. The I.R.S. and the E.R.S. of Allport and Ross.

c. A shortened, 12-item version of the Mysticism Scale of Hood.This scale, partly based on the categories of Stace (1961) aims at measuring, by means of structured questions, the presence of religious (mystic) experiences. Though the use of structured questions in this field may meet with objections (cf. Thomas and Cooper, 1978), the scale of Hood turns out to be very reliable and is also found to have criterion-oriented validity.

However, because the probability of the presence of intense religious experiences is relatively small and dependent on age, it does not seem recommendable to submit the scale to younger age-groups.

d. A 20-item version of a rigidity scale, forming part of a Dutch personality inventory: de Nederlandse Persoonlijkheidsvragenlijst. This scale was included because of Batson's above-mentioned suggestion that an end-orientation, in contrast with a quest-orientation, relates with rigidity.

e. A Social Desirability Scale. According to Batson (1978, 1982) an intrinsic end-orientation, correlates positively with scores on a Social Desirability Scale. In order to get comparable results we made use of the same scale as Batson: a Dutch version of the Marlowe-Crowne Social Desirability Scale.

In view of the objective of our research, a partial replication of the research of Batson, we did not formulate hypotheses. The p-values in the tables are based on two-tailed tests of significance.

Method

The above-mentioned scales were submitted to 70 subjects, all male, most of them married and varying in age between 40 en 60 years (mean age: 50.9).

The order of presentation of the scale items was couter-balanced to prevent any order effect.

The greater part of the subjects were selected from the card-index of a Roman Catholic parish in Eindhoven (Neth.) and further selected in such a way that all of them reported at least a moderate interest in religion.

The sample was relatively homogeneous as far as educational and professional level were concerned. More than half of the subjects (51%)

had at least an education at college-level.

Unlike Batson, we did not make use of student-subjects. One of our objections to Batson's research is that his results are mainly based on the answers of students at a theological seminary and on relatively great numbers of undergraduates. Most of his subjects are in a stage of development in which they relate in a very specific and hardly representative way to existential and religious questions. At this age much is in change and little is integrated. Unless the researchers are particularly interested in developmental problems characteristic for this age, it seems hardly tenable to recruit subjects mainly from lower age-groups or to generalize the research--results to other age-groups.

Results and discussion
The main results of our research are presented in the tables 1, 2 and 3.

---

table 1 Reliabilities, means and standard-deviations on the five religious scales (means are on the seven-point response scale; 1 = strongly agree, 7 = strongly disagree)

N = 70	Reliability (alpha)	Mean	Standard deviation
Extrinsic	0.65	3.41	1.11
Intrinsic	0.84	3.51	1.31
Internal	0.89	2.92	1.32
Interactional	0.67	4.12	1.21
Mysticism	0.91	4.49	1.47

table 2	Correlations among the seven scales.					
N = 70	Intr.	Intern.	Interact.	Mystic	Rigidity	Soc. des.
Extrinsic	-0.31**	-0.27*	0.00	-0.21	0.22	0.24*
Intrinsic		0.80*	0.73**	0.57**	-0.16	-0.15
Internal			0.51**	0.49**	-0.15	-0.07
Interactional				0.42**	-0.14	-0.11
Mysticism					-0.10	-0.08

*p < 0,05; **p < 0,01, two-tailed.

table 3	Principal components analysis with varimax rotation	
N = 70	Factor 1	Factor 2
Extrinsic	-0.12	0.96
Intrinsic	0.92	-0.20
Internal	0.82	-0.25
Interactional	0.85	0.22
Mysticism	0.70	-0.21

They speak more of less for themselves. In the first place it must be remarked that the reliabilities of the E.R.S. and of the Interactional Scale are not very satisfying. As for the Interactional Scale, we have the impression that the same holds good for the results of Batson. His original version of 9 items was reduced to a 6-item version, because 3 items "were found not to relate especially well to the other items of the scale" (1983: 43). We had to make a similar decision for the Dutch version of the scale: One item (Batson's item 2: I do not expect my religious convictions to change in the next few years) correlated not especially well with the scale as a whole. For this reason we omitted this item in our final analysis.

Particularly table 2 presents a number of intriguing discrepancies between our results and those of Batson. Of importance are the correlations between on the one side the Interactional Scale and on the other side the I.R.S. and the Internal Scale: With Batson these correlations were respectively .07 and .09 (in the sample of theology students these correlations were even negative) and with us positive on a very significant level: .73 and .51. The correlation between the Interactional Scale and the Mysticism Scale was lower, but still very significant.

In the same table are presented the correlations with social desirability and rigidity. Rigidity correlates negatively with all religious scales, except the E.R.S. High scorers on the Interactional Scale are not less rigid than high scorers on the I.R.S.: the correlations are all negative and on the same level. The same holds good for social desirability. While Batson (1978) reports a positive correlation (.36) between social desirability and the I.R.S. and a negative correlation (-.10) between social desirability and the Interactional Scale, with us both correlations were negative and on the same level.

Table 3 presents the results of a principle component analysis of the five religious scales.(1) The eigenvalues of the scales permitted only a two-factor solution.

The second factor received a single very high loading from the E.R.S., the first factor received high loadings from the other religious scales. Of course it is always possible to extract more factors, but in this case a third factor would have been dominated by the Mysticism Scale and a factor structure similar to that produced by Batson's subjects could not be obtained.

Our conclusion must be that, at least in the Netherlands and in other samples than student samples, the four scales loading on the first factor are in certain aspects fairly similar but that there are no reasons to prefer the Interactional Scale. Intrinsic religiosity as measured by the I.R.S. appears to relate with Batson's quest-orientation and likewise with the experiential aspect of religion as measured by the Mysticism Scale.

While the Mysticism Scale might be an alternative for subjects who do not participate in institutional religion, the Interactional Scale shows a number of serious shortcomings as a measuring instrument.

In the first place, the face validity of the items does not seem to be very convincing; a number of items might be differently interpreted by the subjects. As a consequence, the reliability of the scale is not high.

Second, a factor-analysis of the scale produced two different factors; the items 1, 4 , and 6 (It might be said that I value my religious doubts and uncertainties. My religious development has emerged out of my growing sense of personal identity. Questions are far more central to my religious experience than are answers) loaded on the first factor and the items 3 and 5 (I have been driven to ask religious questions out of a growing awareness of the tensions in my world and in my relation to my world. God wasn't very important to me until I began to ask questions about the meaning of my own life) on the other factor.

---

table 4 Principal components analysis with varimax rotation

N = 70	Factor 1	Factor 2
item 5	-0.02	0.85
item 3	0.23	0.68
item 1	0.78	0.24
item 4	0.64	0.49
item 6	0.82	-0.08

We already mentioned that a number of items of the Interactional Scale seem to indicate an extrinsic religious motivation, in so far as religion is viewed as a means to deal effectually with existential problems of to find meaning in life. In this case religion is identified with one or its possible functions.
Some evidence for this interpretation is presented in table 5.

table 5 Factorcorrelations Interactional Scale and E.R.S.

N = 70	Interactional Scale	Factor 1	Factor 2
E.R.S.	-0.00	-0.16	0.25

$p < 0.05$; two-tailed.

Factor 2 of the Interactional Scale correlates with the E.R.S., though on a low level.

The Interactional Scale, at least the version which we used, turns out to be of a limited value as a measuring instrument. Though Batson is probably right when he contends that the I.R.S. discriminates insufficiently between more rigid and more flexible forms of religiosity, this objection can partly be met when including a rigidity scale in the test-battery.

For the rest, on the basis of our results, we can only conclude that in our sample the quest-orientation is implicitly present in the intrinsic religious orientation as measured by the I.R.S.

Note
(1) Because of the limited scope of our study, which only aimed at a partial replication of Batson's research, we decided to make use of the same statistical techniques as Batson, so that different results could not be attributed to a different way of handling the data. For further research it would however be recommendable to present both the findings of principal component analysis and of common factor-analysis.

Summary
The research reported in this article aimed at a partial replication in a Dutch sample of the researches of Batson c.s. We wanted to verify if Batson's three-dimensional model of religious orientations might be a useful model and, especially, if this Interactional Scale measures a religious orientation which is partially or totally absent in the concept of "intrinsic religiosity" as measured before. Our results turned out to be very much in disagreement with the results of Batson. Probably the differences might be explained by the circumstance that Batson's respondents were mainly undergraduates and students at a theological seminary. As for the Interactional Scale, this scale turned out to be a less satisfying measuring instrument.

Literature

Allport, G.W. The Individual and his Religion. New York: Macmillan, 1950.

Allport, G.W., & Ross J.M. Personal religious orientation and prejudice. Journal of Personality and Social Psychology, 1967, 5, 432-443.

Batson, C.D. Religion as prosocial: Agent or double agent? Journal for the Scientific Study of Religion, 1976, 15, 29-45.

Batson, C.D., Naifeh, S.J., & Pate, S. Social desirability, religious orientation, and racial prejudice. Journal for the Scientific Study of Religion, 1978, 17, 31-41.

Batson, C.D., & Raynor-Prince, L. Religious orientation and complexity of thought about existential concerns. Journal for the Scientific Study of Religion, 1983, 22, 38-50.

Batson, C.D., & Ventis, W.L. The religious experience: A social-psychological perspective. New York: Oxford University Press, 1982.

Hoffer, E. The true believer. New York: Harper, 1951.

Hoge, D.R. A validated intrinsic religious motivation scale. Journal for the Scientific Study of Religion, 1972, 11, 369-376.

Hood, R.W. Religious orientation and the report of religious experience. Journal for the Scientific Study of Religion, 1970, 9, 285-291.

Hood, R.W. The construction and preliminary validation of a measure of reported mystical experience. Journal for the Scientific Study of Religion, 1975, 14, 29-41.

James, W. The varieties of religious experience. New York: Longman, 1902.

Morris, R.J., & Hood, R.W. The generalizability and specificity of intrinsic/extrinsic orientation. Review of Religious Research, 1981, 22, 245-254.

Peloschek, C.P. Generalizability of intrinsic and extrinsic orientations toward work situations.

Unpublished Research Report. Tilburg University: Psychological Institute, 1983.

Proudfoot, W., & Shaver, P. Attribution theory and the psychology of religion. Journal for the Scientific Study of Religion, 1975, 14, 317-330.

Stace, W.T. Mysticism and philosophy. Philadelphia, Pa.: Lippencott, 1960.

Thomas, L.E., & Cooper, P.E. Measurement and incidence of mystical experience: An exploratory study. Journal for the Scientific Study of Religion, 1978, 17, 433-437.

Some characteristics of God's figure as perceived by unbelievers. Conclusions of three first approaches.

E. Bocquet
Catholic University Louvain

The main purpose of this report is to determine which figure of God have unbelievers in our society. Because this is merely an exploratory and empirical study in this area, conducted under the direction of Prof. A. Vergote, these results must be approached with caution. Anyway we are still thinking that some conclusions seem to confirm a certain number of theoretical statements on this difficult and delicate argument.

Our paper is subdivided into three parts. After a short introduction (I), we describe the methods and the samples of the three researches we are summing up. Before giving some general conclusions (III), we present the main results of this study (II).

I. Introduction
1.1. Parental figures and representation of God

It is a well-known fact that over and above certain real cultural differences, the general representation of God among believers is to be found at the confluence of the dual parental dimensions, the paternal and the maternal (Vergote-Tamayo, 1981; Vergote, 1983: 205-222).

The dimensions are so-to-speak subsumed in a tensional harmony in which the paternal metaphor becomes the ideal symbolic pole in the representation of God (Vergote-Tamayo, 1981: 205-222).

1.2. Non-believing and representation of God

Faced with the challenge of unbelieving and leaving aside the sometimes irreconciliable polysemy, our aim has been to examine and study the presence and the modalities of this tension constituting the representation and the idea of God among non believers, by analogy with its determinant role in the believing option.

It appears evident that the majority of non-believers in this part of the world possess a certain representation of God by virtue of their access to the same religious concepts available within a given culture. It is a fact moreover that all the non-believers encountered for the purpose of this research were able to cite a certain more-or-less direct and prolonged contact with the Christian religion (mainly Catholic and Protestant), whether through their education, families or whatever.

It is no more strange to discover that psychological processes underlie the varying attitudes of non-believing to the God reference than is the case within the believing option. This fact does nothing, however, to

225

diminish the somewhat conjectural and incomplete nature of our study at its present, initial stage.

1.3. Hypotheses

A first hypothesis must of course concern the similarity between representations of parental figures by believers and non-believers.

Secondly, as a result of their participation in objective religion, one expects the perception of God by non-believers to be identical with that of believers.

The third hypothesis concerns the gap between the "perceived" and the "desired" God in the case of non-believers. Following the research carried out on doubters by D. Hutsebaut (Vergote-Tamayo, 1981: 125-136) which shows that the "law" factor is perceived as a menace to their autonomy, we put foreward the hypothesis of a rejection of the paternel God conceived in terms of law, judge, authority and a accentuation of the maternel, "desired" God.

N.B. It will be interesting to examine possible cultural modifications in the relationship "parental figures" - "representation of God" as a function of the age factor, sex and socio-cultural category by example.

II. Methods
2.1. Instruments

The principal instrument employed is the French version of the SDPS (Semantic Differential Parental Scale).

Richard's semantic scale on the Sacred (Richard, 1973; Vergote, 1983) has only been employed in one sample (see Chaineux, 1984).

2.2. Samples of non-believers and believers
2.2.1. Samples of non-believers

The results reported are related to three samples dated between 1982 and 1985. (1)

We consider as non-believers those individuals who position themselves on the levels 5 or 4 of the self-evaluation (or self-rating) scale. (2)

The population is French-speaking Belgian. It should be noted that our samples are simple and occasional with a relatively small number of subjects.

The composition of the three samples is as follows:

-- two samples (Bocquet, 1982 and Chaineux, 1984) are identical as far as the population and its distribution according to age, sex and socio-cultural category are concerned;

- the second sample (Prémont, 1983) differs only as to the age group considered.

Sample	Self-rating	Men	%	average	women	%	average	socio-cultural. cat.
Bocquet 82 (85)	14: pos. 4 71: pos. 5	53	62	40.6	32	38	38,8	Upper class University
Prémont 83 (90)	10: pos. 4 80: pos. 5	50	56	25.6	40	44	23.2	"
Chaineux 84 (75)	75: pos. 5	40	53	40	35	47	39	"

Taken overall the final results in this report concern 250 French-speaking Belgian non-believers: 160 between 30-50 year
90 between 20-30 year.

2.2.2. Samples of believers

The sample of believers which served as a basis of comparison is that of Bonami 1966. It was made up of 180 Frech-speaking university students and adults believers whose average age was closest to of the "Prémont 83" sample.

It would be useful and instructive to employ the most recent results based on two samples of French-speaking Belgian believers: "Bocquet 85" sample made up of 100 believers and "Terlinden 85" made up of 84 French-speaking Belgian believers. The particular characteristic of this sample is its socio-political orientation. (We use the term SP) (Terlinden, 1985)

III. Results and discussion
3.1. Parental figures

An initial comparison can be made between the parental representations of believers and non-believers. Taken overall, the two appear similar. Thus, we discover the same major factors, both as regards the mother-figure ("unconditional availibility" and "law and authority") and the father-figure ("law-authority" and "accepted availibility"). Here too, the father figure appears more complex and more conflictual than that of the mother. Father's figure always embodies the two parental dimensions to a higher degree.

Moreover it is of interest to note that the non-believers of 1982 resemble quite strongly present-day believers (Boquet 85) "with regard to the intensity of the attribution of paternal items to the father" (Terlinden, 1985: 52). Bearing in mind the dynamic relationship between cultural models and representations of God, how should we evaluate the mutual influence, on the one hand of the modifications in the representation of God throughout objective religion and on the other, of the considerable changes in the representation of parental figures?

Whatever the line of reasoning adopted, this question of the relationship religion-personality is as relevant as to religious faith as it is to non-believing.

As far as the mother figure is concerned, the same overall isomorphism can be observed as regards believers and non-believers. It is at the most possible to ascertain some slight emphasis in the non-believers sample as to the items "dynamic", "who takes the initiative", "the one who acts", but nonetheless in a maternal context, since these items are to be considered in the dynamics of the affective bond which unites mother and child.

In conclusion it is possible to suggest that, in spite of minor maternal accentuation in the case of the younger non-believer sample (Prémont 84) as also in the case of the more recent believer sample (Bocquet 85 and Terlinden 85), the general configuration of parental figures remains isomorphic for believers and non-believers. Would it signify that the actual crisis of paternity has not exactly the same signification from the parental viewpoint?

3.2. God as perceived by non-believers

3.2.1. Using the same semantic scale (SDPS), non-believers described their representation of God as presented by believers.

We can assert without hesitation that the complexity of the God figure is clearly perceived by non-believers. In the representation of God by non-believers, the paternal aspects turn out to be more marked than in the case of the father figure itself ($Gp_p > Fp$) whilst the maternal aspects are less marked than in the case of the mother figure ($Gm < Mm$). However, this representation has more marked maternal characteristics than has the father figure ($Gm < Fm$) and similarly, the paternal characteristics are more marked than in the case of the mother figure ($Gp > Mp$).

To put in another way, the non-believer perception of God reflects both the complexity of the God figure and a high level of integration of the two parental dimensions.

Furthermore, the absence of a relationship between the order of attribution of paternal items and maternal items to the parental figures and that to the representation of God, reveals a fairly precise understanding of the particular meaning of these attributions, paternal and maternal, as made to God and to the father and mother figures respectively r Fp GPp = -.33; r Gm GPm = -.20 (Bocquet 82). The paternal items principally attributed to God are "power", "who gives the law", "strength", "authority". God is thus mainly perceived in terms of law-giver, judge and power, that is the father figure. The father's authority is more often related to the initiative and dynamic aspects than to the role of law-giving. Simultaneously, however, the non-believer sample tends to stress those items in God's maternal dimension which stress affective intuition ("gift", "always available", "who is always there", "who is always waiting for me").

Hutsebaut had already pointed out that the doubters tend to accentuate the affection dimension of contact with God (Vergote-Tamayo, 1981: 125-136).

In summary the representation of God is always closer to the father figure than to the mother figure; we also observe a slight emphasis upon the specific paternal dimensions (paternal items and law factor). Semantic analysis of paternal items shows a real convergence by unbelievers on a kind of incompatibility between God as lawgiving and the autonomy of man.

3.2.2. Taking the Sacred scale as a base
3.2.2.1. Theoretical pointers

This scale is constructed around two symbolical high and deep dimensions considered as being "the most likely to reveal the meaning of the ideas of "Sacred" and "God" (Vergote, 1983: 150). (3)

It appears that if sacred incorporates to a high degree depth variables and only to a low degree those relatively to height values, "God", on the other hand, incorporates to an approximately equal degree the two dimensions. Here also, the idea of God reveals itself as being more complex than that of sacred. The "height dimension" is particularly characteristic of God, signifying his radical alterity.

Thus, if certains common characteristics can exist between a dynamic sacred and God, this is not sufficient to permit one to postulate a total identity between Sacred and God. Sacred, as defined by Vergote, is "a transitional area between the purely secular world and the religious God" (Vergote, 1983: 152).

This research on the representation of sacred in the non-believer sample was carried out together with the study of the representation of God using the SDPS (Chaineux, 1984).

To speak generally, it is possible to observe that if the non-believer sample perceives God via the two "height" and "depth" dimensions, it is primarily as "sovereign power" and "domination force" that He is seen in his radical transcendance. And the item "source and origine", first attributed on the depth axis, refers to a God who preceeds man.

Based upon the comparison of factors which emerge in the two samples (believers and non-believers) (Chaineux, 1984), there is to be seen an important difference between believers and non--believers. Thus, the N° factor in the case of the believers (36% of the variance) which represents God as "majestic power" (36.9% of the variance) and "dynamic value"

229

(11.4% of the variance). It would also be possible to discover a defensive split between the revealing power of God and his immanent, non threatening presence in Man. This is at least a deduction which we can make in considering the item saturation in the factors of the perceived God.

In fact, we can see that the non believers tend to refuse and to reject the personal transcendance of God while their conception of the sacred is more spontaneous and direct.

3.3. The desired God

A double observation is immediately apparent concerning the three samples:

on the one hand, the maternal accentuation of the desired God as compared with the perceived God: the desired God shows a degree of similarity with the maternal figure: GDm > GPm and GDm = Mm. But we had by the non-believers: r Mm GPm = -.20 (Bocquet 82) and r Mm GPm = .21 (Prémont 83). The same attribution profile is thus not present in these two figures.

on the other hand, the desired God is totally less paternal than the perceived God: GPp > GDp. For example, the accentuation of maternal items in relation to paternal items reflects this proportion in the three samples: $\bar{X}m : 5.30 / \bar{X}p : 3.65$ as against : $\bar{X}m : 5.25 / \bar{X}p : 5.35$ for the perceived God.

God in a maternal context is primarily desired as being "who welcomes me with open arms", "a warm-hearted refuge", "the one who is most patient", "charming" and in a paternal context, "intelligence", "strenght" , "the one who has the knowledge", "dynamic". It should be noted that the paternal items, more highly accentuated in the case of the perceived God are rejected here, i.e. "who gives the directions", "who is the principle", "who makes the decisions", "authority", "the judge". Moreover, the correlation is negative as regards the order of attribution of paternal items in the cases of the desired God and the perceived God.

Thus r GPp GDp =   .003 (Bocquet 82)
          "   =   .056 (Prémont 83)
          "   =   -.081 (Chaineux 84).

It is thus possible to observe that there is no relationship between the paternal dimension of God as the non-believer sample represents Him and such as this sample would accept Him in the believing hypothesis. On the other hand, certain paternal items such as "dynamic", "the one who has the knowledge", "strength", are attributed to the desired God to the same degree as are certain maternal items. In fact, these qualities seem to refer to a sort of impersonal dynamic.

Three factors have been extracted from the different samples by factorial analysis.

In the first two samples (Bocquet 82 and Prémont 83), the three factors are largely similar. The first explains slightly more than 60% of the variance, i.e. the factor "Law-authority". Thus we can see a strong saturation of certain items such as "authority": .86 and .90; "who gives the directions": .82 and .78; "the judge": .75 and .74; "who gives the law": .77 and .67 which have moreover a low average value on the continuum of the attributions (from 2. to 3.), the average of $\bar{X}p$ being 3.60.

From the statistical point of view, this would tend to establish fairly strongly the hypothesis of a vigorous rejection by the unbelievers (the totality of the subjects) of a God "law giver", "judge" and who "embodies authority", a God likely to hinder man's desire for autonomy and happiness.

On the other hand, items such as "dynamic", "systematic mind", "strength" which are strongly attributed are not particularly saturated. God does thus not appear to suffer rejection as an impersonal dynamic!

The second factor entitled "unconditional acceptance" covers 27% of the variance. It is interesting to observe that this factor matches up with all the items of the third factor of the perceived God, with, in addition, "close to whom one feels at home", "who takes loving care of me", "tenderness". Is it conceivable that God could become total acceptance of man, once his paternal demands perceived as intrusive have been eliminated?

The third factor describes God as a presence made of empathy and almost complicity with man.

The following testimony supplied by non believer who was asked how he might desire God to be provides a reasonably good summary of the ambivalent position of a number of non believers when faced with God: "I am not inclined to deny the existence of a God created by and for man, but that of a God who is authority and judge".

We are aware that non believers have no difficulty in perceiving what is at stake in the paternal and maternal representation of God. It is certain that the culture coefficient of the dialectical relationship between parental and divine representation is liable to cause fluctuations which are of greater or lesser importance in the adoption by non believers of certain personal and social attitudes. The stumbling-block is however constituted by a kind of paradox from which arises the alterity of God, near and yet alien at the same time. God meets human desire by being Mother and Father at the same time. He transforms the desire from within to this point when he appears to expropriate it.

Taking this ambivalent, conflictual position towards God as a point of departure, a position which many non-believers could accept as theirs, we may sum up the complexity of non believing and our fragile and incomplete understanding of this latter, from a psychological point of view.

Would it nevertheless be too bold to put forward the idea that the over-accentuation of the specific paternal dimension of God, far from being a mistake based on ignorance, presages a conflict, the severity of which is sometimes capable of evoking the narcissistic wound and disappointment, and at others, the anguished refusal and the revolt in face of the conversion which is required by the desire of the Other and the Alliance in a context of liberty.

But in any case, the more fundamental question remains posed of the transcendantal stamp of human desire in its fundamental dehiscence. This creates an opening for a possible alliance of faith with the paternal and maternal alterity of God, far removed from the dangers of religious alienation. In other words, it appears that certain types of non-believing constitute even for believers a beneficious insurrection against any representation of God which might circumscribe human desire, either by focusing it on its maternal mirage, or by emasculating it in the face of implacable paternal authority.

We do believe therefore that beyond possible cultural modifications both in parental and divine representations, the question of the tension experienced or of the voluntary conversion of believer's desire and representation of God returns in force. The effect is that the believer's wish for attachement and for happiness does not eliminate his listening to God and to God's desire whose law also constitutes a symbolic Presence beyond believer's affirmation and non-believer's negation.

Notes

(1) These three samples form the base material for three first Religious Psychology dissertations on the subject of non-believing, carried out under the direction of Prof. Vergote.

(2) This is the self-rating scale with 5 degrees:
  (1) Absolute belief in the existence of God
  (2) Belief in the existence of God but with questions
  (3) Doubt in the existence of God
  (4) Difficulties in believing in the existence of God
  (5) No belief in the existence of God

(3) One must make a distinction between two groups of symbolical items relative to the "deep" level: those which designate the dynamic qualities of nature ("who is fertile", "who invades one's being"...) and those which qualify the ethical dimensions of human existence ("confess on things a serious and weighty"...). Thus, sacred, contrary to what is maintained by Otto, for whom it represents the "one who is totally Other, signifies rather a dimension of alterity within the world which is not strictly personal. It constitutes a kind of threshol of divine transcendance."

Literature

Bocquet, E. Profils de non-croyance et représentation de Dieu. Unpublished manuscript. University of Louvain-la-Neuve, 1982.

Bonami, M. Le symbole du père et de la mère dans l'image de Dieu. Unpublished manuscript. University of Louvain-la-Neuve, 1966.

Chaineux, M.P. Représentation de Dieu et expérience du sacré chez les Non-Croyants. Unpublished manuscript. University of Louvain-la-Neuve, 1984.

Godin, A. Psychologie des expériences religieuses. Le désir et la réalité. Paris: Centurion, 1981.

Hutsebaut, D. Belief in the existence of God and the representation of God. In: A. Vergote and L. Tamayo. The parental figures and the representation of God. A psychological and cross-cultural study. Leuven, The Hague-Paris-New York: Leuven University Press and Mouton, 1981.

Premont, J. Profils de non-croyance et représentation de Dieu. Unpublished manuscript. University of Louvain-la-Neuve, 1983.

Terlinden, G. Interprétation du rite eucharistique chez des Chrétiens Socio-Politiques Belges. Unpublished manuscript. University of Louvain-la-Neuve, 1985.

Richard, R. Les dimensions de hauteur et de profondeur dans l'image de Dieu et du sacré. Unpublished manuscript. University of Louvain-la-Neuve, 1973.

Vergote, A., & Tamayo, L. The parental figures and the representation of God. A psychological and cross-cultural study. Leuven, The Hague, Paris, New York: Leuven University Press and Mouton, 1981.

Vergote, A. Religion, foi, incroyance. Etude psychologique. Bruxelles: Mardaga, 1983.

Research on belief with the selfconfrontation.

M. de Fraeye
Catholic University Leuven

The purpose of this lecture is to give an illustration, by means of a casestudy, of the kind of research we are working on within the framework of our doctoral project entitled : "Religious development as a process of integration". The actual researchprocess consists of about 20 students of science of religion (1st, 2nd and last year students) who participate in a selfconfrontation about their belief, for a period of 1,5 to 2 years.

First we will deal with the topic of our study which is "belief as a process", to continue afterwards with the specific implications which include our choice to use the selfconfrontationmethod of Hermans, also called method of selfinvestigation. We will be very brief about the method itself, but we will always be very willing to give further information to those who are interested on this matter.

Belief as a process.

The Christian religious attitude essentially consists of a "commitment to" which implies an involvement with God, who transcends the human world (Vergote, 1984, p 171). It is because of this specific core of meaning that a psychology which studies religion, as a given fact within our Western culture, considers its object as a "process". For the message of belief is not evidentally grafted upon human experiences and motivations. It rather occurs as an appeal to man, who answers it according to his own dispositions. The outcome of this interaction is considered to be fundamentally contentious and liable to tensions. The meanings which religious language and tradition introduce do not automatically correspond with human intentions and aspirations. Although man in his religious desires is directed by fundamentally human interests and longings, an authentic answer to the question of belief presumes a working-through and a transformation of that same desire, through a lived confrontation with the present religious meanings.

The integration of the given objective religion into a personal religious attitude is a "process" and properly assumes a nature of "be-coming". Throughout its development the subjective religious life can take different forms. It can grow towards an active refusal, or slumber in indifference for a long time. A moment of delay can be introduced as belief and unbelief question each other, or because of crucial questions which are conscientiously avoided. A given commitment can renew itself throughout those movements and changes towards a more solid belief.

It is this dynamic movement in its critical aspects which we want to study and understand in its psychological proceedings, as they interact with the situational and cultural environment out of which they emerge. We focus here on the essential dimension around which belief and unbelief are structured, namely "the relation to God".

<u>The self-investigation</u> (Hermans, 1974, 1976 & 1981)
The goal of the selfconfrontationmethod of Hermans is to enable the person to reflect on his own valuational life, so as to discern a certain order in it. Two questions are essential : "What is important to me?" and "How do I feel about it?". The whole structure of the self-investigation is based on these two questions.
A first stage consists of the explicitations of the so-called "value areas". By means of a series of general open questions (as for instance about the past, present, future, activity, thinking, and so on; cf. examples in annex I) the person is invited to explore his experiential world, in order to search for those aspects which are most important to him. The ultimate formulation of what he experiences to be important, at that given moment, is called a "value area". In its concrete form a value area can cover a great diversity of things, as for instance an event, a person, a memory, and so on... After the construction of all the value areas, two special ones are added and introduced by means of two questions : "How do you generally feel these days?" and "How would you like to feel?" These respectively stand for the General and Ideal experience.
The whole of the personal value areas organizes into a meaningful system, not only regarding its contents, but also regarding its affective modalities. In order to obtain this information each value area is related to a standard list of feelings (cf. annex II), 12 positive and 12 negative ones. Starting from this affectmatrix (cf. annex III) a number of indices can be calculated, from which a certain hierarchy and organisation can be derived. We will confine ourselves to the most important ones. A first index is the affective quality of a value area (=Q), which is based on the balance of positive (=P) and negative (=N) (cf. annex III). This balance can incline towards the positive or the negative side, but can also show an almost equal distribution of both sides. In that case we talk about an "ambivalent" quality. For example as we look at the contents of Va 1 (cf. annex III), we could speak of a positive experience, although the rating of the feelings gives more accurate information about the ambiguous way this value area is being experienced. Besides the hierarchy of the value areas according to their quality, we can also analyze the relation between value areas ; this in as far as they show either a strong resemblance or a strong opposition in their affective modality (= configuration of feelings). This is especially interesting to determine the degree of homogeneity or

heterogeneity in the way the whole system is experienced. Consequently, a possible dominant modality in the affective structure can be traced, which can reveal information about the nature of the relation between the General and the Ideal experience. We will come back to this in the casestudy.

Typical of the selfconfrontationmethod is that the results, as acquired here, are discussed afterwards with the person himself. In this way he has a chance to look at his valuational system, which he sees before him, from a certain distance and gain an insight into the shades and relations structuring the system as a whole. In this feedback of the data to the subject we notice the own interpretation of the person to be very important.

The most essential of the self-investigation - and in our opinion this is too often omitted in a researchapplication - is that the selfconfrontation, as described here, is repeated entirely for several times. Then we have a "confrontation" with the value areas instead of a "construction", as the existing formulations can be modified or replaced by new ones. Afterwards the value areas are again related to the feelings, with a discussion following. Interesting is that the person, throughout such a series of self-investigations, gets a view of the possible continuities or discontinuities in the organisation of his system. In the period between two confrontations these results can be either confirmed or considered to be in-valid. (Here we also refer to the casestudy). In this way the selfinvestigation not only leads to explicitation of developments in one's personal valuational life, but also tends to stimulate the on-going valuational process.

Adaptation for research on belief

We have made a few changes to the method of Hermans. All open questions have been formulated in relation to "belief for you" instead of "your life" (cf. annex I). This formulation seemed most suitable to us in order to give the participants sufficient subjective space to situate themselves in relation to their own attitude towards belief or unbelief. On the other hand we state that "belief" operates upon valuations which concern the personality as a whole. On the other hand we must be aware of the fact that, in view of our choice of the participants and the circumstances in which the research takes place, "belief" is obviously situated within the context of Christian belief. Nevertheless we leave it up to the participants to explicitate their own associations of meaning in relation to "belief".

Before the first and after the last self-investigation the item-list of L. Vercruysse (Vercruysse, 1972) on the meaning of God is presented to each participant. The answers to the list are discussed in the third confrontation and can induce additional value areas.

Perspective of the method and the foundation of our choice

After this short description we would like to briefly set the method of Hermans in the perspective of the current trends in the psychology of personality and clinical diagnostics ; afterwards we account for the use of the method for research in psychology of religion.

We will not deal with the historical development of the valuational theory as such, but limit ourselves to the most striking statements which characterize the present individualized personality research, to which Hermans is definitely related. First of all the person, as an object of research, is considered to also act as a scientist at the same time. He is appointed to be a co-expert in providing data on his own way of functioning in a given situation. From this point of view, research is usually set up within the so-called "symmetrical" dialoguemodel, and takes the form of a more or less structured person-to-person relationship. Attention is given to the individual experience and feelings, and to the personal way of expressing oneself. So, in the first place one talks "with" the person before giving one's opinion "about" the person. Thus the "local" theory is effectively included within the general scientific theory (Hoekstra, 1978). A second important aspect is the conception of personality as a dynamic and interactional process. The personality emerges out of interaction with the continuously changing cultural and social environment, and is consequently always in motion. This interaction is situation-specific, but at the same time there is a basis of affinity which is assumed in every moment of sharing between two human beings. We acknowledge in this new approach on psychology of personality a revaluation of the person as "meaning-maker" (Van Hoof, 1973) and agent of reorganisation. In our choice of the selfconfrontationmethod as method of research, we were especially guided by these options and their implications about personality-as-a-process. In those we found a remarkable number of similarities with the dynamic view on the phenomenon of "belief", without however disregarding some critical comments. We were pleased with the method because of its dialogical nature by means of which the person is invited to express himself to someone else (who is also called the "helper") concerning his way of experiencing belief or unbelief. It is of basic inportance here that the person can speak freely and that the conversation between him and the helper takes place within a confidential relationship. Still more fundamental is that this "conversation about oneself" is guided by the so-called 'valuational principle", which is induced as a structuring and organizing principle of life. This means for the person that he formulates, in his own words what is important to him in relation to "belief", what he

237

experiences to be meaningful to him, or considers to be of great value. At that given moment we as researchers enter and take part of the personal valuational process concering "belief", in as far as it is explicitated by this method. In our opinion this accent on the valueorientation as the core of personality, as it originates on the crossing of a given meaning and the subjective dispositions, has been worked out very succesfully in this method of self-investigation, and the principles of the valuational theory on which it is based. The valueconcept is exceeded in all its ambiguity and dubious connotations by its operationalization in terms of "value areas" and especially by emphasizing the valuational process as an interactual process of be-coming of the personal identity (Vergote, 1985). We consider "valuating" as a process of creating meaning which assumes a triadic synthetical structure, namely that of cognition, affect and behaviour. "Valuating" means making a choice, which is confirmed in the way this acknowledged value is experienced and integrated in the personal life, with all the consequences it takes; what the self-investigation concerning "belief" aims at, is that the person looks back on himself, in a retrospective view, and reflects on his valuations in relation to his religious life. Experiencing something as significant always implies:
being moved by a meaning which automatically includes an affective component. In his affectivity the person focuses on certain values, but in their turn the values also attract him, because of the meanings they represent. In relating the value areas to the feelings - which is often a rather "confronting" experience - the person's attention is drawn to the nature of those valuations he eventually prefers. In the discussion the person can then discover certain inconsistencies, in the form of contradictions between valuations or tensions between an acknowledged value and the matching pattern of feelings or behavioural commitment. In which way these insights have their effect, can again be considered in a following self-investigation. It is through this series of "instant" surveys that the valuational system of "belief" is studied in its dynamical and potential restructurational process.

The self-investigation as a diagnostic method has particular merit in presenting the personality-as-a-process. Moreover, we can say that the method already preássumes changes and movement! The question which arises here is whether the so-called "confrontation" as it takes its shape in the assumed "symmetrical" relation between the person and the helper, within the structure of the self-investigation, can be considered as a sufficient condition to cause transformations. An additional problem concerns the difference between "periodic revival" and the "structural change" (Hermans, 1981, p. 117). According to Hermans the latter becomes clear in the changing of the general affective modality wich goes along with modifications in the value areas. In order to give further interpretation to these "structural changes" there are no reliable criteria available. We claim that the valuational theory considered as a theory of personality, does not give sufficient fundamental theoretical background to analyse the psychological correlatives of certain modifications in the material of the selfconfrontation. More systematic study on self-investigations which go over a long period, could mean an interesting contribution to this matter.

In spite of these rather critical remarks, we consider the self-investigation to be of a great value to our research on "belief" which is principally defined as a meaningful "process of integration". On the one hand the method appeals to the ultimate organizational forces of the personality which develops itself towards an identity, this by means of the "principle of the valuation". On the other hand the method keeps the openness for the subjective process of valuation concerning "belief" and the way in which "belief" takes shape, at a given moment, in the form of a personal attitude of belief or unbelief.

The casestudy.

The casestudy consists of a female first year student of science of religion. She is 19 years old and is called Ann.

We want to show three "instant" surveys of her self-investigation about "belief". We are presenting this in a very restricted way by only giving those value areas and their modifications which explicitly deal with "belief" and "the relation to God" (cf. annex IV).

At the start of the first self-investigation Ann considers herself "not as strongly believing". When she expresses her expectations towards the selfconfrontationmethod she stated : "I would like to know what I really can believe" and "I would like to get more insight into myself" through which "I could come to God in a better way". Those statements are very typical of Ann's initial situation. In the first self-investigation we come upon some important experiences from the past, through which Ann felt to be "already more believing" (cf. Va 1 and 2 in annex IV). However the current meaning of these value areas has changed. Va 1 shows a relatively high involvement, but the affective quality is divided almost equally between positive and negative. We are dealing with an ambivalent experience. Besides joy, hope, trust and energy, sorrow and guilt are also frequently present. Va 1 was a "fantastic" experience to Ann, but because of the time that went by and the thinking process which started along with it, a question is more strongly rising: "Does God exist at all?" "I would consider it really bad... you are praying ... and to whom?". This reaction is repeated in relation to Va 3. In both cases we initially notice a positive experience of belief, which afterwards arouses doubts, as the feelings and momentary moods cannot be trusted. At the same time a sufficient rational explanation is lacking as she states : "...that is not possible with God".

Va 4 reveals how Ann assesses her own attitude towards belief as a whole. Paradoxically this value area does not show any correspondance in modality with the General experience of belief, but does with the Ideal experience. The confrontation with this apparently rather passive way of distanciating from belief leads to the awareness of : "...In fact I should give more thought to belief....." but as opposed to that she immediately adds: "... still you'll never find out why you are here..." In this way we see her religious commitment entangled in on the one hand the desire to believe, and on the other hand the impossibility to get rational answers to belief questions. This also affects the structure of the valuational system. Remarkable is that the obviously rather positive General experience of belief has very few roots in the formulated value areas, nor does it have any resemblance with the Ideal. Va 7 is the only value area which still generalizes moderately. It focuses on Ann's fundamental doubt. But next to strong feelings of uncertainty and powerlessness, feelings of freedom and hope are also fairly frequent. For freedom is, together with self-esteem, the feeling which is generally used most frequently. According to Ann : "... It is better to doubt God than to believe blindly". "I do feel my freedom in it ... that there is no God which imposes his will...I think that I'll also discover that God... that is why I also feel hope". Disappointment, grief and anger is a cluster of negative feelings which occur in an important number of value areas. They mostly deal with critical remarks about clergymen and the church, because of their hypocrisy, and about the way old people believe, because of their naïvety. We get the impression that in this self-investigation "belief" for Ann still raises more questions than answers can be found (cf. also Va 12), which leaves her divided and insecure. The question about the existence of God is placed on the same line as the question about the meaning of her own existence. But this question is also – so to say – suspended and results in a tendency to have everything come as it comes and wait...

In the second self-investigation (7 months later) Ann's valuational system has changed a lot. Only Va 4 and 21, which were dominantly positive areas, are preserved. However they now show a decrease in quality and involvement. This is a general tendency which characterizes the whole of the areas. The most striking modifications, which can rightly be called invalidations, are shown in Va 1 and 2. Here Ann becomes aware of the illusive nature of these experiences, because of her desire for support and resource, out of which they originate. This explicit recognition causes a change of perspective which transforms the feeling "that God was there" into : "I thought it was God, because I wanted Him to pay attention to me..." "I think that that was something of myself, and that it had nothing to do with God..." She clearly shows her distrust towards her own feelings (and also to those of others) as they result from her own imagination looking for a solution in God's intervention.

Here the representation of God as "interfering" authority in human life, and "by which God is placed on a throne", comes into the forefront. However this representation is strongly rejected because it is "sense-less" and "illogical", and this fixes her critical mind at the present time. This state of : "...not knowing...not even whether He really exists..." is the origine for doubts such as : "...does something exist above us?..." and "...don't we imagine things to encourage ourselves?..." The predominantly negative, but low involved, affective modality which goes along with this, extends to the whole valuational system and also to the General experience. This time the feelings of uncertainty, powerlessness, stress, loneliness and anger exceed the positive feelings. The explicit awareness of the fact that "In fact you can't say anything about it" imposes a negative quality on the system and immobilizes the process at the moment.

The tension between on the one hand the desire to ultimately know "it", and to have proofs of it, and on the other hand the clear consciousness that those proofs do not exist, because God is considered to be "transcendent", has reached its climax here. Va 12 strongly expresses at which point Ann has arrived in her religious attitude namely : the question of a renewed meaning, which at this stage cannot be answered.

The General and the Ideal experience now show a slightly opposite modality. The General experience is most strongly supported by areas which deal with criticism of the church and religious people, who in fact work against human nature and its emancipation. The intolerant and selfisch attitude towards one's fellow-man is also something with which she reproaches her parents, who assert themselves as believers. In our opinion this hides a basis for an even more stronger dissociation from belief, as she experiences it in her immediate surroundings.

At this level we discern an other aspect of tension namely that of belief which is opposed to life. In fact this tension, as experienced within herself, concerns the way she views "belief" and presumes "how a person who beliefs ought to be". This idealistic view on belief contrasts with the experienced imperfection of her own attitude. This tension also activates her severe reproaches towards other believers. Much attention is taken up by this matter, as a consequence of which Ann seems to turn away from the indecision and obscurity within her own religious attitude.

The only value area that corresponds closely with the Ideal experience of belief and which also has the highest quality, deals with people whose belief especially consists of being social. Helping your fellow-man in everyday life is forced to the front as the only value which can still be considered as "worthy to believe in", but it is rather isolated from the other value areas. There are even more value areas that show a reverse idealization-index. About her Ideal Ann says : "I don't long for it...it will come..." It is very peculiar that this Ideal experience still has the highest degree of involvement and a maximum quality, although its modality does not have enough potential to positively affect the whole system.

The third self-investigation (4 months later) shows clear modifications in the affective structure of the valuational system. Positive feelings as trust and solidarity increased strongly, while loneliness, grief, anger and uncertainty decreased in frequention. Energy is now by far the most frequently used feeling. There is also a general increase of the quality, together with a progressing involvement. A great number of areas, which mostly deal with one and the same topic namely : the link between belief and life, split up the system into very positive and very negative areas. People who accomplish this link are those who put social commitment on the first place (next to the possibility of a supreme being), and aim at the emancipation of man (as for instance the liberational theologists). People who do not respect this link are priests, the pope and persons who only measure belief through external criteria. Typical for the first mentioned areas, which are experienced very positively, is their strong correspondance in modality with the Ideal experience; through which they induce a dominant positive pattern of feelings into the system.

The General experience still remains on low potentials, but this time it just reaches above the ambivalence. General and Ideal do correspond now, however on a very low level. Much uncertainty and the absence of security are again characteristic of their discrepancy. Va 12 keeps the prominent function in the system, with the highest degree of generalisation. However this area, together with some others, did evolve from dominanty negative to ambivalent, with an increasing involvement. The representation of God as interfering in what happens here, has been considered very explicitly with all the mixed feelings which go along with it; and on which the General experience seems to be fixed. Uncertainty remains next to freedom and energy.

Even the imaginative representation that tangible proofs exist (cf. Va 6) and that there is no more uncertainty, is experienced as very ambivalent. This ambivalence is of a very specific nature. There are some feelings of rest and fairly many of security, but there is also a great deal of powerlessness and incertitude, and anxiety remains moderate. Ann states : "I would rather have no proofs ... because if there are any there is no more freedom. God seems to be so ready-made then". "I would accept it because it is so ... but I would not be happy with it". Va 6 is also isolated in relation to the General and Ideal experience of belief. Ann comments :

"...this is also because I do not really long for those proofs. On the one hand there is no more freedom, on the other hand your belief becomes a fact and there is no more doubt... It is difficult to imagine, because in fact you know it will never happen..."

Va 25 (1) is completely different because it shows a remarkable number of connections with the General and the Ideal. "God" in the twofold meaning, as an answer to the ultimate questions of life and as the actual judge of man, is experienced predominantly positive. There is very much energy and trust, and a lot of joy and hope. This representation of God, as stated conditionally here, seems to fit positively – to a certain degree – within the whole system. However the dominantly positive modality which presently supports the system, is not yet a sufficient condition for further generalization and improvement of the process.

The fundamental tension which we gradually discern in the course of the self-investigation is situated around a growing recognition of God as being "the other" and being "more"; and at the same time the confirmation of God as actual judge of man. Especially the distance between God and man is implicitly stressed here. The strong concern for keeping human freedom, which goes along with this reveals, in our opinion, a tension concerning the human autonomy as opposed to the commitment which the religious attitude implies. This inner conflict between autonomy and dependence which is actually experienced in a multitude of oppositions between belief and life is still activated and strengthened by representations of God given by religious people from the immediate surroundings.

Questions about life and death (actually concerning the possible decease of her grandmother) remains an important source of negative feelings throughout the three self-investigations, but also insists on an answer to the question of the meaning of God which presently remains open.

In this lecture we have tried to especially present Ann's own way of dealing with certain religious meanings, as this occured throughout her valuational investigation concerning "belief". The initially confirming experiences were questioned by a rising distrust in her own feelings. Tangible proofs of the existence of God became a necessity to be able to believe, but at the same time they were considered to be impossible and afterwards even undesirable. The demand for a renewed meaning and creation of an acceptable significance became very important.

In this casestudy we assume to have revealed a number of psychological lines of force that are fundamental to the dynamic process which belief induces, and which also operate upon the valuational life of other persons, although in an ever changing constellation. The transformations we presented here are not of a very spectacular nature, but we consider this rather slow developmental character of the process to be proper to all serious and fundamental human problems.

Note
1. Va 25. was induced by the presentation and discussion of the answers on the itemlist of L. Vercruysse in the third self-investigation. It is added at the end of the list of value areas.

Literature

Hermans, H.J.M. Waardegebieden en hun ontwikkeling, Amsterdam: Swets en Zeitlinger, 1974.

Hermans, H.J.M. Value Areas and their Development, Amsterdam: Swets en Zeitlinger, 1976.

Hermans, H.J.M. Persoonlijkheid en Waardering, Amsterdam: Swets en Zeitlinger, 1981.

Hoekstra, H.A. Waarderingstheorie en Attributietheorieën : verenigbaar? Nederlands Tijdschrift voor de Psychologie, 1978, 33, 464.

Hoof, J.J. van. Symbolisch interactionisme. Mens en Maatschappij, 1973, 4, 434.

Vercruysse, L. The meaning of God : a factoranalytic study. Social Compass, 1972, 19, 347-364.

Vergote, A. Religie, Geloof en Ongeloof, Antwerpen: Nederlandse Boekhandel, 1984.

Vergote, A. Waarden in psychologisch en pedagogisch perspectief. Een commentaar vanuit de psychologie. Leuvens Bulletin Lapp, 1985, 34, 55-61.

PAST
Has there been, in the past, a person(s), an experience, or a circumstance that greatly influenced "belief for you" and still appreciably affects your present existence?

FUTURE
Is there a goal or object of which you expect it to play an important role concerning "belief for you".

ACTIVITY
What is the most important activity in relation to "belief for you" in which you are strongly involved?

PERSON; UNITY
Is there a person who is important to you in relation to "belief for you" and to whom you feel closely related?

SOCIETY
Is there an aspect of the society that is of great importance or influence in relation to "belief for you"?

ANNEX II

STANDARD LIST OF FEELINGS (= 12 POSITIVE AND 12 NEGATIVE)

Please indicate, by means of a number rating, for each feeling the extend
to which in your present life, you experience this feeling in connection
with the aspect stated in the label (= value area).

If the feeling occurs very often, you are to rate it 5

often	4
fairly often	3
sometimes	2
rarely	1
not at all	0

1. joy
2. powerlessness
3. self-esteem
4. anxiety
5. happiness
6. worry
7. stress
8. enjoyment
9. affection
10. self-alienation
11. uncertainty
12. guilt
13. solidarity
14. loneliness
15. hope
16. trust
17. inferiority
18. security
19. anger
20. grief
21. energy
22. disappointment
23. inner calm
24. freedom

ANNEX III

AN EXAMPLE OF AN AFFECTMATRIX (selfconfrontation 1 of the casestudy)

Va = value area
P = sum of the scores on the positive feelings
N = sum of the scores on the negative feelings
I = involvement = P+N = degree of affective involvement
with a maximum of 120(= 24 x 5) and a minimum of 0

Q = quality = $\dfrac{P \times 100}{P + N}$ = the percentage of the positive feelings on the total, with a maximum of 100 and a minimum of 0

G = generalization-index = correlation between the row of affectscores on the General experience and the row of affectscores on the given value area.

I = idealization-index = correlation between the row of affectscores on the Ideal experience and the row of the affectscores on the given value area with maximum correlation of 1.00 and minimum of -1.00

Value areas	Feelings 1+ 2- 3+ 4- 5+ 6- 7- 8+ 9+ 10+ 11- 12- 13+ 14- 15+ 16+ 17- 18- 19 20 21+ 22+ 23- 24+	P	N	I	Q	G	I
Va 1. Personal confession through which I have found support in God.	4 2 2 3 2 1 2 5 3 2 4 4 1 3 3 4 4 3 2 2	36	29	65	55	0.27	0.34
Va 20. My friend.	4 0 3 1 4 2 1 3 4 5 1 1 3 0 2 4 1 2 2 1 1 2 1 4	35	12	47	74	-0.04	0.74
Va 22. If you do not go to mass, people gossip	0 5 4 0 0 1 1 0 0 0 1 1 0 3 1 0 2 0 5 4 0 5 0 4	8	28	37	24	0.46	-0.29
General experience "belief"	2 3 3 1 2 2 1 0 0 0 4 3 1 1 5 1 3 1 3 2 4 3 0 4	23	26	49	47	1.00	0.03
Ideal experience of "belief"	3 0 4 0 1 4 4 0 0 0 5 0 4 4 0 4 1 1 5 1 2 5	48	4	52	92	0.03	1.00

SELFCONFRONTATION

	I	II	III
General information:			
General experience	Q 67 I 48	Q 32 I 31	Q 57 I 37
Ideal experience	Q 92 I 52	Q 100 I 47	Q 100 I 52
Correlation Gen.-Ideal	0.03	- 0.27	0.26
Means	Q 49 I 49	Q 42 I 33	Q 64 I 48

Va 1. Personal confesseion through which I have support in God.

    Q 55   I 65

Va 1. I thought God was there, but I have invented it myself because I needed some-one who was listening to me.
    Q 39   I 33

Va 1. Eliminated.

Va 2. The statement : "God believes in you" as an answer to my statement : "I do not belief in God".

    Q 60   I 42

Va 2. I can not believe any longer in that statement : "God beliefs in you" because I really want proof of it.
    Q 32   I 25

Va 2. Eliminated.

Va 4. I tend to go on living without lingering on belief.
    Q 64   I 56

Va 4. Preserved.

    Q 53   I 38

Va 4. Preserved.

    Q 78   I 37

Va 5. I find it difficult to believe that God can interfere with what happens here. I ask myself if it is possible.
    Q 42   I 31

Va 5. I find it difficult to believe that God can interfere in what happens here.

    Q 54   I 37

Va 6. I would want there was someone who could explain it in-tirely, and than it is your duty as a man to belief in it.
    Q 41   I 34

Va 6. If there are tangible proofs, I could belief in God.

    Q 47   I 43

Va 7. I happen sometimes to doubt the existence of a certain God.

    Q 40   I 52

Va 7. One can invent everything about God but you do not know anything about it, and not even if He really is there.
    Q 25   I 32

Va 7. Preserved

    Q 65   I 34

Va 12. To think about God.

Va 12. It is difficult
for me to believe that
God has something to
tell us here, wich
meaning can I still
give to God?

Va 12. Preserved.

   Q 45   I 51   Q 23   I 35   Q 50   I 40

Va 21. Belief is something
individualistic.

Va 21. Preserved.

Va 21. Eliminated.

   Q 65   I 48   Q 54   I 37

Added : Va 25. If there is a God, I think he
is the answer on the ultimate questions of
life and that He judges man according to
his deeds in the hereafter.   Q 79   I 33

The transmission of religion in family situations in Finland.
A preliminary report.

N. G. Holm
Åbo Akademi

The significance of the family for the child's religious attitude in adult life has been stressed by various theorists in both psychology and sociology. Emphasis has been placed, on the one hand, on the psychological learning process that occurs when a child learns to say its prayers and perform other devotions in the home; prominence has also been given to the emotional ties which arise between mother/father and child. The latter aspect has above all been studied by depth psychology. In addition, we may mention social psychology which speaks of primary socialisation in the family circle. Hjalmar Sundén, who likes to combine a number of ideas from depth psychology with insights from social psychology, has also emphasized the significance of the parents, particularly the mother's role, in the development of the religious dimension of the child. He thus speaks of a total transmission of tradition and of a purely verbal one. Purely verbal transmission occurs when a parent on certain occasions tries to transmit religion to the child by means of oral accounts. The child does not then obtain an overall view of religion and religiosity. If however transmission is total, the child learns its devotions even before the acquisition of language. The verbal explanation then has an experiential reference within the child itself.

But Sundén is also conscious of the importance of emotional ties for the successful transmission of tradition. He therefore speaks of mediators of tradition who are: confident, lacking in confidence, and over-confident. The confident ones are those who manage to transmit religion to the child in an optimal manner. The lacking in confidence ones are aware of their own limitations and often mediate purely verbally. Over-confident mediators, on the other hand, bind a child's religious experience excessively to emotional contact with the partent. Religion, in other words, becomes a means available to parents for making children obey and follow their will. In this case, so-called affective anthropomorphism readily occurs in the child. The concept of God and religion as a whole thus acquire prominent features from the personalities of the parents. In this category we may include those who Swedish psychology of religion has often called "God's grandchildren". These are people who have grown up in strictly religious environments with a sharp distinction between children of God and children of the world. Parents have an intense desire for their children to become God's children in the same way as they themselves feel they are. But at the same time there is an emotional disturbance which means that the child does not obtain direct access to religion, but the latter is instead communicated only on the parent's terms. They become, in other words, second hand practitioners of religion, God's grandchildren.

In the light of what has been said, it is thus quite clear that the parent-child relationship is an extremely important area of research for the psychology of religion. Some time ago, therefore, I began a project in my department at Åbo Akademi which would pay particular attention to this relationship. Five to six of us began working on the project, the majority of those involved still being undergraduates. Well aware of the comprehensive nature of the task before us we began by "brainstorming", that is we tried to produce as many angles of approach as possible to transmission of tradition. The first concrete task then became the construction of a questionnaire which was to be sent in the first instance to students. The questionnaire was quite comprehensive with a number of fairly "difficult" questions, but as we intended to administer it to student, we calculated that they would have a relatively large capacity for answering questions. The questionnary was sent out to students in both Turku and Helsinki, both Swedish and Finnish speakers. We have received 1.002 answers, of which 334 or 33% were from Swedish speakers. Just over 50% returned the questionnaire, which is not a particularly good figure but nevertheless fairly satisfactory in view of the nature of the questions.

The questionnaire first included the traditional background variables such as sex, age, civil status, etc. These were followed by a number of adjectives, with the respondent asked to decide to what extent they were applicable to his/her own personality. There were 11 terms such as warm, ready to judge, open, understanding, just and gentle. There were then a number of questions about home upbringing and attitudes to parents during childhood. These included largely the same terms as those employed for assessing personal character traits.

A subsequent block of questions dealt with religiosity, Church membership, prayer activity and bible reading. Questions were also included about parents' religious attitudes. There were then a number of attitude questions, dealing with religion but also with individual personalities. Here we included questions on extrinsicality, intrinsicality and bible views. These questions had been used before in research conducted in the Scandinavian countries and originate in tests constructed in the United States. At the end of the questionnaire we included a number of claims about God and Jesus. Here the respondent was asked to indicate how he conceived these figures on the basis of given statements on a seven point scale. Last of all in the questionnaire there was a slightly facetious question. Respondents were asked to record to what extent the qualities of different animals resembled their own. The list included eagle, swan, butterfly, lion, rabbit and gorilla. This question was intended to shed some light on sexual identification with animals which could be regarded as either male or female.

I present below some quite preliminary results from the processing of the material. Much remains to be done as the variables are as many as 172, often with several alternative answers. I am also waiting for two students to produce the results of analyses, before proceeding with work myself.

If we first consider personal qualities of the respondents and their parents (according to the respondent's own evaluation) we find a fairly strong correspondence. Qualities bunch together in such a way that respondents either regard themselves as ready to judge, strict and hot-tempered or as warm, open and gentle. The same qualities are also correlated with judgement of parents. A tendency for the mother's qualities to influence the daughter more than the father's and for the father's to influence the son more than the mother's may be found in the material. We must of course be very cautious about pronouncements about to what extent the father's and mother's qualities have affected the children, as we not not have any purely objective criteria with which to compare. But in any case, we must say that the child's self image has points of coincidence with the image of the parents.

If we inquire about parent's transmission of religion to their children, we find a general phenomenon: if the parents exhibit a religious attitude, the children also have a religious orientation. This is in accordance with general socialisation theory and nothing remarkable in itself. If, however, we break the phenomenon down into its different components, transmission emerges as something far more interesting.

In the first place we may state that 31% of respondents in the study said they were critical towards the Christian faith. 12% are indifferent and 4% only dissociate themselves from Christianity. There are 53% who have an

252

entirely positive attitude towards Christianity or think that it suits them very well. What may seem surprising here is that as many as 31% say they are critical. In earlier studies we have not obtained such high percentages for this answer. In my study of school pupils it was the alternative "I am indifferent to the Christian faith" which obtained 32%. I assume it is the respondent group, students, that has influenced the result. One may suppose that students reserve the right to be critical towards any ideology to a greater extent than other groups in our society.

The questionnary includes questions about the extent to which the respondent's own religious position coincides with that of his/her father and mother. If we contrast these questions with the variables for religiosity we find that in those cases where a person has become religiously oriented, he/she regards their attitude as not being in conformity with the father's. On the other hand, it is in conformity with the mother's. This reflects the self-evident fact that in our culture the mother is considerably more religiously oriented and also the one who most strongly transmits the religious tradition. Children are aware of the mother's attitudes in a quite different way than they are of the father's. This also emerged clearly in the schools study I completed in 1978 for Swedish Finland. But it is interesting that in those cases where women's attitudes are in agreement with those of the father, it is a question of areligious attitudes, or at least ones without clear church orientation. For men there are no clear connection with appreciation of the father's opinions. Religiously oriented men, on the other hand, are readily able to distinguish agreement with the mother. On this point there is potential for further analysis.

Generally speaking, it may be stated that this study produces a pattern suggesting that if the relationship to both parents is a good one, then the child also adopts the parent's life view fairly unproblematically. If, however, only the relationship to the mother is a good, there is a great chance that the child will acquire a religious orientation, although this is not as clear as in the previous case. If only the relationship to the father is good, the chances of the child becoming religiously oriented are not particularly great. It appears that conflicts in relation to parents can jeopardize the mediation of tradition decisively. It is in any case clear that the emotional relationship has greater importance than whether the parents are religious or merely regarded as religious.

If we consider the attitude questions we find that those persons with a rigid view of the bible (largely fundamentalist) also admit to having strict and censorious personality traits. God and Jesus are regarded to a higher degree than they are among other people as strict and ready to judge. God is also regarded as male to a greater extent than among other respondents. If we relate this to the slightly facetious question at the end about animal identifications we also find almost incredible correlations with animals such as the eagle, the lion and the gorilla. This is also true of women!

If we consider correlations between animal qualities two patterns clearly emerge: one for the more femine animals, which include swan, butterfly and rabbit, and one for the masculine ones, eagle, lion, bear, elephant and gorilla. The femine pattern shows a high correlation almost throughout with questions measuring traditional religious outlook. The masculine pattern, on the other hand, correlates with variables for dissociation from traditional Christianity. If we only consider the women in the material this pattern emerges particularly clearly. Those women who have stated that they can identify with male animals have also in other respects adopted attitudes which are male and a-religious. They thus conceive God as a delusion to struggle against and as a theoretical concept without significance. Jesus emerges principally, as a historical person or as a mythical one. The material therefore exhibits a personality type which is characterised by self-sufficiency and which does not seek security in religion. Among women this type is particurlarly polarised against the traditional woman's role.

To summarise these preliminary results, we may therefore state that the personality features of respondents are also found to a very high degree in the parents. At least, the respondents are prepared to find them there. Rigid personality variables correlate with ideas of God and Jesus as strict and sensorious beings. The father's role as mediator of religion once again turns out to be modest. In cases where he emerges as the bearer of tradition, it is mainly in the capacity of someone who has dissociated himself from traditional Christianity. This attitude finds its clearest manifestation in the female sex. Somewhat surprisingly, the facetious question about animal identification acquired a clearly decisive role. The feminine qualities correspond with religiosity and the male ones with an a-christian attitude. If one only considers the women in the material, the patterns emerge among them too. We must quite logically reckon with both attitudes in men, too, even if it has not yet been possible to deduce these from the material.

254

In the future I would like to analyse the emotional ties between parent and child more deeply where religion is concerned and thus come to grips with the question of unconfident and over-confident tradition bearers. Nowadays one must assume that there is a considerably larger number of unconfident tradition bearers than confident ones, not to mention over-confident ones. The a-religious attitude which appears to correlate with unconfident mediation of tradition is perhaps in the long run not alien to religious experience but only to a sort of Churchjargon and mentality. At this point, huge areas of search open up, but for these the present questionnaire material is in no way sufficient. At least in depth interviews with a larger number of individuals are now required.

Jesus Christ as identification-model for the adolescents.
Report of several studies.

J.M. Jaspard
Catholic University Louvain-la-Neuve

A few years ago, the character of Jesus came into the limelight suddenly and literally conquered the screen as Superstar and the stage in one or other Godspel. Nobody could have missed him. Everyone, to begin with the young people, admired him, found him fascinating, was carried away by this being. He was full of life, overflowing with free vitality, he was a hero. He overcame every prohibition and also fear. He turned all feelings of love into a victory, even beyond death. The only question in the debate which divided young and old people, rightwing and leftwing, clergy and non-clergy, was the problem of the "likeness" or even "the likelihood". Was this Jesus-Superstar, this Lord, the man of Nazareth and of the Gospels or was he the hero of a tale adopted to the tasks of the day? Or a passing hero whose face was remodeled in the mirror or our century's hopes?

In any case this Jesusrape is enough to measure how much our contemporaries can identify with this Jesuscharacter. All he has to do is highlight some specific features with the help of colourful lighting and a rich rythmical sound-track to attract his followers who have now deserted "His House" massively.
Is it a question of fashion? of style? of presentation? of redecorating the front? Or is it a question of disguise? Shadows hiding the light? Adorning the character and his message?

Whatever the answer and in spite of some encouraging evidence that was given by the elite of the christian young people (1), recent sociological polls in Belgium (2) and in Europe (3) have shown that religious faith and the values attached to it are not the young people's main concern in their search for self-realization. Everywhere the place given to religion in life is smaller the younger the age-group.
The European study of which Stoetzel gives an account tends to show that religious indifference is only superficial and is related to the forms of religious practice and to the institutions, but not to the belief in God nor to the "religious search" for a meaning to life.
One study on adolescents, made by Prof. Reszohazy (sociologist at Louvain-la-Neuve), shows nevertheless that religious interest is insignificant among the realities which they and their parents care for. The religious dimension seems greater and more integrated in the teachers' objectives. But this passes unperceived by those whom they wish

to interest. Here we can cease very clearly (and this study confirms many other ones) how slight the moral influence of the teachers is compared to the parents'. And if 20 years ago, average small and bigger children were more religious than their parents, nowadays this average is reversed as regards faith and religious practice. And one can notice even that if the parents have dropped the practice whilst remaining believers, their children link non-belief to the absence of family practice. This reversal is explained sociologically by the disappearance of a large social frame, which affects the young more than the adults. But the indifference seems even deeper when one notices that religious faith is always at the bottom of the scale of the values which the young people consider the most important, the things which make life successful, the realities that are spoken about, parent's expectations as regards their children, the most precious things we owe to our parents or to school... Most valued are freedom, love, harmony with oneself; a successful life consists mainly in linking on accomplished family-life to personal growth. This wouldn't be new if it weren't for the fact those values and criteria are not related at all any more to the principles at the basis of the christian faith such as self-sacrifice, generosity, unselfish involvement, the search for brotherhood, equality, beauty. And also the ethical correlates of the christian faith seem to detach themselves from the youth's quest for happiness.

This kind of picture of the young people's aspirations nowadays doesn't encourage one to investigate further into our first question : do the adolescents find an identification model in Christ? But yet, it seems sufficient to stimulate them slightly by highlighting the founder of Christianity to notice immediately that his character doesn't leave them indifferent. To prove my statement I'll refer to a few recurrent studies done between 1960 and the end of the seventies in our two Centers of Psychology of Religion at Leuven and at Louvain-la-Neuve (4). The result of which reveal a surprising stability no matter the area where they took place (in Belgium, flemish or frenchspeaking, and in Spain); only slight differences occur between the adolescents depending on their age, sex and type of secundary studies (humanistic, studies, technical or professional). Let us see what these studies reveal concretely, before reflecting upon the identification-types the character of Christ offers an adolescent in his personal growth and in the growth of his faith.

I. A first type of study showed young people between 12 and 18 two series of 20 pictures from the christian iconography. The first one represented Christ suffering on the cross (close-up), the other one Christ not suffering. Each serie included pictures chosen by specialists in a progression from the most symmetrical, hieratic – representing "transcendence" - to the most realistic - representing theoretically "immanence". The adolescents were invited to choose or reject some pictures according to their likes or dislikes; explain their choice and describe in a few lines how Jesus was perceived by his contemporaries. The results were obvious : dislike for the "transcendence" images, sympathy for the "immanence" images. And the comments are as obvious : they prefer in the pictures of Jesus a gentle face, a human look, expressive and inviting eyes, manly and strong features, mixed with tenderness. They don't like a distant, ascetic character, an inhuman look, hard, stern or disapproving, or unmoved, without feelings, seeming indifferent, out of the world. The essays confirm these choices : Jesus was essentially a good person, loving and open to every one.

The younger ones compare him to a good father in whom one can have confidence, the children's friend. The older one are struck by his perfect likeness to other people. It seems as though they reacted more strongly against a message stressing his difference. A boy of 17 says: "I find that Jesus' divineness is not written on his face". His divineness is mentioned very little. And as regards his "transcendence" it can only be confirmed and attractive when they can make sure that it stays on a human level. So, Jesus must be an extraordinary human being, a fascinating personality, surprising in his love. He was the bearer of an exeptional message of love. But they don't really liken him to God, or then - but only the younger ones -- in an impersonal way, using the dogmatic formula of the catechism. In fact, they don't reject necessarily Jesus Christ's divineness, but they obviously don't know what to do with it; it remains a outward word that gives Jesus an accessory sign that doesn't add anything to the interest he awakens.

II. The second type of study offered the adolescents a selection of 40 short excerpts from the Gospel to criticize ; they were presented textually and followed by a brief sentence explaining what they were supposed to criticize on a scale ranging from the utmost sympathy to the utmost dislike.

E.g. text : He who loves his father and mother more than me, says Jesus, is not worthy of me. He who loves his son or his daughter more than me, is not worthy of me.

sentence and appreciation : The fact that Jesus demands from his disciples to prefer him to their father and mother,... makes me feel very friendly, friendly, indifferent, unfriendly, very unfriendly.

Those 40 extracts from the Gospel offer a wide range of images of Christ, that stress alternately his condition as a human being, his unselfishness and the way he relates to other people, his strong demands, his privileged relationship with God, his share in some godlike qualities and the terms he sets on those who wish to follow him. Whatever the time or place of the study, Christ is invariably the most lovable when he shows his altruism or his human sensitivity. He is the most hateful when he claims faith in his person and selfdenial to follow him. They love Jesus when he welcomes the small, the humble, the rejected, the dropouts of his time. Jesus who considers the smallest of his children as himself, who gives courage to the adulterous woman, Jesus who forgives his executioners, who considers himself as everyone's servant, who defends his disciples during his arrest. They worship him when he shows deep human feelings in important situations: when he is moved, when he undergoes agony, the fear of suffering, when he needs his friends' help and also when he is faithful to his mission and his Father in spite of difficulties, exhaustion even on the cost of his life.

But they dislike the Jesus who asks his followers to choose him above their father, mother, children: to forsake their career and possessions. Hateful is Jesus who demands impossible things, such as unconditional forgiveness or love for the enemy; or who turns over values by representing poverty as a source of happiness. Hateful too is he when he flows up in anger to defend the sanctity of the Temple, when he bullies Peter who wants to make him avoid his fate, when he shows a preference for some disciples, when he criticizes harshly the Pharisees' ambiguous religiosity.

Particularly the older ones disapprove when he calls himself Master and cuts himself off from the others by saying he is sinless, by speaking with authority, by promising freedom to those who obey him, by calling himself the Bread of Life that gives eternal life... Some features arouse mixed feelings, especially with the younger ones, those who give him a certain power and the possibility to do miracles.

It is embarrasing for him to cure a blind man because, although they appreciate the fact that he helps someone, they don't like it when, because of this, others cannot compete with him. They appreciate the fact that he doesn't use this gift too much ; but they find it artificial that he remains passive in the face of the humiliation of his suffering or that he let himself be led into temptation. The older ones remain more different to this question either because they evade it more easily, or because they accept a certain ontological difference in Christ. In fact, the purely religious aspects of Jesus' life and mission don't attract the young's attention very much. They appreciate the fact that he was faithful to the mission his father gave him. But that he is really united to God, that he renders importance to God's glory, that he promises his disciples that they will be glorified with him... all this just seem words or abstract realities.

They don't know what to think of Jesus' total submissiveness to his Father: for the younger ones alienation? for the older ones confident selfdenial?

Let us point out two more contradictory observations, which we will discuss subsequently.

1° The rejection of Jesus evangelical demands and the admiration for Jesus when he puts them into practice (love for his ennemies, forgiveness for his executioners for instance).
2. A very strong dislike for Jesus when he behaves too humanly (in casu his marked preference for certain disciples) contrasts strikingly with the wish to see Jesus sharing fully the human condition.

These contrasts and the global orientation of the results of this research bring us to the heart of the discussion about the position of Jesus as a possible identification model for the young people, now and also in the past.

1. We have noticed that the most spontaneous and most frequent tendency (whatever the age, sex, socio-cultural position) is to liken Jesus' person to one's own situation and to give him an ontological identity that is as similar as possible to one's own. The identification process always starts with <u>a work of assimilation</u>: the distance and the differences are suppressed. Christ interests them less than the concrete person Jesus, when he belongs to his other world, namely the world of God. The latter proved how rooted he was in the human world through his sharing of all human experiences; including these (well known from adolescents) of the need of understanding, of the loneliness, of suffering, of the comfort of friends. But there are breaches in the likeness which awaken suspicion. His possibility of doing miracles and his reputation of being sinless (flawless) make him unmatching and thus suspect.

2. This leads us to the second tendency of the identification process : <u>idealization</u> whereby attachment to the model is stirred up. It is the phase where the other person, the model is identified to the Ego Ideal. One recognizes oneself in this flawless being and one wants to be like him. For this reason the model-individual becomes a fantasy. It loses its reality and its representation is purified from each aspect that doesn't correspond to the projected ideal. Usually a groupsolidarity around the same perception of the model tends to give it a certain appearance of reality, which accounts for the feeling that the perception is objective and that the attachment is justified socially. And this is the usual process for all Jesus' features which infatuate

our adolescents. They are chosen carefully and all together they create the profile of a person who has succeeded particularly in developing in himself, at the same time, qualities of openness, understanding and service that should distinguish all the adults around them, and on the other hand willpower, courage, sense of justice, constance, freedom to act and speak, the audacity to take risks and to challenge the authorities in the name of the great values... All these qualities belong to the real hero, ready to overcome hardships. But as we have seen this ideal picture must not be disturbed in any way (no particular friendships when one preaches equality) and the hero must not give himself the palms of victory, nor use his natural leadership to impose or print the faith people have in him.

3. And this is where the identification process with Jesus ends. Most adolescents refuse to follow the master there were they have never imagined to go.

Their significant negative reaction to the evangelical demands and the renouncement Jesus requires as a condition to follow him shows clearly that they don't make the step from an imaginary and narcistic identification with Jesus' person to a symbolical and dynamic identification to Jesus' project. They renounce at that precise moment when the person they have created as a reflection of the perfect hero of their ideal would like to be their guide in a more realistic way on the more difficult road to a not yet experienced happiness.

This, the third phase – nevertheless the only fruitful one – of the ideal-process is realised only by a minority. They dare give back to Jesus the complexity of his person and take the risk of following him in a dynamic identification to his project, to cooporate to the true realisation of a brotherly, just and loving humanity that Jesus could only imagine as linked to the acceptation of God as a Father.

Only these were able to appreciate the fact that Jesus asks people to give up their security and important human ties to follow him and to be confident in him to perceive a promise of happiness and freedom in privation and unconditional forgiveness. A few of the more believers among our adolescents had done this step.

Some reflections in order to end and to widen the question.

Would we find many more among those who call themselves adults and even Christians adults? We discover here at the end of our discussion a real psychological question the significance of which reaches far beyond the mere fact that it is embedded in the adolescent phase of human development: the question of the specificity of the religious relationship aroused by christianity and of the overtaking of the first humancentred identification movements demanded by christianity.

261

Christ himself had little illusions about this 2.000 years ago. He had warned his disciples about the difficulties of the way.

Unconsciously, even with the best will in the world, the human being stops following Christ as soon as his Truth and his Way don't belong anymore to the common human life. The "Kingdom of God" remains another world and God remains really the Other one with whom one cannot identify : the first step to assimilation is impossible and the second step to idealization to a short-circuit because of one's narcistic attachment.

The way Jesus opens consists in leaving the ideal of self-conservation of the ego (that, without the constant denial of reality, would easily be seduced by the delusion of the divine almight) to take part in an adventurous project that is thought according to the divine Wisdom on the structural basis of filial and brotherly ties on the scale of the Whole of humanity.

Identifying to this project gives coherence to all "evangelical demands" and makes them necessary. But will the human being be able to give up his fundamental anthropocentricism to perceive that it is a matter of being saved... ?

Jesus didn't let himself be taken in by the psychological stakes and thus by the resistance the recognition of his message would meet, but God's patience itself lived in him... He never forced anyone... "He who has ears, may he listen".

Notes

1. Cfr. J.F. Six, Les jeunes, l'avenir et la foi, Paris, DDB, 1976 ;
J. Valery, Ma foi, oui... ma foi, non, Bruxelles, CJC, 1978
2. Par exemple, R. Rezxohazy, Les jeunes, un profil social, politique et religieux, Louvain-la-Neuve, Service de Diagnostic Social, 1983 ;.
R. Boulet, R. Depri, M. Maury, J.Nizet et P. Tobie, Le cours de religion dont ils rêvent, Namur, Ed. LICAP, 1982.
3. Cfr. J. Stoetzel, les valeurs du temps présent, une enquête européenne, Paris, PUF, 1983; P. Delooz, Une enquête européenne sur les valeurs, La Revue Nouvelle, janv. 1984, 80-101; R. Rezsohazy, La désaffection religieuse en Belgique, Revue Théologique de Louvain, 1984, 15, 184-206. C. Camilleri et Cl. Tapia, Les Nouveaux Jeunes, Toulouse, Privat, 1983.
4. Centre de Psychologie de la Religion, UCL et Centrum voor Godsdienstpsychologie, KUL, Mémoires de Licence en Psychologie ou en Sciences Religieuses, inédits.
Deux articles ont été publiés sur trois des premières recherches par J. Claerhout et M. Declercq, L'idée du Christ chez les adolescents, Bruxelles, Lumen Vitae, 1970, 25(1), 67-88 ; M. Deblaauw-Plompteux, l'attitude des adolescents et des jeunes adultes envers le Christ, in Social Compass, XIX, 1972/3, 415-430.

Bibliography of researchs.

Clearhout, J. and DeclercqQ, M., L'idée du Christ chez les adolescents, <u>Revue Lumen Vitae</u>, 1970, 25, 67-88.

Deblauw-Plompteux, M, L'attitude des adolescents et des jeunes adultes envers le Christ, <u>Social Compass</u>, 1972/3, 415-430.

Dache, M., <u>L'image du Christ chez les adolescentes</u>, Mémoire de licence en Psychopédagogie, Louvain, U.C.L., 1969.

Lavens, De affectieve reacties van adolescenten ten opzichte van bepaalde eigenschappen van Christus. Licentieverhandeling Psychologie en pedagogische wetenschappen. Leuven: 1977.

Lecoq, G., <u>L'image du Christ chez les adolescents</u>, Mémoire de licence en Psychologie, Louvain-la-Neuve, U.C.L., 1978.

Linard, H., Suivre Jésus, est-ce l'imiter?, <u>Revue Théologique de Louvain</u>, 1984, 15, 5-27.

Martin Jimenez, S., <u>Contribution à l'étude expérimentale de l'attitude envers le Christ</u>, Mémoire de licence en Psychologie, Louvain, U.C.L., 1966.

Refoyo, S.F., <u>L'image du Christ chez les adolescents. T.1: Garçons: T.2: Filles</u> (échantillon espagnol), Mémoires de licence en Psychologie et en Psychopédagogie, Louvain-la-Neuve, U.C.L., 1978.

Espen, D. van, <u>L'image du Christ chez les adolescents</u>, Mémoire de Licence en Sciences Religieuses, Louvain-la-Neuve, U.C.L., 1977.

A social psychological model of the individual meaning system.

M. H. F. van Uden
Catholic Theological Faculty, Heerlen

1. Introduction

At our last symposium in August 1982 I presented a case-study from my research project on the role of religion in bereavement (Van Uden and Berger, 1983). One major conclusion was that only by looking at the individual as a totality, an insight into the role of religion in grief became possible. We saw how man chose from his religious tradition that which fitted him best and how he used that for coping with his grief. If one is to understand the function of religion in grief, religion must be placed in a broader frame of reference: the total meaning system of this personality.

In this paper I would like to present a model of what I call: the "Individual Meaning System". I furthermore will deal with the place of traditional religiosity within this system, and the relation between several components of this system. In doing this, we make use of ideas from the theory of Symbolic Interactionism. The use of the term "Primary Self-Other System" will be of great significance in this context (for more details, see Van Uden, 1985).

2. Secularization and Meaning System

2.1 Secularization

Defining religion as a meaning system does not mean that other systems cannot function as meaning systems as well. As our case-studies showed, it is preferable to define religion as one of many possible meaning sources. If we want to elucidate the role of religion in bereavement, religion must be studied in a frame of reference in which other sources of meaning also function. In the proces of secularization the traditional religiosity has lost its taken-for-granted role of source for all meaning.

In the sociology of religion quite some research has recently been done on these issues. According to Luckmann (1967) the central question of the sociology of religion today is whether there are "institutionally non-specialized social forms of religion" and what he calls: "invisible religions".

This private invisible religion consists out of a collection of meaning systems, gathered by the individual out of what is available on the "market" of ideologies. From this perspective of "invisible religions" research on meaning systems was done mainly by American sociologists (e.g. Yinger, 1969 and 1977; Machalek and Martin, 1976; Mc.Cready and Greeley , 1976 ; Wuthnow, 1976).

Still the meaning systems they write about, are hard to reformulate on an individual psychological level. We will now try to give a more psychological oriented formulation of the concept of "Meaning System".

2.2 A psychological formulation of the concept "Meaning System".
For the concept "meaning system" we find several labels in literature: "systems of meaning", "meaning structures", "world views", "invisible religions", "symbolic universes", "systems of ultimate values", etc.
Leaning on the philosopher Kruithof (1968) and the sociologist Schoovaerts (1981), we choose the following descriptive definition for the concept of "meaning system":
A **meaning system** is a cognitive complex of beliefs, attitudes, values and norms, that the individual constructs during his personal history in a continuing process of interpretation, systematization and legitimation of himself, others and events, by which the individual structures himself as a totality and transcends his immediate life situation, gives meaning to his life and acquires a relative subjective security.

This meaning system can be regarded as a part of the cognitive system of man. The cognitive system helps the individual to recognise and label experiences. The meaning system has a specific controlling and integrating function within this cognitive system. Characteristic of the meaning system is that it deals with "existential questions", questions that transcend day-to-day experiences.
Let us now deal with the three aspects contained in our description of the meaning system:
   a. aspects regarding the nature of its constitutive elements
   b. aspects regarding the process of development
   c. aspects regarding its function for the individual

ad a. A meaning system is a cognitive complex of beliefs, attitudes, values
           and norms....
The concept of meaning system could be misleading if by system we meant a logical coherent pattern. The structure we intend, is rather somewhat hierarchical than coherent, closed and strictly organised. We speak of a complex of interdependent parts. During his life the individual acquires a growing knowledge that this complex of gathered meaning sources is in fact a totality, belongs to him and constitutes his identity.

ad b. ....that the individual constructs during his personal history in a
           continuing process of interpretation, systematization and
           legitimation of himself, others and events.....
The individual today is confronted with the task to integrate his

segmented life into one identity or "Self" (in the terms of G.H. Mead, 1934). He chooses from what is available on the cultural market. This choice is dependent on socialisation-processes in the broadest sense.

Within this meaning system there is a continuing process of adaption to changing circumstances. The loss of work, the death of a spouse, will be followed by changes in the complex components of the meaning system. Certain parts may disappear or be exchanged. Apart from this dynamic aspect in the meaning system, there is also a constant factor involved. In every individual a "primary factor" can be discriminated, usually not subject to change. This factor enables the individual to see himself as one person, despite his involvement in many areas in as many partial identities. In the next paragraph we shall label this factor with Charles Estus as the " Primary Self-Other System".

ad c. ..by which the individual structures himself as a totality and
        transcends his immediate life situation, gives meaning to his life
        and acquires a relative subjective security.
From the viewpoint of the individual, the function of the meaning system is to integrate the various domains of existence. It integrates the many sources of meaning into a totality of meaning. By means of his meaning system the individual transcends single experiences. The immediateness of a "part" is transcended and the individual is enabled to perceive himself as a "unity". Diversity becomes unity for this individual. Thanks to his meaning system, this individual is enabled to discriminate between meaningfull and meaningless. This renders him a certain amount of peace and security.

3. Estus' contribution
Until now we did not deal with the precise place of the traditional religiosity in this meaning system. Nor did we handle the question, how to understand this "somewhat hierarchical" structuring in the meaning system. To shed some light on these matters, we will now briefly, probably too briefly, go into the ideas of Charles Estus, as he worked these out in his dissertation from 1966.

3.1 Starting points
Estus starts by claiming that reality manifests itself in the relationship between the "Self" and the "Other" (in the terms of George Herbert Mead). What is religious for a person or group, is also stated in terms of a relationship. This relationship however is primary and functions for the person or group to enable the attribution of meaning to all of experience. The religious he defines as a "Primary Self-Other System" which, again following Mead, manifests itself in the "I-Me" dialogue of behavior. It

266

ttern for this dialogue. The religious --in this sense- is the
ymbolic organisation of behavior. "Self--Other "linkages are
ıtity "claims" or commitments in relation to their sources of
since identities are realised through social interaction.
Self-Other System" is the final or ultimate commitment of
claim about its identity. A specific identity linked to any
ınceptualised so as to maintain that commitment to the
ity. Role enactments in any situation are organised and
modified about role requirements so that this primary identity may be
realised. The religious therefore is a dimension of all behavior, a
dimension that does not manifest itself exclusively in traditional religious
practices. The question should be in that context: which "Primary
Self-Other System" is realised by engaging in certain religious practices?
What primary relation is confirmed by this involvement in traditional
religious activity? In order to answer these questions Estus tried to
develop a personality model with concepts from Symbolic Interactionism.
He called this the "Self-System" model.

3.2 The "Self-System" model
   In this model various components can be differentiated. The personality
is looked at as an accumulation of several "Selves", according to the
several "Others" the individual is related to. The relations between the
"Self" and these "Others" are constitutive for the behavior of this
individual.
   Mead later differentiated between "specific" and "generalised Others".
"Specific" refers to a relation with one "Other", "generalised " to a relation
with an "Other" who represents a group of reference figures.
   This results in a complex "Self-System" with components referring to
relations with for example "father", "mother", "family", "friends",
"neighbourhood" or "church".
   So a model of the "Self" develops, in which the individual is characterised
as if he acts with a number of "Others", available in his mind. He calls on
these "Others" to attribute meaning to his actions.
   First of all the "Self-System" is a collection of partial identities ("Me's"),
called upon by the "I" to achieve certain goals in particular situations. In
this model of the "Self" two levels can be differentiated:
a. the level of the "Primary Self--Other" relation
b. the level of the various "Self-Other" relations
   On both levels the relation to the "Other" can be to a "specific" or
"generalised Other". So we can distinguish four types of "Self-Other"
relations.
   a. At the primary level:
      1) The "Primary Self-Specific Other-System " e.g. the relation

267

"Self-Mother" (assuming that the relation to the mother is the pri[...]
structure of this individual).
2) The "Primary Self-Generalised Other-System" e.g. the relation
"Self-Family".
b. At the non-primary level:
3) The "Self-Specific Other-System", e.g. the relation "Self-Neighbour"
4) The "Self-Generalised Other-System", e.g. the relation
"Self-Neighbourhood".
Whether in the relation of the "Self" to an "Other" the "Other" is
"generalised" or "specific", is of minor importance for the development of
the "Self-System" model; of crucial importance is the assumption that only
one "Primary Self-Other" relation exists. This relation enlightens the
commitments of this individual to other "Self-Other Systems".

Estus' perspective implies that behavior is organised around one identity
enclosed in one "Primary Self-Other System". The task is to discover in
each individual case this organising principle which appears as the
"Primary Self-Other System".
One general class of indicators of the "primary" character of a certain
"Self-Other System" has to do with "intensity". It is clear that concepts
like "most important", "most significant", "most intense" and "ultimacy"
(remember Tillich's (1959) "ultimate concern" in this context), are used by
individuals to refer to the "depth" of experience when such an identity
("Self-Other System") is expressed and/or questioned, threatened or
transformed. To be committed is to care about, to be committed in this
primary sense is to "care most about".
James (1893) expressed such commitment in the following: "The most
peculiar social self which one is apt to have, is in the mind of the person
one is in love with. The good or bad fortunes of this self cause the most
intense elation and dejection" (p. 294).
An ultimate commitment will be that point at which self-objectification
ceases, in the sense that it represents the final location of meaning for all
experience; the final standard of judgement; it can not be transcended in
any other context of meaning.
So far a brief introduction of the "Self-System" model Estus developed.
Let us now represent several ingredients and ideas together into what we
call a model of the "Individual Meaning System".

4. The model of the "Individual Meaning System"
As stated earlier we regard this "Individual Meaning System" as a part of
the cognitive structure of man. Within this "Individual Meaning System" one
can distinghuish various "meaning sources", in Estus' terms "Self-Other
Systems", e.g. work, family, politics and traditional religiosity. These

"Self Other Systems" develop during the individual life history from an interaction of the "Self" with "Significant Others" (generalised or specific).

In this complex of "Self-Other Systems", the aforementioned two levels must be differentiated: 1. the level of the "Primary Self-Other System" and 2. the level of the various "Self-Other Systems".

The "Primary Self-Other System" has an integrative function within the "Individual Meaning System". It integrates the segmented world with its various meaning sources and at the same time affirms and realizes the "Primary Self-Other System" in the partial identities that are enacted in the various life domains. So there is no oneway direction. We speak of meaning sources from which we gain meaning and of life domains to which we attribute meaning.

The "Individual Meaning System" can be regarded as a complex of gathered meaning sources. In the process of secularization, traditional religiosity has lost its role of "Sacred Canopy " (Berger, 1967). Every individual collects his own "Sum of Meaning Sources". This idea of the meaning system can be represented as a circle filled with smaller circles of different size depending on the individual life history. These smaller circles represent the various meaning sources. Meaning sources as for example work, family and traditional religiosity.

INDIVIDUAL SUM OF MEANING SOURCES

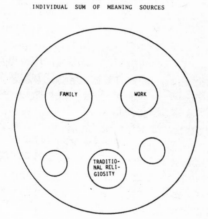

If we now add the crucial ingredient: Estus' idea of the "Primary Self-Other System", we come to the follcwing representation of the "Individual Meaning System".

269

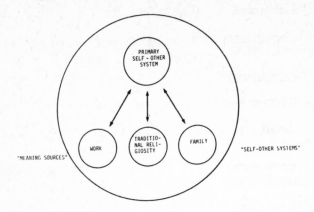

In this representation the internal structure of the "Individual Meaning System" becomes clear. It furthermore emphasizes our idea of the organising principle of the "Primary Self-Other System", we assume to be present in each meaning system.

In this representation we chose three meaning sources: work, traditional religiosity and family. It will be obvious that in many individuals other "Self-Other Systems" than these three are relevant and that the sizes of the circles that represent these "Self-Other Systems", can vary as well.

5. Final Remarks

The model thusfar developed, helped us to understand several aspects of our case-studies. It helped us to understand why and how people selected from the traditional religious arsenal. They selected those elements that enabled a maximal enactment of their "Primary Self-Other System". The model gave insight into the indirect role of traditional religion in grief. Religion does not help a person in grief, the individual in the crisis of bereavement does something with his religion. To understand this, we must have a close look at this persons "ultimate concerns", concerns that frequently are not found in the traditional religious domain of life but for example in the relation to one's mother, spouse or neighbourhood. Therefore I would like to end my paper with a plea for what might be called: "ultimate diagnostics". Or with Anselm Strauss (1959) we should look for answers to the following question: "To what, for what, to whom am I committed"?

270

Litoroturc

Berger, P. The sacred canopy. New York, Doubleday, 1967.

Estus, C.W. Selected factors in the decision- making of members of religious organizations. New York University, 1966. (Dissertation)

James, W. The principles of psychology. New York: Henry Holt and Compagny, 1893.

Kruithof, J. De zingever. Hilversum: Paul Brand, 1968.

Luckmann, T. The invisible religion. The problem of religion in modern society. New York: MacMillan, 1967.

Machalek, R. and Martin, M. "Invisible" religions: some preliminary evidence. Journal for the Scientific Study of Religion, 1976, 15, 311-321.

McCready, W.C. and Greeley, A.M. The ultimate values of the american population. Beverly Hills, London: Sage books, 1976.

Mead, G.H. Mind, Self and society. Chicago: University of Chicago Press, 1934.

Schoovaerts, F. Zingevingssystemen van jong- volwassenen in een geseculariseerde cultuur: een onderzoeksontwerp. Paper gepresenteerd op het congres van de A.I.E.M.P., 1981.

Strauss, A. Mirrors and masks. Glencoe: Free Press, 1959.

Tillich, P. Theology of culture. New York: Oxford University Press, 1959.

Uden, M.H.F. van, and Berger, W.J. Religion and grief. In: Proceedings of the Second European Symposion on the Psychology of Religion. Nijmegen: Psychologisch Laboratorium, 1983.

Uden, M.H.F. van, Religie in de crisis van de Rouw. Een exploratief onderzoek door middel van diepte- intervieuws. Nijmegen: Dekker en Van de Vegt, 1985. (dissertation)

Wuthnow, R. The consciousness reformation. Berkeley: University of California Press, 1976.

Yinger, J.M. A structural examination of religion. Journal for the Scientific Study of Religion, 1969, 8, 88- 99.

Yinger, J.M. A comparative study of substructures of religion. Journal for the Scientific Study of Religion, 1977, 16, 67- 86.